PRISONER OF THE WORD

A Memoir of the Vietnamese Reeducation Camps

PRISONER OF THE WORD

A Memoir of the
Vietnamese Reeducation Camps

LE HUU TRI

Black Heron Press
Post Office Box 95676
Seattle WA 98145
www.blackheronpress.com

Jacket Design: Joy Pascoe
Sketch maps: Le Huu Tri

ISBN 0-930773-60-8

Black Heron Press
Post Office Box 95676
Seattle, Washington 98145
www.blackheronpress.com

For my wife and children

Nguyen Thi Phung
Le Ba Nghi
Le Hoang Tram

I would like to thank Ron Wambold for helping and advising me in the early stages of my translation from Vietnamese, in which *Prisoner of the Word* was originally written, to English.

My heartfelt thanks to Joy Pascoe who corrected my English. I am also grateful for her assistance in my search for a publisher.

As for Jerry Gold, my publisher and editor, I can't thank him enough for the time and energy he spent editing my book. Working with him, I learned a great deal about writing.

My wife, Nguyen Thi Phung, helped me to keep my dreams alive. While we lived under the Communist regime in Vietnam, she assisted me in keeping my writing secret by burning the chapters I had outlined on paper. The details of the book were safe in my memory. When I was searching for a publisher here in the United States, she gave me the strength and the courage not to give up.

The contributions of all the people I have mentioned have made this book a reality.

Contents

Sketch Maps

Preface

Dear Reader,

  The following memoir shows how rumors that appeal to basic desires such as freedom or security can be used to control people. The Communists used political techniques involving rumors to govern southern Vietnam after the war ended in 1975. They used these techniques to get former South Vietnamese officers concentrated into what they euphemistically called "reeducation camps," but which were actually labor camps. I had been an officer in the South Vietnamese Army and was imprisoned in the reeducation camps for more than five years.

  Those in charge of the reeducation camps were called cadre. The cadre controlled the prisoners by several different tactics. Sometimes, when they wanted to reinforce a rumor, they increased our food rations. Then, after we grew hopeful from our belief in the rumor's veracity, they decreased our rations.

  At times, they imprisoned us in high-security camps, surrounded by barbed wire and carefully guarded. When we were confined in this way, they sometimes beat us and forced us to work. This type of confinement made us feel trapped, so we looked for ways to get out of working. The cadre also used rumors in the high-security camps to discourage us from escaping and to encourage us to work harder. They provided us with partial truths or acted in a way that supported the rumors, thereby leading us to believe them even more. Usually the rumors appealed to us, and we hopefully discussed each one.

  Sometimes we were imprisoned in camps with no fences and with little or no supervision. The cadre left us to supervise ourselves in these camps, and we were allowed to visit civilian zones during the day. The cadre rarely beat us, and we worked voluntarily. It was usually the hope of being released and the fear of getting punished that kept me from escaping from these low-security camps.

Eventually, I began to ask myself why the cadre changed their attitudes and behavior towards us so frequently. For about six months, I reviewed in my mind all that I had experienced over the previous two years. It became clear to me that the cadre had planned everything from the start. Their plans varied, some lasting a few weeks and some a few months, but I developed a method that revealed their true intentions. I have thus organized the book by what I call periods. Each chapter, or period, represents one of the cadre's plans and the goal that it accomplished.

First, I determined the cadre's intent. What did they intend to accomplish in this period?

Second, I determined their action plan. What camp rules did they enforce? What type of work did they have us do? What news and information did they choose to announce to us, or allow us to overhear? What rumors did they spread? What did they do to reinforce camp rules and rumors?

Third, I determined the prisoners' reaction. What did I and the other prisoners think? What did we say? How did we behave?

Last, I asked if we had reacted in the way the cadre intended us to. Usually we had.

While I was in the labor camps, and later when I was confined to the custody of my family, I recalled these incidents. Each night, before I slept, I reviewed a few of them in my mind. I determined to write this book as soon as the opportunity arose, because I did not want my experiences and insights to be lost.

One

APRIL 30, MAY and JUNE 1975

I had been stationed about 25 miles northeast of Saigon during the Vietnam War and was a lieutenant in the South Vietnamese Army. My job was to train officers and NCOs in the use of weapons at the Armor School in Long Thanh.

On April 27, 1975, North Vietnamese army units attacked the Armor School. My unit defended its position as best it could, but was no match for them.

On April 30, we withdrew to Saigon. By this time our forces were in chaos and the chain of command was broken. When I arrived in Saigon, I thought, "In a few more hours, the Communists will enter this city. More bloodshed will not solve anything. It is better for me to return to my family." I left my unit, changed from my uniform to civilian clothes, and started home.

As I walked I thought about the fall of South Vietnam. I was depressed and, at the same time, I was afraid. I had heard stories that whenever the Communists took over, they imprisoned or killed anyone who had worked for the previous government. They cut off their heads or drowned them in the river. I decided not to go straight to my house and, instead, hired a motorcyclist to take me to Cholon Crossroads. From there I would check my neighborhood. If it was safe, I would go home; if it was not, I would wait and watch.

When I came to Cholon Crossroad, I was startled by a civilian truck passing by, flying two Communist flags behind the cab. I met some soldiers who were changing into civilian clothes and listening to General Minh make an announcement on the radio.

"The Communists are entering Saigon, aren't they?" I asked.

14

"We've already surrendered," they answered, as they pointed to their radio. I walked over to the radio and listened for a few minutes. When I looked up the soldiers were gone.

I walked on to the Xom Cui neighborhood, where civilians stood in their doorways and looked out onto the streets. People walked quickly on the sidewalks. An old man on top of the Nhi Thien Duong Bridge raised a Communist flag and a group of about 50 children and teenagers gathered around it. While they walked, they shouted and waved their hands and greeted people along the road. I could see the shock on people's faces to see the Communist flag flying in Saigon. They stood there silently, their mouths open and their eyes wide.

I became frightened, so I hid among a group of people on the corner of Xom Cui Market. I waited for the Communists to pass. An old woman next to me shouted hysterically, "Jesus! Mary! Oh my God! We will all die! The Communists are coming! Here they are! We will all die!"

After they passed, I walked over Nhi Thien Duong Bridge where some Communist soldiers stood guard. After I passed over the bridge I was in my Binh An neighborhood.

As I entered my family's home, three men passed by. They were my neighbors who had been secretly working for the Communists during the war. One of them carried an AK-47. One carried a B-40. The third made an announcement over a loudspeaker.

"Hello! Hello! Today you know for sure which side is just and which side is unjust. The American Empire and the Old Government have failed. The Revolutionary Government is victorious...."

When I heard his words, I became afraid again. I avoided the three men, went to the back of my house, and entered through the kitchen. As I entered, I noticed Mr. Ninh, my neighbor who was a policeman. He was also afraid and had hidden in the pig sty next to our kitchen.

Mr. Ninh looked at me and shook his head. "We will die! The Communists have come. Surely we will die! They will not forgive, so take care of yourself. If something happens, especially at night, run! They will knock on your door, catch you, and take you away." He shook his head again and sighed. I also worried about what the Communists might do to us.

Suddenly, a frantic voice cried out, "Where is he? Where is Tri? Where did Tri go?"

My brothers and sisters also called me, "Brother Tri! Brother Tri!"

Mr. Ninh panicked. He jumped up and said, "Death comes already! The Communists have come to catch you! Take care! Run!"

While he spoke, he jumped out of the pig sty and ran away. I was afraid too. I quickly looked for a hiding place. I did not want the Communists to catch me. I ran out my back door and hid in the narrow gap between my house and my neighbor's house.

After a moment I regained my courage. I realized the person calling me was not a Communist, but my mother's friend, Mrs. Suu. I left my hiding place and went towards her.

As soon as she saw me, she smiled and said, "Hurry up, or you won't get any rice! Civilians are breaking the warehouse doors. The strong can take as many sacks of rice as they want. Go now! If you are late, they will have taken it all and you will have nothing."

I thought to myself, "I am depressed and tired. Besides, I just came home and have not changed my clothes yet." I thanked Mrs. Suu, but refused her invitation.

Later that day I saw many people who had worked for the Old Government walk past my house. They told me that they were on their way to the Ward Office to report themselves to the Communists. I felt panicky and feared that the Communists would arrest me. When I saw so many people going to report themselves, I thought it would be safer to go with them, so I followed. I had to report my name, rank, and address to the Ward Office, then I was allowed to go back home.

I met several other officers before I returned home. We made an agreement that if any one of us heard any news about our situation, he would inform his relatives. His relatives would then warn the rest of us. As I said good-bye to them, they advised me to be cautious, in case the Communists tried to abduct me.

When I returned home, I went to two of my neighbors, Mr. Ninh, the policeman, and Lt. Dien, an officer for the Old Government. I had intended to discuss with them what we should do if the Communists came for us in the middle of the night. I was not able to see them, however. Their wives told me that they were in hiding.

Before I went to sleep that night, I prepared my escape plan. If the Communists came for me, I would be ready. However, no one came, and I slept safely until morning.

May 1, 1975, was the second day of Communist control over Saigon. At 8:00 AM, one of the Communists walked past my house. He announced over a loudspeaker that all the men in our ward had to report for a meeting at the Ward Office.

I saw many of my friends who had worked for the Old Government there. They all said that they, too, had taken precautions against being abducted by the Communists last night, but that nothing had happened. Nevertheless, we were still afraid they would come to our houses and take us away, and decided it would be best to remain alert.

I talked to my friends for about five minutes, then a Communist cadre addressed our group. He wore civilian clothes and held a loudspeaker. He told us to sit down on the lawn in front of the Ward Office.

In a humble and courteous manner he said, "Now, even though the Revolutionary Government has been successful, we are still in a weak position. We need help from everyone. We will not discriminate against anyone for their religious beliefs or political tendencies. This union will make the Revolutionary Government victorious. So, now, how many of you are behind the New Government? Raise your hands, please."

We all raised our hands. The cadre said he was happy to see this agreement among us. He then suggested that we applaud. Everyone clapped their hands and a spirit of unity began to emerge.

He continued, "Would you please consider that we have only four Communist cadre and our ward population is over 10,000 people. There are many services we want to provide to the people, but cannot. We hope you will participate in the New Government. If you contribute to our efforts now, while we are still in a weak position, we will report it to our superiors. Those who are most helpful will become main cadre in the New Government later. So, who wants to participate in the New Government? Stand up, please."

The cadre waited a minute. When the first man stood up, the cadre suggested we applaud him. Other people saw the man being applauded and were encouraged to stand up also. With everyone continuously clapping, it was not too long before about 50 people stood up. The cadre then invited the people standing to come to the Ward Office. Those of us who were still sitting returned home.

The cadre gave the people in the Ward Office jobs. Youths were formed into armed groups, and they guarded the Ward Office, the bridge, and the schools.

On May 2, the Communist organization began to work in the ward. The new staff voluntarily worked all day and night. Among them were people who had worked for the Old Government as well.

My friends and I remained alert against abduction for four nights, but none of us were taken.

On May 4, I heard a rumor that everyone who had worked for the Old Government would be required to study Communist policies for a short period and would then become civilians. We would not be harassed or abducted.

I was relieved to hear this and visited several of my

friends to give them the good news. They all said that they had already heard the rumor and were hoping to study the policies soon. Since the Communists had not bothered or abducted anyone, we believed the rumor and did not feel it was necessary to protect ourselves any longer.

On the evening of May 7, the cadre announced over the loudspeaker that all officers of the Old Government and members of the political parties of the Old Regime had from May 8 to May 14 to report to the District Office. I felt it would be better to report right away so that I could study Communist policies and return to civil society as soon as possible.

The next morning I went next door to Lt. Dien's house. I intended to invite him to go the District Office with me, but his wife said that he and Mr. Ninh were still in hiding. I left for the District Office and met some other friends along the way.

The cadre told us to complete a form asking for our name, rank, and the duties we performed for the Old Government. We also gave them our identification cards. When we finished, they gave us certificates showing that we had reported to them.

Lt. Dien and Mr. Ninh observed the rest of us reporting and saw that we were not being punished. They came out of hiding and presented themselves to the cadre. Within two weeks, the Communists had a complete list of all Old Government military and civilian personnel as well as members of the political parties.

On May 9, soldiers from the regular North Vietnamese army came to my neighborhood. None of them wore insignia of rank. This was a common Communist practice. Even when we fought them in war, we could not tell what rank they held.

At first, the soldiers stayed in schools or churches or warehouses. After three days, their commanders visited every family. They asked if they could put a few soldiers in each house. If the owners agreed, soldiers would stay in their home.

If the owners did not agree, soldiers would not stay there. The soldiers brought their own food and cooked for themselves, and they did not impose on their hosts in any way.

For the first few weeks, my neighbors and I observed the soldiers. We noticed that they did not eat well. Their meals consisted of rice, vegetable soup, and salt. Some of my neighbors tried to give them more food but the soldiers would not take anything. They kept their sleeping areas clean. If their hosts' house was dirty, they would clean it up for them. They were very courteous. In the first two months they stayed in our neighborhood, no one had anything stolen, none of the women or girls were raped, and no one saw them drinking alcohol or making any trouble.

Nevertheless, these soldiers had some characteristics that the civilians made fun of. It seemed to us that their standard of living in North Vietnam was lower than ours. In order to conceal their inferior status, they often boasted about their finances. However, their lies were often revealed to us.

On one occasion, I saw several soldiers watching television. I asked, "In North Vietnam, do you have a TV?"

They answered, "There are a lot of TVs. Many families have two or three televisions in their homes."

"Is it expensive?"

"It is very cheap. If a person works for one month, he can buy two or three televisions."

"What kind of TVs do you usually buy—American or Japanese?"

The soldiers responded defensively, "American and Japanese TVs aren't any good and often break. Only Russian TVs are good. If the power is switched off, Russian TVs will keep showing pictures for two or three more days, but American and Japanese TVs will stop right away."

At other times when I sat and talked to them, I asked, "In North Vietnam, do you have motorcycles such as Hondas or Suzukis?"

They answered, "The roads are covered with motor-cycles, and many families own two or three."

"Do you have refrigerators or electric fans?"

"In North Vietnam, these items are common. Each family has two or three refrigerators and four or five electric fans."

The soldiers claimed they had everything, but when I came to Quach Thi Trang crossroads in front of the Ben Thanh Market, I saw something that made me think otherwise. Civilians had gathered around the soldiers there and were trying to sell them old watches at inflated prices. Many sellers advertised a watch by putting it in a cup of water for several seconds. Then they lifted out the wet watch and explained that it was still good because the hands continued to move. The soldiers watched the demonstration and bought the watch.

I went home and checked all the drawers in my home and found two old watches. They did not show time accurately but I cleaned them up and made them shiny again. I took them to Quach Thi Trang Crossroad and sold them.

My neighbors told me several stories about watches, radios, toilet bowls, etc., and invented funny stories about the soldiers.

During the first few days of June, the cadre announced that all of the noncommissioned officers and soldiers for the Old Government had to participate in a political program. This reinforced the rumor that everyone who worked for the Old Government would study Communist policy for a brief time, then would return to civilian life. The noncommissioned officers and soldiers reported to nearby classrooms and studied Communist policies for three days. A week later, each of them received a graduation certificate. They were happy and believed they had been forgiven by the Communists. I and the other commissioned officers observed how the Communists had treated the others and hoped that we, too, would soon study Communist policies.

A week after the noncommissioned officers and soldiers received their graduation certificates, the newspapers and radio announced the time and place for all commissioned officers to report.

Junior grade officers such as myself had to report for classes on June 25 and 26. Each district had one place to report. I was in District 7 and reported to 91 Tran Hoang Quan Avenue. General and field grade officers had to bring with them money and clothing for one month, junior grade officers enough for 10 days.

At 1:00 PM on June 25, I reported for the study program along with my friend, Mr. Tuong. A cadre told us our curriculum requirements were complete, so we gave him our personnel documents and paid him for our food. He assigned us a group number and we were dismissed.

After we left his office, I visited the place that I thought would be our school and met many of my friends there. We all agreed that since we would be here for 10 days, it would be better to be assigned to a well ventilated classroom. There were 10 people in our group. That afternoon, a truck from Duong Chau restaurant brought us food.

Early the next morning, several more former junior grade officers arrived at our school. One of them was my friend, Mr. Dinh. He looked at me, shook his head, and said, "If I had known what was going to happen last night, I would have reported in yesterday. At 1:00 AM, while my family was sleeping, the Communists came to my door. I was interrogated about why I had not reported in yet, so I promised to report in today. I was worried that my family might be harassed, so I left home first thing this morning."

On June 26, our second night, a loudspeaker was put in our window while we slept. At 11:00 PM, we were awakened to the order: "Please get up and prepare your luggage. The Revolutionary Government is taking you to a new place to study. Don't worry about your families. Your neighbors will take care of them."

Fifteen minutes later we gathered on the concrete

school yard. Thirty of us climbed on board each Molotova, then the drivers covered the back of each truck with thick cloth so that we could not see outside.

Two soldiers with AK-47s guarded each vehicle. One was at the front, the other stood in back. After a few minutes had passed, the soldier in the front said, "Anyone who wants to eat, please do so now." A few people took their bread out of their bags and began eating.

A minute later, the soldier in the back ordered, "Stop eating! Nobody eat anything! We will wait until we arrive at the new place. Then you can eat." A few people who were chewing bread spit it out and put their remaining bread away.

At midnight, while civilians slept, the convoy moved along the streets of Saigon. We passed through Bay Hien Crossroads, Cu Chi District, and Tay Ninh Province. About half an hour after we drove through Cu Chi, the vehicles stopped.

Someone asked, "Could we please get off the truck to urinate?"

The soldier in front said, "One by one, you can get off the truck. When the first person finishes and returns to the truck, the next person can go. Stand at the roadside and don't go far."

The person next to the soldier went first and returned to the truck. I and a few others stood up, intending to go next. It had been more than six hours since we last urinated and everyone needed to go.

Suddenly, the soldier in back ordered, "Stop! No one urinate anymore. We are close to our destination. Wait until you get there. Then you can go. Now please sit down, and nobody go anywhere."

I needed to urinate very badly, but held it back and sat down. The man next to me could not hold it and he urinated on the floor.

At 7:00 AM we arrived at Trang Lon in Tay Ninh

Province, which had been the Old Regime's base for Division 25. One of the cadre came out to meet us. He wore military clothes without rank.

Two

JULY through SEPTEMBER 1975

Seven trucks parked in front of Section 2, in Camp 2 of Reeducation Regiment 1. As we disembarked, the cadre informed us that there would be 210 "reeducation students" living here. The cadre did not want us to realize that we would be imprisoned, so they did not call us "reeducation prisoners" yet.

The cadre showed us to our quarters. A barbed wire fence surrounded our section, which sat on about two and a half acres of land. A large trench ran down the middle, with a few small houses on either side of the trench. Several jack trees with a well nestled between them grew just outside the circle of houses.

My group stayed with another group, and a total of 20 men lived in each 350-square-foot house. These quarters had been used during the war as temporary housing for American soldiers. A scalloped tin roof covered its wooden walls and concrete floor. Sandbags, left over from the war, still lined the roof and outside walls.

I swept my sleeping area, then looked for a piece of plywood to put under my sleeping mat to keep it clean. I believed we would stay here for only 10 days, so I did not think to repair anything. The cadre brought us rice and we divided it between our two groups. We found some iron ammunition boxes and used them for cooking pots. At noon, we ate the rice and some of the food we had brought with us.

Later that afternoon, some cadre gave each group soap, clothes, and mosquito nets. No one in my group took the clothes, so I took a few pieces. Some people had not brought their own mosquito nets, so they took the nets provided. Again, we believed we would be here for only 10 days, so we did not think we needed to take more.

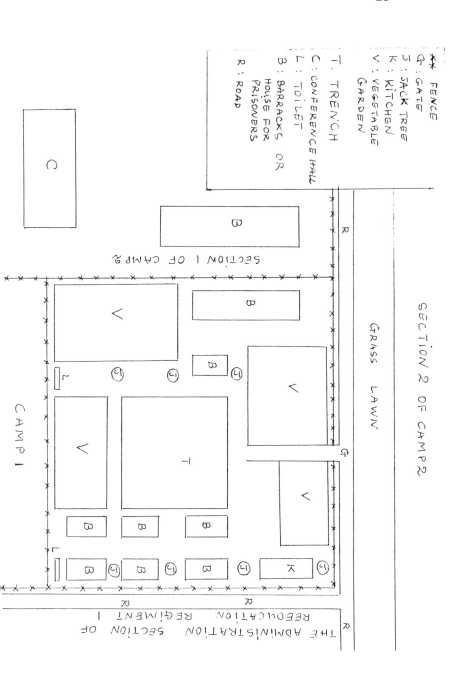

Legend:

- ** FENCE
- G : GATE
- J : JACK TREE
- K : KITCHEN
- V : VEGETABLE GARDEN
- T : TRENCH
- C : CONFERENCE HALL
- L : TOILET
- B : BARRACKS OR HOUSE FOR PRISONERS
- R : ROAD

Map labels:

- SECTION 1 OF CAMP 2
- SECTION 2 OF CAMP 2
- GRASS LAWN
- CAMP 1
- THE ADMINISTRATION SECTION OF REEDUCATION REGIMENT 1

At night, my section attended a meeting in which one of the cadre announced the rules for the camp. We had to repair our quarters, build more houses, build a kitchen, construct a toilet and dig some wells. We had to stay inside the fence. No one was allowed to leave his section.

The cadre also chose from among us a Section Leader and a Deputy Leader. The Section Leader was responsible for telling us what work needed to be done, and he reported our progress to the cadre. The Deputy Leader dispensed our supplies. Every afternoon these two men had to attend a meeting at the Camp Administration Section. They reported to the cadre who gave them our new orders, which they later announced to us.

On the second day, my group began digging fresh wells. The other groups in my section were assigned to one of the other tasks. We all finished in a week.

As soon as we were finished, the cadre ordered all food to be cooked in the new kitchen. Each group would no longer cook its own food, but would now take its turn cooking for the entire section.

About this time, my friends and I started to become uneasy. The Communists had said that the period of study would be for 10 days. We had already been in the camp for eight days, yet we had heard nothing about the study program.

At noon the next day, one of the cadre came to my section. I thought he would give us good news about the study program, but he didn't.

He said, "Please collect 10 more days of rice for your groups."

I watched everyone's eyes widen. I looked at my friends. They looked as shocked as I felt. As I left with my group to get rice, I was too stunned to speak. No one said anything.

When we returned, the cadre said, "We sent a man to bring back a pig for your section."

I immediately thought that this pig must be for our

graduation party. My friends believed this also. We became hopeful again that we would be returning home soon. Everyone appeared to be excited. I heard some people shouting, "Here is the pig! Here is the pig!"

Everyone ran to see the pig. I nudged my way through the crowd. As I got close enough to see it, my heart sank. I expected to see a 70-kilogram pig, but instead I saw a piglet just weaned from its mother and only as big around as my thigh. Confusion and disappointment were on the faces of those around me.

One man asked, "How can this pig feed 210 people?"

The man carrying the pig answered, "The cadre want us to raise this pig until it is big. Then we will kill it and eat it."

The man's words thundered in my ears as if a lightning bolt had struck. It would take a very long time to raise this piglet to a size big enough to feed our section. I suddenly realized that the Communists had lied to us and that we would be imprisoned here for much longer than 10 days.

On July 6, 1,000 reeducation students from my camp attended a meeting in the conference hall. We sat packed together as one of the cadre spoke. He introduced himself as Mr. Luan, the Camp Political Officer. He complimented us on the previous week's work.

Then he said we had, "one leg inside the door and the other leg out." He meant that we wanted to stay, but wanted to go home, too. He also warned us that the cadre were intelligent. Though they did not talk, they knew what we were doing and thinking. Political Officer Luan then announced the camp rules.

First, we were not allowed to go outside the gate or visit other camps.

Second, we were not allowed to beat each other. Anyone caught fighting would be tied up and placed in a discipline cell.

Third, each section would hold a meeting every night.

During our meetings, we had to critique our work for the day and sing revolutionary songs.

Fourth, we were not allowed to sing any Old Regime songs. Political Officer Luan considered these songs to be bad and considered only revolutionary songs to be good.

Fifth, we had to plant a vegetable garden.

Sixth, we had to do calisthenics every morning.

And seventh, each group had to meet every weekend and critique its own members. We had to comment on each other's good and bad points and at the end of the meeting we had to elect one outstanding man. We also had to give the cadre a written report containing the minutes of our meetings. The cadre would then consider all the outstanding men. Those who most often received the outstanding award would be called "progressive men" and would become eligible to be the first to return home.

After the announcement, I knew that if I wanted to return home soon I would have to obey the camp rules and work hard. I decided I would participate wholeheartedly in all of my section's activities. Everyone else seemed eager to participate as well.

That afternoon, my Group Leader showed us the area in which we were to plant a garden. We immediately furrowed the dirt and planted vegetables. We were finished in a few hours.

Afterward, I turned to my friend, Mr. Tuong, and said, "It seems a waste to plant vegetables now. I think we will be gone before we are able to harvest this garden."

Mr. Tuong answered, "Never mind. If we want to return home soon, we have to obey the rules and plant vegetables now."

The next day, we began a new routine. At 7:00 AM a bell woke us. The kitchen did not supply breakfast and there was no work to do, so I played chess and dominos with my friends.

The kitchen served lunch at noon. We ate, then took

a nap. When I woke up, I played chess and dominos some more.

At 5:00 PM we ate dinner. Then we all spent 15 minutes watering our garden.

At 7:00 PM my section participated in a two-hour meeting. First, we sang a song that exalted the revolution. Then our Section Leader announced our new orders. Next, a few people suggested things that needed to be done in our section. We ended our meeting by practicing several more Communist songs.

One of the cadre attended our section meeting the next day. He recommended that we exercise every day to improve our health. Immediately several people raised their hands and suggested we do calisthenics as our exercise program.

One man said, "When the bell rings, the Group Leaders could wake everyone up; then we could all run outside and line up for our calisthenics." A couple of members of my group volunteered to help the rest of us improve our health by instructing us in the Japanese and Korean arts of fighting.

When the bell rang the next morning, the cadre exercised with us. All 210 of us showed up to do calisthenics that day.

On the following morning, no one overslept. We all did our calisthenics again, but the cadre did not show up.

The next morning, the cadre did not inspect us. I noticed some people began to lose their enthusiasm for exercising and the number of people doing calisthenics decreased.

On the morning after that, the number of people who turned out for calisthenics had dwindled to about 100. The day after that there were 50. The people who had volunteered to teach us Japanese or Korean martial arts were the first to drop out. By mid-July, there were only 10 people still doing calisthenics, and finally there were none.

By this time, people began to worry that a poor group critique would affect when they could return home. At our group meetings, whenever someone made an unfavorable comment on another's behavior, the two men would first politely debate back and forth, then they would end up quarreling.

At the end of our group meetings, we always elected one outstanding man. We thought the outstanding man would return home soon, therefore everyone wanted to be elected. We all agreed not to reelect anyone who had been previously elected; that way everyone would get elected at least once.

Everybody obeyed the camp rules. No one fought or sang any Old Regime songs. Although the gate door was left open and unguarded all day, no one tried to leave. Everyone waited for the Communists to tell us when we could return home.

On August 1, I attended a camp meeting in the conference hall. We began by singing a Communist revolutionary song, then Political Officer Luan reviewed our previous month's work.

At first, Political Officer Luan mentioned the calisthenics. He said we started out strong, many people showed enthusiasm by offering to do extra work, and we all participated one hundred percent. One week later, however, no one participated and we all slept through the morning bell. He concluded by stating that we acted like "an elephant's head and a mouse's tail."

Political Officer Luan then complimented us on how well we sang Communist revolutionary songs each night, on how large our vegetable gardens were, and on how well we obeyed the camp rules. Even though there were no soldiers guarding us, no one had tried to leave their section. He also read the lists of outstanding men for each week of the month. My name was on one of the lists, so I stood up. The other outstanding men stood up also. Everybody applauded us.

Finally, he told us that the cadre were very pleased with our progress and believed us to have taken our first step. If we continued at this rate, we would be released soon. Everyone clapped louder and harder. I felt hopeful about returning home soon.

As the days passed I began to grow hungry, but I did not complain. I didn't want to hurt my chances of becoming a "progressive man" and being released. At 10:00 each morning, my stomach growled and hunger pangs dominated my thoughts. The kitchen did not serve breakfast and none of us had any more of our own food, so we had to wait until lunch to eat.

For lunch and dinner, the kitchen served us 500 grams of uncooked rice and small portions of vegetables and dried fish. The cadre called it our "standard food rations." It was not enough, and I was still hungry after eating.

At the beginning of August, the cadre supplied us with tobacco, cigarettes, sugar, and soap. These items were worth 2.4 piastres at the time. The cadre explained that each month we would each be supplied with these items, which they called "two point four piastres of extra supplies" or "two point four piastres."

One evening, one of the cadre attended my section meeting. He said, "According to the camp rules, no one is allowed to visit any other camp. This means that you are not allowed to see or contact anyone from the other camps. I realize that only a barbed wire fence divides Camp 2 from Camp 1, and we sometimes see people from our camp standing at the fence, talking to people in Camp 1. These people are not obeying the rules, and I suggest that those of you who are not correct yourselves immediately."

Even after the cadre's announcement, I continued to see some people from my section standing at the fence, talking to their friends in Camp 1.

A week later, we received orders from our Section Leader to build another barbed wire fence three yards away from the existing fence between Camps 1 and 2. At the same time, Camp 1 also built a fence three yards away, but on their side of the existing fence. After we finished both fences, the cadre told us that it had been done for our own good. Some of the people in Camp 1 had caught an infectious disease, so the cadres wanted to build the extra fences to keep the bacteria from spreading. I was amused when I heard this story. A few of my friends made fun of this explanation. Mr. Tuong said, "The infectious bacterium is probably as big as a cow, so the cadre will use fences to stop it."

The next week, I visited some friends in my camp whose quarters were only about four yards away from the new fence. While there, I saw some reeducation students standing at the fence. I could hear clearly what they said to their friends in Camp 1, but the cadre didn't complained about it anymore. I guessed that the cadre had built the fences to keep us from discussing escape plans with anyone from Camp 1. If anyone planned to escape, he would obviously have to keep it a secret and whisper only loud enough for his friend to hear. Now that the two camps were separated by six yards, someone talking to a friend in the other camp would have to speak loudly enough where anyone near him would hear, too.

Shortages of food and supplies continued throughout August, and problems arose in my group. Before, we put all our food in one place, each of us helped himself, and no one complained. Now we were hungry and selfish. Many people complained that this man ate too much or that man ate like a pig. We divided into groups of two or three people each and divided the food equally. I ate with my friend, Mr. Tuong. I observed that other groups continued to divide their food into individual portions rather than apportioning it to groups, as we did.

We were desperate for more food, so Mr. Tuong and I decided to make some mouse traps. We cooked and ate mice but we were still hungry. At night I walked around my section and saw other people in my group had set out mouse traps too. We were all determined to get through the next few months when we believed we would be released.

By September Mr. Tuong had contracted beriberi. He became bloated and sick. Over half the people in my section had the disease. I was one of the lucky ones and had not contracted it, but I worried as I watched them suffer.

Towards the end of September, we attended our camp meeting. Political Officer Luan reviewed our last three months: planting vegetable gardens, repairing our quarters, building new facilities, digging wells, obeying the camp rules and singing Communist revolutionary songs. He told us that we had done a good job and were all progressive men. Even though no one guarded our camp, none of us had tried to escape. We were all waiting for the day we would be released. When he finished, he and the other cadre applauded us.

Three

OCTOBER through DECEMBER 1975

On the first day of October I attended a camp meeting in the conference hall. Political Officer Luan announced that we would begin studying Communist policies next month. We applauded because we thought this meant we would be released soon. He also described a new program that would encourage us to make improvements in ourselves and in our camp. We were to compete against each other during the month of October. The cadre would then choose those of us who were best at obeying camp rules, repairing our houses, cleaning our quarters, supplying the kitchen with vegetables, and singing revolutionary songs.

Political Officer Luan told us each group would meet that evening to make plans for our contest. Each group would read their resolutions at our next meeting in the conference hall.

That afternoon, the cadre began organizing us into groups of 23. One man in each group was assigned Group Leader. Three groups made up a company. Each company was led by a cadre. Cadre Hoan was in charge of my company. I did not know what rank he held because he was not wearing military insignia. Cadre Hoan chose two men from my company to be our Company and Deputy Leaders.

At our group meeting that night, we decided to repair our living quarters, build a dining room, build a toilet, dig a well, supply a double amount of vegetables to the kitchen, and faithfully obey the camp rules. We also decided that each of us would learn to sing two revolutionary songs.

The next day, we attended another meeting in the conference hall. We all sang a revolutionary song. Political Officer Luan walked to the podium and gave a speech on the importance of improving ourselves and our camp. The cadre ordered several groups to read their resolutions. When it was my group's turn, our Group Leader spoke for us. While he read, we stood in two lines. When he finished, he turned to us and asked, "These are our group's resolutions. So, now, are you determined to achieve them?"

We raised our clenched fists in the air and shouted, "We are determined! Determined! Determined!"

Everyone applauded our enthusiasm, then our Group Leader took our resolutions to the cadres. The Reeducation Regiment Commander told us, on behalf of all the cadre, that they wished us success in obtaining our goals. He also said a lot of us would return home after this period of study. I was very happy when the meeting was over. The message from the Reeducation Regiment Commander greatly motivated me. The other reeducation students appeared to be pleased with this news as well.

The following evening, I attended a company meeting. Our Company Leader had received new orders from the cadre. Next month, our standard of rice would increase from 500 grams to 600 grams of uncooked rice.

The next day, the cadre brought 14 large pigs to each section of camp. They told us that we would eat these pigs in a few months. Later in the evening someone said that it was a Communist tradition to make their prisoners fat just before they released them.

At the end of the first week of October, a special crew came to my section and prepared documents for all the reeducation students. They put our pictures and fingerprints on the documents. That same day I heard another rumor that the cadre were preparing our documents for our release.

My group began working on our resolutions. We built a large plywood platform in our living quarters. We slept on it at night and used it for our meetings during the day. We cleaned the walls and wrote slogans on them like: "Chairman Ho Chi Minh is the teacher of the Vietnamese Revolution" and "Chairman Ho Chi Minh lives long in our useful works" and

"We are determined to follow the Communist ways".

We dug a well and built a dining room and a bathroom. During our group meetings each night, it was usually suggested that one person sing a revolutionary song. Everyone prepared two songs and sang when they were called on. Everyone obeyed the camp rules.

My group was unable to harvest the double amount that we had committed ourselves to because we had no room to plant more vegetables. We had to stay inside the fence around our quarters and had already planted as much of the surface as was possible. We fertilized our vegetable gardens with ashes and urine. We watered the vegetable furrows several times a day. We all had our own private vegetable furrows as well, so we added our own vegetables to the group's. Before we weighed the vegetable bundles, we put them in water to make them heavier. All of this was still not enough to produce the double amount of vegetables.

My group wanted very much to fulfill our commitment. I said to Mr. Tuong, "We fertilized the vegetable garden and did everything else possible, but we still cannot grow enough. I think I can make them weigh more by putting pieces of iron in the middle of the vegetable bundles. That will make them weigh enough right away."

Mr. Tuong whispered back to me, "Don't talk like that. If the other members hear you, they will say you are cheating on the contest."

In November, all the reeducation students in my camp began studying Communist policies and our standard of rice increased to 600 grams, just as the cadre had promised us. We still received the vegetables and dried fish, too. Before our lesson, we sang a Communist song, then a cadre lectured us from the podium. He spent eight hours addressing our first lesson, "The American Empire's invasion of Vietnam," then he assigned us several discussion questions.

My group sat in a circle inside our living quarters. A cadre sat near us, but outside the circle. He observed our discussion, but did not participate. Our Group Leader led the discussion. We sang a song, then raised our hands. The Group Leader called on someone, and that man expressed his opinion. We used points that the cadre mentioned in his speech, and we gave examples from our personal experiences. Each question took from one to one and a half days to discuss. At the end of each day, the Group Leader noted how many times each of us spoke. He then reported this to the cadre. I wanted to show the cadre how well I had studied, so I frequently raised my hand to speak. Everyone else did, too.

At the end of each lesson, the cadre explained to us any issues we did not understand. He then gave us a test on what we had learned.

We spent from four to 10 days on each lesson, depending on the importance of each topic, and a total of one month on all five of the following lessons:

1. The American Empire's invasion of Vietnam.

2. The Old Government—tool of the USA.

3. The Old Armies—tools of the Old Government.

4. How Communist policies will apply to Old Government employees.

5. The duty of Old Government employees.

After the first week I was not hungry anymore. The increase of food was enough to sustain us, and the number of mouse traps in my section decreased. Cases of beriberi decreased also. By the end of November only three people in my group still suffered from it.

At 5:00 AM, on December 1, a cadre came to my quarters, looking for some of the reeducation students in my section. I and a few others heard him say they were being released and could go home. After the students left, we immediately spread the news of their release to everyone else in our section.

Two hours later, 10 released reeducation students passed my area. When I saw them I ran to the fence and looked out at them. As they walked by, they raised their hands and waved good-bye to us. I thought to myself, "How happy those men must be!"

At mid-morning everybody was called into the conference hall for a meeting, and the camp political officer reviewed our studies for November. He mentioned the released reeducation students and called them "progressive men." He said these men were allowed to return home so soon because they had reported a lot of important things to the cadre. For example, one of the released students had an older brother who had been a major in the Old Government and who had not reported to a reeducation camp. The student turned his brother in to the cadre who reported it to the local authorities. His brother was then arrested and put into a camp.

Another reeducation student had reported a concealed weapons storehouse. The cadre reported its location to the local authorities and they confiscated the weapons.

A third student reported he had been part of an organization secretly working with the Americans in Vietnam. The cadre gave his report to the local authorities and they arrested all the other people in that organization.

The camp political officer said that many of us would be released after this period of study. The group of released men would be so large that the cadre would have to use a Molotova convoy to take us back to Saigon.

When I returned to my quarters after the meeting, I saw a truck carrying vegetables, fresh fish, fish sauce, soy sauce, oil and other foods and condiments to our kitchen. One of the cadre entered our kitchen and told the cooks, "From now on you will cook one large pig for lunch and fresh or dried fish for dinner."

For lunch that noon, we ate pork, vegetable soup, and rice. For dinner, we ate fresh fish, vegetable soup, and rice. The food tasted delicious.

The next morning the cadre gave us 2.4 piastres' worth of extra supplies. Each of us received 20 sugar cubes, half a can of milk, 200 grams of tobacco, one kilogram of soap, and one pack of 20 cigarettes. That afternoon, one of my group members said, "The cadre are making us fat because they intend to release all of us soon."

A couple of days later I heard a rumor that the cadre would release another group of reeducation students during the second week of December.

On December 8, 10 more reeducation students were released. Later that morning some cadre came to my section. They sat on the floor and said, "The ten released students were 'progressive men.' They reported truthfully to us and were rewarded by being released sooner than the others."

They continued, "We are looking for honest people whom we can release to their families. The local authorities want honest people they can use in their organizations. The wrong works done for the Old Regime are in the past. We do not care about them, but we want only honest men in our organizations. Therefore, a small number of people will be imprisoned until they die, because they reported falsely."

The cadre gave us extra supplies again, but this time the portions were larger. We each received 40 sugar cubes, one can of milk, one pack of 20 cigarettes, and 200 grams of tobacco.

The next day I heard that during their last meeting the cadre had put in a request for a Molotova convoy to take us back to Saigon. I believed this because it was reinforced by increasing our supplies and by releasing some of the reeducation students. I thought the cadre were choosing all the honest people and would release a large number of us soon. I intended to prove my honesty to the cadre.

I attended a camp meeting in the conference hall. The camp political officer announced that the cadre wanted to determine our level of progress since we entered this reeducation camp five months ago. He ordered each of us to complete a written assignment. Part of it was to be an autobiography, starting from infancy and going to April 30, 1975. He told us to focus mainly on the time we spent working for the Old Government. This part was supposed to help us realize how our previous actions had opposed the Communists. The second part of our assignment was a list of all our relatives: names, ages, addresses, and jobs. We worked on our assignments for three days, then each of us read his own at our group meeting. We all added on to each other's reports, so that it would be complete.

I thought the cadre would release the honest people, therefore I reported truthfully and completely. Some of my group members wanted to show more honesty and enthusiasm, so they completed an additional report and privately took it to the cadre. I turned mine in and thought the cadre would consider me to be honest and would release me soon.

After our assignments were completed, the cadre no longer killed any pigs for our camp. We were no longer supplied fresh fish, vegetables, or pumpkins. The extra supplies stopped as well. We still received 600 grams of uncooked rice each day, but the only vegetables we ate were those we grew ourselves. At the end of the month no one else was released.

A year later, when we studied "The 13 Points of the Reeducation Policies", I discovered that the reeducation students who had been released were actually Communists. They had been spies in our old armies and were planted in reeducation camps to encourage us to report truthfully. The special assignments the cadre had us complete was what they secretly used to decide how long each of us was to be imprisoned.

Four

JANUARY 1976

On the first day of January, Mr. Nghia, one of the reeducation students, was escorted through our camp. His hands were tied behind his back and two armed soldiers walked behind him. About one week later, the Communists chose one person from each reeducation company to observe his execution. The observers reported back to the rest of us what they had seen.

"We sat in many lines, and behind us was a line of armed soldiers. In front of us were two poles, four and a half feet high.

"Two soldiers escorted Mr. Nghia to the poles. A look of surprise came over his face as he realized he was about to be shot. He begged the cadre to forgive him, but they refused. They tied him to the poles and shoved rags into his mouth. Then they tied his mouth closed and covered his eyes with a piece of cloth.

"One of the cadre read the judgement for Mr. Nghia, who hadbeen a South Vietnamese artillery lieutenant for Division 25. Thecadre had caught him trying to escape in a Communist soldier's uniform. They sentenced him to death by firing squad."

Following Mr. Nghia's execution, I attended a camp meeting in the conference hall. Political Officer Luan explained Mr. Nghia's case. My friends and I all agreed that it was too dangerous to escape now. We felt it was better to wait until the Communists released us.

We studied the policy on "Labor". We were told, "It is the responsibility of employees for the Old Government to perform manual labor for the Communist government."

The next day there was a rumor that the cadre intended

to release us, but their superiors wanted each of us to have a good profession first. That is why we had to leave the reeducation camp and go to a labor camp, to be trained there for a short time. Those men the cadre considered to be progressive would be the first to go to a labor camp and the first to be released.

One of my group members told me, "It's a Communist tradition for a man who is in jail for six months to work an additional six months before he is released. This is to repay for the room, board, clothes, and money he received during the six months he spent in jail."

My friends and I discussed this rumor and the topic of Labor. We came to the conclusion that we could not avoid the labor camps. We also believed that whoever was first to be sent to the camps would be the first to be released. I hoped to be one of the first to go. I wanted to be prepared, so I picked up a sandbag that was lying around my section and made a kitbag out of it. I also looked for an iron ammunition box to carry my water in. My group members did the same.

At the end of January, a cadre came to my section. He gathered everyone together and told us, "Many of you will leave this camp today. You will go to a new camp to begin Labor." He read a list of names. When I heard my name called, I was neither happy nor sad. I had prepared myself and accepted my situation.

Fifteen minutes later those of us who were going grabbed our luggage, gathered in a group, and left the section. I waved good-bye to the people staying behind, and I walked over to the Camp Administration Section.

Each of us was assigned to a new group of 10 people. I looked at my new group members and realized they were all strangers to me. No one in my group knew anyone else. All of my old friends were also put into groups where they did not know anyone. The cadre checked our luggage, and collected our hammers, knives, and any sharp metal tools. We then left the Administration Section and walked to the parking lot. By separating us from our friends, the cadre reduced the possibility that we might escape somewhere along the way.

Before we boarded the vehicles the Camp Commander gave us a speech. He told us, "During the past seven months, the cadre have identified all of you as progressive men. That is why you were chosen to be taken to the labor camps first. I wish you all well and hope you will be released soon." There was a loud round of applause. I felt a sense of relief. I was sure that I would be released soon and was determined to work hard.

We boarded the vehicles in crews of 30. The cadre lowered the back cover, and we were completely covered inside the vehicles. Two soldiers guarded each vehicle.

We arrived at a dock within the city limits of Saigon around midnight. As the last vehicle entered the parking lot, I saw a large boat docking nearby. It had the numbers "501" in large print on both sides of its hull, and I assumed that this was the name of the boat. Several soldiers were standing around, guarding the parking lot.

I heard a man in our vehicle say, "Here is the boat. We will probably get on it."

No one else said anything. I understood that we would leave by boat. Still, I wondered, "Where will we go? Will we be taken to North Vietnam?"

Each vehicle backed up close to the boat, then we walked off the vehicles and into the hold. We proceeded to the bow and sat close together on the floor. Each group of 30 people received one box of dried rice and salted, shredded meat. These had already been prepared for us.

The boat began to move. We could not see anything outside. Towards the middle of the boat was a bulkhead dividing the bow from the engines and crew quarters. A soldier watched us from the top of a staircase leading from the bow to a compartment door in the bulkhead.

A few hours had passed when I felt the boat being rocked hard by the waves, and I guessed that we were moving far out to sea.

The hatch above our heads was covered by several large pieces of wood, and sunlight passed through the gaps in the wood. I looked at the sun beams and wondered, "Where are we going?"

At first we moved east. We then turned south, and I guessed we were moving to Con Son Island or to Phu Quoc Island.

On our first day at sea, we realized that we needed water to drink and to prepare our food with. Two men who had been South Vietnamese sailors were familiar with this boat. They switched on the faucet, but it broke. They could not switch it off again and water poured out onto the floor.

There were no restrooms on the boat so on the first day we gathered all the rice boxes and put them at the end of the bow. When we moved our bowels or urinated, we put the stool or urine in a plastic bag. We closed the bags tightly and put them in the rice boxes. Nevertheless, there were too many people. I estimated about 1,000 of us were in the bow of the boat, and by the afternoon of the first day all of the boxes were full.

By the morning of our second day at sea, the bow was flooded with three to four inches of water. We had to stop putting our stool and urine bags in the boxes because there was no more room.

We put our luggage on the floor and sat on it. Our feet hung into the water. When we relieved ourselves we put our stool or urine bags next to our feet. It was very uncomfortable. Later, whenever I had to be transported by boat, I always remembered this experience.

On January 31, we landed at An Thoi on Phu Quoc Island. We took a bath in the sea, then were taken to Camp 18. The camps on this island had held Communist prisoners during the days of the Old Regime. The Communists had been released, and now the camps imprisoned us instead. There were a lot of reeducation prisoners already there when we arrived.

Five

FEBRUARY 1, 1976 to MARCH 14, 1976

On the morning of February 1, one of the cadre came to our quarters. He called us together and assigned a group of ten people to cook in the kitchen. Everyone else was allowed to rest because this was the beginning of Tet, our Lunar New Year Festival, and we did not have to work.

There were 480 of us in Camp 18. We were divided into four companies. Each company consisted of 12 groups, with 10 reeducation students in each group.

The cadre prepared rice, dried fish, salt, pumpkins, and a large pig. They set out large pans and firewood for us to cook with and distributed food containers to each group.

Metal cups and dishes were gathered at one corner of camp. These had been used by those who were imprisoned here during the reign of the Old Regime. We were allowed to take what we wanted from the pile.

Early in the morning on the day before Tet, the cadre gave us tobacco, milk, sugar, tea, and soap. Each of us was issued a pack of 20 cigarettes. One can of milk was apportioned between five of us. Though it was not much, we did have something to celebrate our Lunar New Year Festival with.

In the afternoon, some of us decorated the conference hall for a talent show to be held that evening. The show would include music and poetry. Those of us who wanted to participate had to audition in front of the cadre and have their skit approved.

At 8:00 PM, the show began. The cadre sat on the left side of the stage. Except for the Camp Commander and the Camp Political Officer, the cadre did not wear any sign of rank, so I could not tell what positions they held. I sat in front of the stage with the other reeducation students. Everyone who auditioned was authorized to perform: they played musical instruments or recited poetry.

The show ended just before midnight. It had been very entertaining; everyone enjoyed it. At midnight, we heard a New Year speech over the radio from the Chairman of Vietnam. After that, one man, on behalf of all the reeducation students, wished the cadre a happy New Year. The Camp Commander said he hoped we would be released soon.

On the morning of the first day of Tet, everyone wished each other a happy New Year. We drank tea or milk and smoked our cigarettes. A pig was killed and we ate a delicious lunch, but our dinner was our standard food ration—a little dried fish, vegetable soup, and 500 grams of rice.

On the fourth day of Tet, we attended a meeting in the conference hall. The Camp Political Officer began his speech by telling us that we had violated the law by fighting against the true government, and so we had been brought to this camp to study in the Communist Reeducation Program. Now we were the "reeducation prisoners." He described the Reeducation Program as a manual-labor training course. We were allowed outside the barbed wire fences only when we went to work, and the cadre would train us until we had mastered each manual skill. Those of us who worked hard and obeyed the camp rules would be considered progressive men and would eventually be released. I was unhappy yet determined to obey the camp rules and work hard, because I still hoped to be released soon.

The next day we began working. Every morning we gathered in our quarters to receive our orders from one of the cadre. Each day we were given different orders.

Our first orders were to cut thatch so the cadre could use it to make cottages. Each of us took a yoke and sickle. We collected at the gate, then walked in two lines to the thatch field. Five soldiers guarded us.

We each cut two bundles of thatch about nine inches in diameter. None of us were used to this type of work, so it took us a long time. I spent two hours cutting and tying my two bundles.

We left the thatch field in two close lines, soldiers guarding us on both sides. I walked with the bundles of thatch yoked on my shoulders. I was not accustomed to the weight and my shoulders hurt. I often shifted my yoke from one shoulder to the other. I saw other prisoners readjusting their yokes also. As we walked to camp the bundles of thatch would break, and we were constantly stopping to retie them.

Outside the camp gate the cadre counted us, then we walked through the gate and unloaded our bundles. My shoulders were red and sore. Other people in my group also complained of sore shoulders. We decided to put pillows under our yokes next time.

When the cadre saw us with the pillows, they smiled and said, "Don't put pillows on your shoulders. Endure the pain for a few months. Then you will be used to this work and will not feel it anymore." At the same time, they trained us on how to properly bundle the thatch.

Our second task was to collect firewood. The cadre led us to a forest about three miles from camp. I put a pillow over my shoulders and placed a piece of wood over the pillow and carried it back to camp that way. The pillow did not help much though: my shoulders still hurt. My legs also ached for the first few days.

We had to hoe furrows on the farms. My hands blistered. Several of us wrapped towels around our hands, but it didn't stop the blistering. When the cadre saw us, they told us, "Don't worry about it. In a few weeks your hands will become callused and will not hurt anymore."

Camp 18 was very different from my last camp. Here, we mustered three times a day. The cadre counted us in the morning, at noon, and in the evening. We were surrounded by barbed wire and guard posts. The cadre counted us several times when we worked outside of camp. The soldiers' rifles were loaded, ready to fire.

Nevertheless, our work was relaxed. We worked at our

48

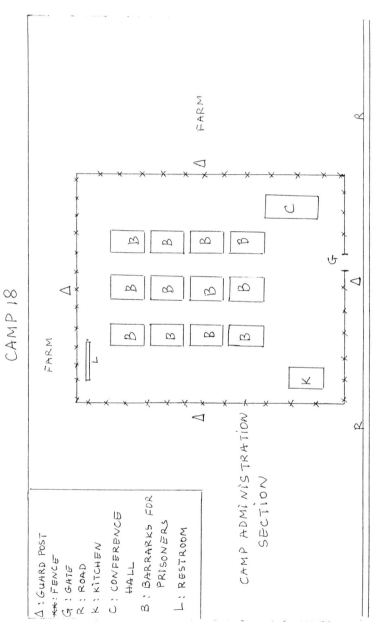

CAMP 18

FARM

FARM

FARM

FARM

△: GUARD POST
✗✗: FENCE
G: GATE
R: ROAD
K: KITCHEN
C: CONFERENCE HALL
B: BARRARKS FOR PRISONERS
L: RESTROOM

CAMP ADMINISTRATION SECTION

own pace and capacity. The majority of us did well, but a few did not. They made small bundles of thatch and carried small pieces of wood. However, the cadre did not force anyone to do any better. They only said at the end of the week that some of us were too lazy and their bundles of thatch or pieces of wood were too small.

I was in Camp 18 for three weeks, then 100 of us were moved to Camp 10 for another three weeks. The policies of Camp 10 were the same as those in Camp 18. Though I experienced physical discomfort and pain, I did not feel mistreated. The cadre did not pressure us. I was certain we would all be released soon. During this time no one even tried to escape, because we still trusted the Communists.

Six

MARCH 15, 1976 to APRIL 30, 1976

On the morning of March 15, all the prisoners in our camp were moved to Camp 9. The cadre checked our luggage and confiscated everything valuable—our gold rings, our watches, and our money. I guessed the cadre were being cautious and took these items to keep us from using them to escape.

Next, the Camp Political Officer addressed us. Hostility seethed from his voice as he spoke. "You were the military officers for the Old Government. You served the Old Regime and were the tools of the United States. You killed a lot of Communists. Now the Old Government has been defeated. We did not kill you, but you will be required to participate in the reeducation program. You must repent for your transgressions by working hard to rebuild what you have destroyed."

He announced the camp rules. He told us that if we worked hard and obeyed them, the cadre would consider us to be progressive and would release us soon. I had the feeling that life in this camp was not going to be easy.

The Camp Political Officer assigned us to new groups and companies. I was assigned to Company 4. Cadre Vien, Cadre Vuong, Cadre Hong, and Cadre Dung were in charge of my company. They wore military clothes and acted like military personnel, but they did not wear any insignia on their collars, so I could not tell what their ranks were.

The cadre showed us to our new quarters. I prepared my sleeping area, then I walked around camp. I saw several prisoners who had obviously been here for a while. The camp sat on about four and a half acres of land enclosed by barbed wire and guard posts. Forty prisoners occupied each

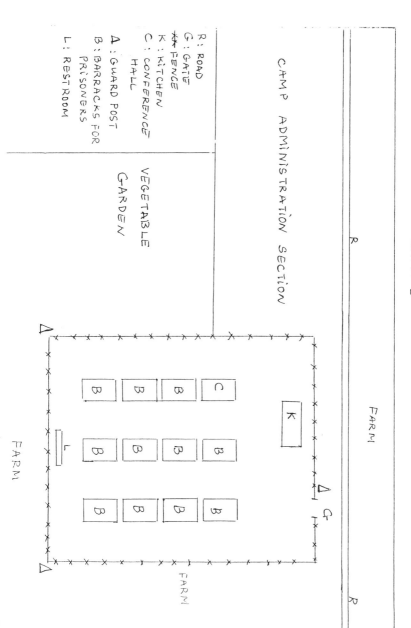

51

of several small tin houses spread over the grounds. We slept on mats placed over concrete floors. There were electric lights inside the houses, but none outside or in the conference hall.

We began working outside camp. My company was sent to a thatch field. We walked in four files. Five armed soldiers and one cadre walked on each flank. When we reached the fields a cadre counted us, then we each cut two bundles of thatch. The cadre would later use the thatch to build cottages for themselves. Before we left the field, the cadre counted us again. He then checked our bundles and made a note of anyone who carried an exceptionally small bundle.

When we mustered that evening, the cadre counted us, then he read a list of prisoners who had been cited earlier in the day. These men stepped forward, and the cadre cursed loudly at them. The cadre announced that these people had been the tools of the American Empire in the days of the Old Regime. Now these prisoners continued to be stubborn, lazy, and unwilling to work in the reeducation program.

The next day we walked about three miles into the forest to fetch firewood. Before we left the forest the cadre checked each piece of firewood. If anyone carried small pieces, he made a note of it. That evening those men who were written up were called forward and yelled at.

The following day my company hoed the fields of a farm outside our camp grounds. If we became tired and rested for a moment, the cadre and soldiers yelled at us. They forced us to hoe continuously for the entire labor period. At the end of the day we were exhausted and blisters covered our hands.

As I returned from working in the fields one day, I saw a prisoner kneeling at the camp gate. I recognized him, though he was not in my company. I asked someone from his company what had happened and was told that this prisoner saw a friend while walking to the fields that morning, so he raised his hand and said "Hello." The cadre were punishing him for talking.

At the end of the week, my company attended a meeting in the conference hall. One of the cadre reviewed our work, then read the list of prisoners who had been cited that week. These prisoners stepped forward and the cadre cursed at them once more. The same prisoners then had to stand in front of their respective companies and say they were sorry for their laziness or their mistakes, and they had to promise to correct them.

After our first weekly meeting, I felt depressed. I did not want the cadre to yell at or punish me. I planned to make big bundles of thatch and carry heavy pieces of firewood and to hoe the fields without resting.

During the next week, I began carrying heavy loads. I pushed myself as hard as I could. I noticed that the cadre often led us farther away from camp than was necessary. Even though there were places to gather thatch and firewood nearby, the cadre would not take us there. Instead, they would lead us three or four miles away.

Walking back to camp each day, my clothes were wet with sweat. My legs felt so heavy that each step took every ounce of strength left in my body. Several people fainted from exhaustion, but I couldn't help them. I was so tired myself that I could only try to keep moving.

Two weeks after our arrival at Camp 9, Cadre Vuong led my company to one of the minefields to look for and pick up live mines left over from the war. The minefields were full of plants and trees, and the maps were lost. I was afraid to perform this dangerous work, but I was more afraid of what the cadre would do to me if I refused.

Some of the other companies were already doing this work. Mr. Manh, who was in another company, had a mine explode in his face and was blinded in one eye.

As we mustered in front of the field, Cadre Vuong said, "In the Old Regime you set mines here with the intent to kill Communist soldiers. Now, you must take them out and return this land to the civilians."

Immediately, reeducation prisoner Nho stepped forward. He asked permission to be excused from this job, since he had worked for the military's Justice Department and had not been trained on guns or mines.

Cadre Vuong responded by loading his gun with bullets and aiming it at Nho. The cadre's voice shook with anger as he shouted, "You were in the Army, so you had to know about guns and mines! Now—are you going to do it or not?"

At the same time, five armed soldiers about 20 yards ahead aimed their AK rifles at us. We stepped into the minefield, but I did not know how to accomplish this task. None of us had any tools, so I asked a couple of my group members for advise. They explained to me how to look for the mines without setting them off.

I found one long, thin stick shaped much like a chopstick. I pushed it into the ground at an angle so that it hit the side of the trap and not the top. When I felt the stick hit something hard, I called over the prisoners who knew about mines. They came and picked it up and disarmed it. Fortunately, the soil was mixed with sand, and the ground was soft. This made it easy for me to use the stick. The first morning my company worked in the minefield, no one was hurt.

When I returned to my quarters at midday, I was afraid to go back into the minefield again. I decided to try and get out of this dangerous work by pretending to be sick.

Before we went back to work that afternoon, my company mustered in front of the gate to be counted. I and several other prisoners stepped out of line to report being sick. We asked if we could rest in our quarters for the remainder of the day. Normally there were only a few patients. Today about 30 patients stepped forward.

Cadre Vuong asked the first prisoner, "What is

wrong with you?"

The prisoner pulled up his pants leg and showed the cadre his knee and said, "I have a sore on my knee and it hurts. It is very hard for me to lift my leg up, so would you please allow me to rest in my quarters?"

The cadre bent down and looked at his sore, then he said, "Your sore is very small and is already dried up. Never mind about it. Now, please go back to work."

The second man said, "I have a toothache and a fever. Would you allow me to go back to my quarters?"

Cadre Vuong answered, "Today we will work with our hands, not our teeth. Never mind about your teeth. Please go back to work."

The third man wore three coats and a blanket. He reported to the cadre, "I have a serious fever. Would you allow me to stay in my quarters today?"

Cadre Vuong said, "Never mind about the fever. Please return to your quarters, take off your blanket, and go back to work."

When I heard the cadre refusing the third man, I could not help but smile. I looked around and saw many other prisoners smiling also. We all knew that he had taken a bath at the well that afternoon. He had been stripped to his waist, smoking tobacco and talking loudly just five minutes ago. Now he suddenly had a serious fever and covered his body with three coats and a blanket.

When the fourth man took his turn, the cadre looked at the long line of "patients" and saw some more prisoners putting on blankets. He said, "No one else report any more illness. Return to your quarters, take off your blankets and go back to work."

The prisoners who were still in formation smiled at the cadre's response, but I and the other would-be patients sadly got back in line.

We were working in the minefield for 15 minutes when suddenly I heard a mine explode. A man cried out,

"Oh my God, I'm dead!"

I stood up and saw reeducation prisoner Liem lying on the ground. He thrashed about, holding on to his foot, part of which had been blown off. He was rushed to the emergency clinic. After that, I became very depressed and stopped working. No one else in my company worked either. Cadre Vuong saw this, so he ordered us to stop. He then moved us to another area where we weeded grass. When we returned to camp, the news about Liem had already spread.

I was in a dangerous situation and I did not know what to do. That night, I went to the conference hall to relax. In the dim light, I noticed something different. Normally there would have been a few people relaxing in here, but tonight the number had increased to about 70. The prisoners had gathered in small groups of two or three and were praying to God. There were several people around me praying, and they thought I was praying, too.

Reeducation prisoner Loc came up to me and said, "Excuse me, are you Catholic?"

"Yes, I am."

"Please, pray with me. Surely Jesus and Mary will not forsake us. They will rescue us from this horrible situation."

I agreed to pray, then watched him walk over to some other prisoners. He said the same thing to them. The other prisoners prayed too.

Several people outside the conference hall were praying. They clasped their hands in front of their chest, bowed their heads, and bent over. Then they straightened up and looked at the sky and prayed. I guessed that they must be Buddhists.

As I was watching them, another man came up and said, "We are in a dangerous position and have no way out. Please believe in our God. Our Lord is compassionate. He will surely help us."

I answered, "I do."

He walked over to another group of prisoners and said the same thing to them.

After Liem lost his foot, my company no longer had to work in the minefields, but the other companies did. Because the work in the minefields was so dangerous, some prisoners avoided it by secretly reporting private conversations to the cadre. The cadre gave these prisoners work in the Camp Administration Section. We named these people "the antennas." One of the reeducation prisoners from my company, Mr. Tuy, had criticized some of the cadre's actions. Mr. Tuy spoke just loud enough for his friend to hear him and no one else. However, his comments were mentioned at a camp meeting. The cadre did not see or hear what we did in private, but they somehow found out. Since I did not know who "the antenna" was, I had to be careful about everything I said.

A week later, the cadre stopped all work in the minefields and began preparing to take us back to the mainland. By this time, I was very hungry. Our meals consisted of rice, some dried fish, a small bowl of vegetable soup, and sometimes a little fresh fish. The cadre had told us our ration of rice would be 530 grams per person per day. In fact, I asked one of the prisoners who cooked our food about this, and he said that we really only received about 400 grams each.

One day, I saw some of the cooks burying smelly fish and other rotten food. They told me, "When the cadre buy pumpkins and cassava roots, they keep them in the storehouse until they begin to rot. Then they give this half-rotten food to the kitchen. So when we fix it, we have to throw away as much as 50 percent of it. When we receive fresh fish, we cook only the good fish. We bury the spoiled fish. The cadre deliberately create a food shortage."

We were all hungry. When we got our food from the kitchen, my group divided it into 10 individual portions and numbered each portion. We wrote the numbers one to 10 on pieces of paper, folded the pieces of paper and mixed them up in a cup. We each picked a number out of the cup and that determined which food portion we ate. When we divided our food this way, no one complained.

After each meal, I was still hungry. I drank a lot of water, until I felt full, but soon I would be hungry again.

Once when I was ordered to work in the Camp Administration Section, my crew passed a pigsty. Three of us walked towards some rice and vegetable scraps set out to be fed to the pigs. None of the cadre were there, so the prisoners stole some of the pig food and ate it.

In addition to our food rations each month, we also received 2.4 piastres of sugar, soap, and cigarettes. Everyone received one pack of 20 cigarettes, but some people were very addicted to smoking and finished their pack within the first two days. These people then craved tobacco for the rest of the month. They picked up cigarette ends that the cadre and soldiers had thrown away. They cut the cigarette ends into tiny parts, each as big as a green bean seed. When they wanted to smoke, they put one part into a pipe and lit it.

I did not smoke, so many people asked me for my pack of cigarettes each month. They would pay me with clothes, lighters or other things. I often agreed because there was no safe place to store them. Several people gave up their honor when they were too eager for cigarettes. They could not control themselves and were caught trying to steal them.

At the end of April, the Camp Political Officer announced that we would be leaving Camp 9. We would move to another camp and wait there for a short while, then we would be taken back to the mainland. Everyone clapped their hands at this announcement. I was very happy. The cadre here were hostile towards us, and I wanted to leave as soon as possible.

Seven

MAY 1, 1976 to JUNE 28, 1976

Camp 9 closed. The Camp Political Officer told us we would go to a holding station in Camp 8, wait there a while, then be taken back to the mainland. One hundred forty reeducation prisoners transferred from Camp 9 to Camp 8 that day.

At first, we stayed in the conference hall of Camp 8. When we arrived the cadre did not check our luggage, and we were allowed to keep our money.

After I prepared my sleeping area, I met the other reeducation prisoners who were already here. I realized that they had been noncommissioned officers for the Old Regime and had come to this island a few months before us. They told me the cadre were very good to them, especially the Camp Political Officer. For instance, the first few times they carried firewood, several prisoners carried long, heavy pieces. The Camp Political Officer saw this and stopped them. He said they still had a long time to go in the reeducation program and the cadre did not want them to carry anything that was too heavy. However, the cadre did not want them to be lazy, either. They only wanted the prisoners to protect their health and work at their capacity.

On another occasion, the Camp Political Officer passed by while they were cutting thatch near some barbed-wire fences. He ordered them to stop working there and moved them to a new place because he was concerned that they were in danger of being hurt or killed by mines left over from the war.

On still another occasion, a prisoner collected his group's food from the kitchen and fell down on his way back, dropping the food on the ground. When the Camp Political Officer saw this he helped the man up, brought him back to the kitchen, and made sure he received additional food for his

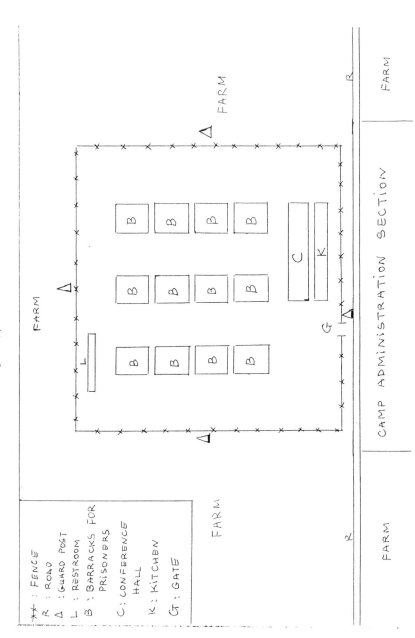

CAMP 8

CAMP ADMINISTRATION SECTION

FARM

FARM

FARM

FARM

x : FENCE
R : ROAD
△ : GUARD POST
L : RESTROOM
B : BARRACKS FOR
     PRISONERS
C : CONFERENCE
     HALL
K : KITCHEN
G : GATE

group.

The Camp Political Officer also inspected all the food delivered to Camp 8. If the fresh fish or vegetables were not good, he ordered the spoiled food to be returned. Every time the prisoners were served rice or fish, the Camp Political Officer made sure they weighed it themselves so they always received their full ration.

When the Camp Political Officer spoke to a prisoner, he was humble and courteous. If a prisoner reported a problem to him, he helped him to the best of his ability.

I heard many of the reeducation prisoners in Camp 8 say they liked the cadre, and out of all the cadre, they liked and respected the Camp Political Officer most.

On my first day in Camp 8, the Camp Political Officer told us that if we wanted tobacco, we could give some money to the cadre and they would buy it for us. Many people were eager to smoke, so they were glad to hear this.

For our first meal, we were given much more food than we were used to receiving. The amount of dried fish was five times as much, and the rice and vegetables were more plentiful, too. After I had been in Camp 8 a few days, we began to get fresh fish. At each meal, everyone got two to three fresh fish. It was delicious, too.

We worked in the mornings and afternoons. We carried firewood and tore down buildings in vacated camps (the prisoners had already been moved back to the mainland). We piled up the discarded material, which would later be picked up by trucks and loaded onto boats headed for the mainland. We all worked steadily, but at a relaxed pace. The cadre did not force us to work any harder.

After the labor was done, we went back to camp. We mustered twice a day inside camp, once in the morning and once in the evening. When we went outside camp to work, we mustered before we left the gate and again just before we entered the gate. We also mustered when we arrived at the work area and when we left. Along the way soldiers guarded us, but they did not force us to walk in columns.

About two weeks before my company left Camp 8, the Camp Political Officer had each group of 20 people make a tin barrel covered by a lid. These barrels would contain stool and urine bags, which we would use during our trip in the boat.

On June 26, I and all the other reeducation prisoners in Camp 8 carried our luggage four and a half miles to a large boat called a 503. Plywood and other pieces of wood were put on the floor of the bow for us to sit on. We were on the boat for two days, and it was a clean place compared to the 501 I was on when we left the mainland six months earlier.

After two days and nights, we arrived at a dock called New Port, inside the city limits of Saigon. At 10:00 PM, we got off the boat and onto Molotova vehicles. The convoy took us to Long Giao Reeducation Center in Long Khanh Province. Along the way I reflected on the last two months and realized that no one had tried to escape when we were at Camp 8.

Eight

JUNE 29, 1976 to SEPTEMBER 30, 1976

At two in the morning on June 29, the convoy arrived at Camp 13 in the Long Giao Reeducation Center. It was completely surrounded by barbed wire, as were all the other camps inside the Center. Upon our arrival, one of the cadre escorted us from the camp gate to our new quarters.

We mustered at 8:00 AM and a cadre assigned each of us to a new group and company. I was in Company 1, consisting of 12 groups of 10 reeducation prisoners each. My new camp held a total of four companies. Companies 1 and 2 each had 120 prisoners. Companies 3 and 4 had 200 prisoners each.

After the cadre divided us into our new groups, he announced the camp rules. Out of the long list, I only remembered a few. He said we had come to this camp to study the Communist Reeducation Program. Part of this program would be to farm the small patches of dirt which lay between the camps. We would not be allowed outside the barbed-wire fence unless the soldier guarding the gate gave us permission first. Camp 13 had only one gate and one guard post, and there was one soldier guarding the gate at all times.

The cadre also told us that if we obeyed the camp rules and worked hard, we would be considered progressive prisoners and would be released. He then ordered us to return to our barracks and prepare our sleeping mats.

As I walked back to my quarters, it dawned on me that we had been brought to an old military base that had previously belonged to the South Vietnamese Army.

On my second day in Camp 13 our labor program began. The kitchen did not supply us any breakfast, so I went to work hungry. At 7:30, my company mustered just inside the gate. One of the cadre counted us, then two of the soldiers led us outside to the Camp Administration Section. There we

64

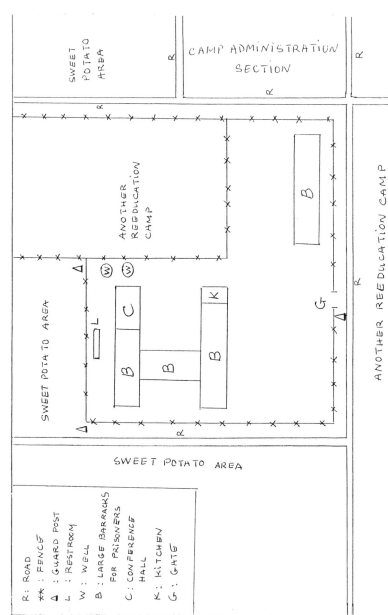

CAMP 13

SWEET POTATO AREA

CAMP ADMINISTRATION SECTION

ANOTHER REEDUCATION CAMP

SWEET POTATO AREA

ANOTHER REEDUCATION CAMP

SWEET POTATO AREA

R : ROAD
×× : FENCE
△ : GUARD POST
L : RESTROOM
W : WELL
B : LARGE BARRACKS FOR PRISONERS
C : CONFERENCE HALL
K : KITCHEN
G : GATE

repaired and built houses that cadre and soldiers would soon occupy.

At 11:30 we stopped working and returned to our barracks for lunch and a nap. At two o'clock one of the cadre came to my company and counted us again. Then two soldiers led us back to the work area.

At 5:30 we stopped working and returned to our barracks for dinner. At 7:00 my company mustered out front and a cadre counted us once more. At 9:00 the cadre turned out our lights and we went to sleep.

Two days later two soldiers led my company to an area inside the fenced Reeducation Center, but outside our camp fence. We weeded grass, dug furrows, and planted sweet potatoes. When we took a break, I overheard two prisoners talking. They said that the Communist government had recently announced their new Reeducation Policies, and that the reeducation prisoners would remain in the camps for three years.

This took me by surprise. I did not believe what I had heard. I thought to myself, "Surely we won't have to be imprisoned for three years. Did they hear wrong?"

Later, when I returned to camp, I discussed this rumor with my friend, Mr. Tien. He told me that his group had been working at the Administration Section where all the guards lived, and one of the soldiers there had said the same thing.

After talking to Mr. Tien, I returned to my quarters where I overheard several of my group members discussing the same rumor. Some of them said they believed it, others said they did not. There was an air of uneasiness throughout the camp that afternoon.

In the evening one of the cadre came to count my company, and addressed a short speech to us. "Over the last few days, the majority of you have worked hard. However, a few have been doing poorly. If these lazy people do not improve their work habits, they will not be released after the three-year reeducation period."

When I heard this my heart sank, as I realized the rumor had been true. I couldn't sleep that night. Depression overwhelmed me. If I worked hard or was lazy, it didn't matter—I would still be imprisoned for three years. I thought about how many times the cadre had told us to obey the camp rules and work hard so we could be nominated an outstanding man and be released. I had done well for a year now and still had not been released. The cadre had lied! Now I thought it would be a waste of energy to work hard. I would be imprisoned here for another two years, no matter what I did or did not do.

The next morning my company worked on a farm near camp. We weeded grass and planted sweet potatoes. Again we had not had breakfast, so I was hungry and sluggish. When the soldiers watched me, I worked with just enough enthusiasm to get by. When they were not looking, I sat down and rested. I saw most of the other prisoners doing likewise. About 20 prisoners worked continuously, and the remaining 100 of us rested whenever the soldiers weren't looking.

In the second week of July, my company again weeded grass near the center gate, but outside our camp fence. Two prisoners from my company, Mr. Thach and Mr. Phuong, slipped away when no one was looking.

On the morning of July 15, we attended a camp meeting. The Camp Political Officer reviewed our work over the last two weeks and said, "There are some of you who continue to oppose the Communists. These people do not want to study in the Reeducation Program. When they go to work, they are very lazy. Some have tried to escape. Some have already escaped, like Mr. Thach and Mr. Phuong. The cadre will deal with these stubborn people."

In the afternoon, I overheard a prisoner in my company saying that the cadre planned to implement a visiting policy soon. They were also going to allow us to receive supplies from our relatives. When I heard this, my mind raced. I thought about seeing my parents and brothers. Then I thought about the food, medicine, clothes, and money they could bring me. I was filled with excitement.

Later in the evening, I discussed this rumor with my group members. They, too, had heard it and were hoping to see their relatives. Some of them were married and had not seen their wives or children for over a year. They talked about how much they missed them and how worried they were about them. Even though I did not have dependents to worry about, I understood their anxiety.

The next day four new cadre came to our barracks and told us they were in charge of the company. Cadre Nhi, Cadre Dan, Cadre Trong, and Cadre Suc were all military officers. Cadre Nhi was a first lieutenant, while the other three cadre ranked as second lieutenants. These four cadre sat in our barracks and spoke to us in a humble and courteous manner.

That evening, when the cadre checked our numbers, one of them made an announcement. "The cadre held a meeting to discuss your situation. We realize that you have been far from your families for over a year, and that you must miss them very much. Therefore, the Camp Administration will allow you to write one letter a month to your families. When you finish your letter, you will have to show it to the cadre. We will check the letter, then we will mail it for you. We will pay for postage. If you write letters that encourage your relatives to follow Communist policies, then they will be mailed. However, if you write anything bad about the reeducation camps, then you will be written up for it and your letter will not be mailed. When your relatives mail letters back to you, we will check them, as well. Any letters that do not encourage you to obey us or to work hard in the camps will be confiscated and you will not be allowed to read them."

I was glad when I heard this. I immediately went to my area, brought out a pen and paper, and began writing a letter to my family. When I went to bed that night, I thought about the letter I had written. I hoped they would receive it by next week. I was eager to let them know where I was now, since they had not heard from me in over six months. I thought they might be worried about me, and I wanted to know how they were doing as well.

A day later I overheard some prisoners from my company saying, "The Communists have begun a visiting policy in the reeducation centers in Bien Hoa Province, Tay Ninh Province, and Long Khanh Province. All the reeducation prisoners there have had their relatives visit." That evening, I and a few other prisoners from my company asked Cadre Nhi about this rumor. He said the cadre would allow our relatives to visit us in a few months and to bring us supplies then.

After Cadre Nhi left, I noticed many of the prisoners in my company sitting in small crews, excitedly discussing the visiting policy. No one talked about the three-year reeducation period anymore. I realized then that the cadre had used the visiting policy to make us forget about the reeducation period.

On the morning of July 18, my company mustered outside just as we did every morning before work. Today, however, we did not go to work. Instead, one of the cadre told us to collect all our luggage and report out front again so the cadre could check it.

One of the cadre confiscated a small knife from my luggage and the wood yoke I used to carry it with. I watched the cadre inspect the other prisoners' luggage as well. They collected all the knives, hammers, iron rods, wood yokes, and sharp metal tools that they could find. We stayed outside as the cadre went inside and checked our barracks. They confiscated the same kinds of things in there, as well.

I thought to myself, "The cadre must be taking precautions in case we become angry about the three-year reeducation period and decide to oppose them in a demonstration or rebellion."

The following morning there were some changes. There were no longer two soldiers guarding my company, but five. We had to walk out the camp gate in four columns, with the armed soldiers on either side of us. The soldiers watched us as we worked. I thought to myself, "There is no way to escape while they watch us so closely."

We stopped working at noon and headed back. As we approached camp, I noticed another change. Instead of one guard post and one barbed-wire fence surrounding Camp 13, there were now two additional barbed-wire fences and two more guard posts (built above ground level). When I saw them, I realized that there would definitely be no way to escape.

We were given breakfast the next day. Because I had eaten, I had a different attitude when I got to the work area. I no longer felt hungry or sluggish, and I had energy to work.

After about 15 minutes, I observed an angry soldier approach Mr. Long, a prisoner in my company. The soldier yelled at Mr. Long and accused him of being lazy. The soldiers yelled at other prisoners before we took our morning break.

We stopped working at noon. When we reached our camp, I talked to a prisoner in Company 3. He told me that four prisoners from his company had been beaten that morning. I visited Mr. Tien, who was also in Company 3 and asked him about this. He said the soldiers who guarded his company were watching them more carefully. They yelled at or beat anyone who did not work as hard as the others. Mr. Tien verified that four prisoners in his company had been beaten and several others had been harshly reprimanded.

There were so many soldiers in our camp that my friends and I made up names for the cruel soldiers whose names we did not know. We picked names which described obvious attributes such as: Mr. Red Face Soldier, Mr. Black Face Soldier, Mr. Fat Soldier, and Mr. Big Eyes Soldier.

In the morning, the cadre ordered us to bring our luggage out in front of our barracks for them to check. Mr. Lanh took too long, so Mr. Red Face Soldier stopped him and slapped his face several times. Then he shouted at Mr. Lanh and slapped him again.

While Mr. Lanh was being beaten, the Camp Commander, the Camp Political Officer, and all the other cadre watched. Some of them looked at Mr. Lanh for a few seconds, then they disinterestedly looked away. As they turned their heads, I saw smiles on their faces, but they did not say anything. Mr. Red Face Soldier continued to beat Mr. Lanh. That afternoon, our company cadre came to our barracks to console us.

Cadre Nhi explained, "Please try to understand our position. It is uncomfortable for us to see these cruel soldiers beating you. They are stupid men! They are easily angered and often make trouble. We have protested their stupid actions many times at the cadre meetings. They are stubborn and do not try to change. As for Mr. Lanh, we were very uncomfortable but could not do anything. If you see these cruel soldiers when you go to work, try to work hard. Otherwise, they will make trouble for you."

Our cadre sympathized with the prisoners, but had done nothing to stop the cruel soldiers from beating any of us. I thought about the prisoners who were beaten or yelled at and about Cadre Nhi's advice. I realized the soldiers could beat us as much as they wanted. The cadres would console us later, but the lazy prisoners would still be beaten. I decided that whenever I saw these cruel soldiers I would try my best to work hard.

We ate breakfast again the next day before we went to work, so I wasn't hungry. I feared punishment from the soldiers, so I worked hard. The other prisoners worked hard as well. By the end of the day, none of us had been beaten or yelled at.

At the end of July, the Camp Political Officer reviewed our previous month's work at a camp meeting. "In the first and second week of July, a few prisoners were stubborn and opposed Communist policies. They did not obey the camp rules. They were lazy and did not want to work. Some of them escaped. However, these people have corrected their bad habits and now work well. They obey the camp rules. No one has escaped during the third and fourth weeks of July."

Later I realized it was the cadre who had spread the first rumor, that we would be imprisoned for three years. They were testing us, to see how we would react before they officially announced it. Then, when people became lazy or escaped, the cadre increased security and spread another rumor to make us forget the first issue. This worked, and the cadre succeeded in getting us to work hard and in keeping anyone else from escaping.

One morning in early August, my company stood in four lines at the camp gate. One cadre and five soldiers armed with AK-47s guarded each side of the formation. They led us past the reeducation center gate and onto a road, towards one of the civilian zones. Along the way I saw many civilian trucks and buses. The passengers looked surprised to see us.

We walked about a mile and stopped at Cam Duong Village, where the cadre bought some firewood. We formed one line and each of us picked up a piece. We then re-formed into two lines and the cadre counted us. When he finished, we carried the firewood back to camp.

The next day, the same cadre and soldiers led us to a nearby rubber plantation where we cut thatch. When we finished, each of us yoked two bundles of thatch and carried it back to camp. The cadre used it to build cottages for themselves.

During August and September, we sometimes worked inside the Reeducation Center fence. Sometimes we worked outside the fence, in civilian zones. I thought the cadre were probably confident that they could guard us effectively now, and this was why they let us into the civilian zones to work.

At the end of September, during our camp meeting, the Camp Political Officer reviewed our previous three months' work. All the cottages for the cadre were finished and many sweet potatoes had been planted. He continued: "....at the end of July 1976, we realized that all of you were progressive. None of you escaped, and you all worked hard. Therefore, in August and September, we pushed you into the second step of the reeducation plan. We took you to work in civilian zones. The result was that no one escaped, and you all worked well. We applaud you for this...."

Nine

OCTOBER 1976 through FEBRUARY 1977

At the beginning of October, we studied two lessons in the conference hall. The Camp Political Officer spent one hour on our first lesson, "Thirteen Points of the Reeducation Policies". He explained how the Communists used the 13 points to deal with employees for the former South Vietnamese Government.

First, all reeducation prisoners were categorized into several groups. The first group was policemen. The second group was noncommissioned military officers and soldiers. The third group was commissioned military officers.

The fourth group consisted of civilians contracted to work in government facilities such as public schools, factories, hospitals, or offices. The fifth group was composed of public servants such as congressmen, district administrators, province administrators, province department heads, and village leaders. The sixth group was made up of civilians who were affiliated with political parties from the Old Regime.

The seventh group consisted of Communist spies who had worked for the Old Government and had been released in December 1975 (as I mentioned in Chapter 3), and the eighth group of Communists who, during the war, had surrendered to the Old Government and were now living as civilians again. Unfortunately, I have forgotten the other groups he mentioned.

The Camp Political Officer gave us the specific periods in which each group was required to participate in the reeducation program. I paid attention only to the length of time my group, the military officers, had to stay. As I listened to the Camp Political Officer tell us we would be imprisoned for three years, I took this as old news because I had heard it three months earlier.

The Camp Political Officer then spent another hour

explaining our second lesson, "Visiting Policies". We were allowed to see our relatives for one hour and receive supplies from them. Permissible items were clothes, medicine, dried food, cooked food, fresh vegetables, and fresh fruits. We were not allowed to receive any fresh fish, fresh meat, live chickens, or live ducks.

Prisoners who were allowed visitors would be issued "visiting permits" which they could mail to their families. A maximum of three visitors were allowed per visiting permit.

When the Camp Political Officer finished the second lesson, he told us we did not have to go back to work. Instead, we returned to our quarters and wrote letters to our families. I thought about how happy I would be to see my parents and brothers. I also thought about how having more food and supplies would relieve the shortages I was experiencing now. I thought about everything I wanted them to bring and listed it all in my letter.

We finished our letters that afternoon, and the cadre collected them that evening. They screened our letters and mailed the ones they approved of. Afterwards, I saw several large groups of reeducation prisoners sitting on the floor, talking about the visiting policies. One of my friends, Mr. Hao, said to me, "I miss my wife and children. I have not seen them for over a year. I am worried about them, and do not know how they are surviving. I hope I will see them soon."

No one discussed the three-year reeducation period anymore. I came to the conclusion that the cadre had used the visiting policies to distract us from dwelling on the length of our sentence.

The following day when my company was led outside the gate, I saw that the number of guards had changed. Before, when we went to work, there were five soldiers and a cadre. They stood nearby and watched us closely. Today there were only two soldiers and a cadre. While we worked, they sat in the shade of a large tree and talked. We were no longer forced to work hard, and we were allowed to rest when we got tired. They were very courteous to us. The soldiers who had beaten or yelled at us before were gone.

At noon, when we returned to camp, I saw several reeducation prisoners standing in front of a blackboard near the kitchen door. The blackboard read: "From now on, the standard food ration of rice will increase from 500 grams to 600 grams. The trucks will deliver vegetables, soy sauce, fish sauce, dried fish, and fresh fish to our camp daily."

After that, we had rice and dried fish for breakfast everyday. For lunch and dinner we had fresh or dried fish with rice and vegetable soup. The amount of food we received was much greater now and I was no longer hungry.

A little later, we received 2.4 piastres of extra supplies, and the amount of these items increased as well. Each of us received 20 sugar cubes, two pounds of soap and one pack of 20 cigarettes. Also, four prisoners shared one pound of tobacco. The cadre offered to buy other items for us, such as sugar or beans. They said we would continue to get these supplies on the first of each month.

Several days later, my company held a meeting. Cadre Nhi announced that the cadre had begun choosing prisoners who had obeyed the camp rules and had worked hard enough to receive the "Outstanding Man" award and visiting permit. He then read the names of 15 men from my company. He said the cadre noticed that these men had done well over the last three months. He handed each of them a visiting permit.

He added that the visiting houses were next to the Reeducation Center gate, and the Outstanding Men's relatives would be allowed to visit in about a week. At the end of our meeting, the cadre told us that this was just the first group of men to be allowed visitors. There would be many more opportunities for the rest of us, and eventually we would all receive visiting passes. All the prisoners who received visiting permits wrote letters to their families and enclosed the permit. The cadre read and mailed their letters.

That night my friends and I discussed the day's events.

We agreed that if we wanted to see our relatives soon, we had to work hard and obey the camp rules. This was necessary to get the Outstanding Man award. I wanted to see my family, so I set my mind to earning this award.

The next day I tried to impress our cadre by working hard in the fields. I hoped he would recommend me for the Outstanding Man award. I looked around at the other members of my company. Even though the cadre and soldiers sat in the shade and did not force us to work, no one stood idle or rested. Everyone worked hard.

It was now two weeks since the cadre increased our food and supplies, and transferred the cruel soldiers. They were treating us much better now, and no one was beaten. I felt more comfortable about my situation, so I did not try to escape, and I worked on earning a visiting permit. None of my friends talked about being hungry or about the prisoners who had been beaten. I thought that everyone must be so excited about the visiting permit that they had forgotten about all the bad things.

On October 14, everyone attended a meeting in the conference hall. The Camp Political Officer said: "The cadre have been preparing for your visitors over the last two weeks. We built visiting houses at the Reeducation Center gate, and that is where you will meet your relatives, beginning tomorrow. We will let you know when they arrive. If you want to give them anything like clothes or shoes, bring these items with you to the camp gate. There the cadre will check everything and escort you to the Reeducation Center gate. You can visit with your relatives for one hour. When you leave, carry the supplies your relatives gave you back to the camp gate. We will check them there, then you can take them back to your quarters."

The next day, we collected firewood. Whereas last week, two soldiers and a cadre guarded us, today the two soldiers guarded us, but they walked in front of instead of beside us. Also, we walked in one line instead of four, while the unarmed cadre walked behind us. The soldiers led us about two miles to the edge of a rubber plantation. The cadre told us to enter the plantation, look for a piece of firewood, and return in two hours. We were allowed to roam while the cadre and the soldiers sat at the edge of the plantation and waited for us to return.

I walked about half a mile looking for firewood. I found a piece, then rested at the foot of a rubber tree. When I saw my company returning, I followed them. The cadre counted us when we had all returned. We formed one line, then carried our firewood back to camp. The cadre and the soldiers walked at the end of the line.

At noon, a few reeducation prisoners had relatives visiting. The men followed one of the cadre to the Reeducation Center gate where their families waited. They returned to camp with two heavy bags of supplies yoked over their shoulders. The bags were filled with noodles, cooked meats, fruit, sugar, peanuts, etc. I thought, "How much delicious food they have! How happy they are! If I am visited, I will have such food too!"

The cadre continued to issue visiting permits twice a month. Each time, about 15 percent of my company were issued permits. When a prisoner was visited, he invited his friends and group members to join him for a meal. Everyone brought their own rice, and he shared some of the food his family gave him. While they ate, he talked to us about his family's situation.

By mid-November, several people in my company had been visited and we had plenty of food. Before the visits started, each group of six people were given one container of food from the kitchen, which we divided into individual portions. Now we no longer divided our food and we put the container for our group in a central place. Each man helped himself. Many who could not finish their food would announce: "Whoever wants more, please come and help yourself." A small barrel had been placed outside the kitchen door. Those who did not finish their food put it in the barrel and it was fed to the pigs. By afternoon, the barrel was full. I thought about how much food was left over and realized that everyone in my camp must be getting enough to eat now.

At night, the cadre turned on the conference hall lights. Several prisoners sat in there playing chess or dominos, or just watching others play. Some prisoners read newspapers that the cadre had put on the tables.

I finally received a visiting permit. I anxiously wrote to my parents and sent the permit with it. I asked my friends who had already been visited what had happened on their visits.

Mr. Thang told me his mother had looked at him and cried out, "How thin you are now!" She sat down and wept for the whole hour. They did not say much to each other, and then their time was up. When his mother left, he regretted not asking her any questions. There were many things he wanted to know which were not suitable for him to ask about in a letter, but her tears caused him to forget to ask.

Another friend, Mr. Hien, told me about his wife and children. The children were a little taller, but thin. He was so overcome by emotion when he saw them that tears welled up in his eyes and he forgot all that he had wanted to ask. When his family left he, too, regretted not asking any questions.

Mr. Hao told me that he worried about forgetting to ask all the important questions. Therefore, he wrote them on a piece of paper and asked them first. Then his wife asked him some questions about living in the camp. This way he found out everything about his family, but he still felt that one hour was much too short.

I thought about my friends' experiences, and decided to follow Mr. Hao's plan. I made a list of questions in my mind, intending to ask my family these questions first.

My mother and two younger brothers visited me in the middle of January. I was very glad to see them. I explained that I had only one hour, so we would have to speak quickly. I asked them all the things I wanted to know. When I finished, my mother asked me what it was like living in the reeducation camps. I considered the little time we had left to talk, and I quickly summed up my present situation. "The cadre give us 600 grams of rice and three meals of a little dried fish and vegetable soup each day. They also supply us with soap, sugar, tobacco, cigarettes, and other stuff each month. We hoe the ground, grow sweet potatoes, cut thatch, and collect firewood."

My mother and brothers left with the impression that conditions in the reeducation camps were not too bad. They felt comfortable about my being here. As I lay under my mosquito net that night, I couldn't sleep. I kept thinking about my family and how much I missed them.

After my visit, I no longer worked hard. I didn't consider it necessary, since I knew I would not be getting another permit for a while.

I felt very lazy. I often stood leaning against my hoe, resting. I observed about half the people in my company doing the same thing, and about half of them actually working.

In the last week of February, four reeducation prisoners from Company 3 escaped while collecting firewood in the rubber plantation. One of the escaped prisoners returned to camp the next day. The other three were arrested by village bush fighters who lived nearby. All four were punished. The cadre placed them in four dark rooms, called discipline cells. They were still in the discipline cells when I left this camp, almost a month later.

At the end of February, the Camp Political Officer reviewed our previous five months. "The cadre recognize that in October, when we announced the visiting policy, you were all encouraged about it. Everyone worked hard and obeyed the camp rules. Even when you were taken to civilian zones and the cadre allowed you to work unguarded in the rubber plantations, no one escaped. Nevertheless, after your relatives visited, some of you became lazy or planned to escape. Four have already tried. The cadre will deal with these stubborn prisoners."

Ten

MARCH 1, 1977 to MARCH 24, 1977

The next morning, when my company was led outside the camp gate to work, five soldiers and a cadre guarded us. Two of the five soldiers, Mr. Black Face Soldier and Mr. Big Eyes Soldier, were known to be cruel. As we passed other companies, I noticed that the number of guards watching them had also increased. All the cruel soldiers who had disappeared five months ago had now reappeared.

My company worked on the farm today. The soldiers watched us closely. We had been working for about 10 minutes when Mr. Black Face Soldier yelled at a prisoner in my company, Mr. Hoa. The soldier accused him of not working as hard as the rest of us, because he rested for a few minutes. The cruel soldiers then yelled at other prisoners.

I thought to myself: "If I am lazy, I will be yelled at or beaten. Therefore, I must work hard." I quickly glanced at the other members of my company. Everyone was working hard. No one was resting.

The following day, my company walked out the Re-education Center gate in four lines and headed for the civilian zones. Again, one cadre and five soldiers walked on either side of our procession, their rifles pointed toward us. At first I thought the cadre would lead us to the rubber plantation to look for firewood. Instead, we were led to Cam Duong where the cadre bought firewood from the villagers. We carried the wood back to camp in two lines, still carefully guarded.

A week later we were studying in the conference hall. Our topic was "The Labor Production" and consisted of two points. The first point was that we had to participate in a program called "The Production Battle." The second point was that we would receive several benefits from working in this program. Every day each person would get 700 grams of rice.

We would also receive .48 piastres to purchase additional food. Whenever we became sick, we would be treated at a camp or civilian hospital. Last, men who received the "Outstanding Man" award most frequently throughout the year would be released the soonest.

When we finished this lesson, I thought about how hungry I had been over the last 20 months, how hunger pangs had gnawed at my stomach as I worked. By participating in The Labor Production I would receive 700 grams of rice each day and my stomach would be full. I would not have to worry about being hungry anymore. I would be better off in The Labor Production.

When I returned to my quarters, I noticed my group members were discussing the lesson. Everyone agreed that if we went to the labor camps and participated in The Labor Production we would no longer be hungry.

Seven days later, I saw something strange as I walked out the camp gate. All the cadre and soldiers were arranged in parade. Normally, there would be a cadre and five soldiers guarding a company of prisoners. Today, the Camp Political Officer, the Camp Commander, all of the cadre, and all of the soldiers stood outside the gate. Chinese dragon dancers, a dragon head, and a drummer stood at the head of the parade. The Communists' national flag and banner came next in line. The banner read "BE EXCITED ABOUT THE LABOR MOVEMENT TAKING ON THE PRODUCTION BATTLE."

We stood in four lines at the end of the parade. Company 1 was first, then Company 2, then Company 3. We were ordered to put our hoes on our left shoulders and let our right hands swing free. The cadre and soldiers stood in a line on our left side.

When everyone was in place, the departure ceremony began. At first, the drum played and the Chinese dragon crew danced. While they danced, they moved forward. The flag and banner followed the dragon. All the cadre and soldiers and reeducation prisoners followed the banner and flag. One prisoner had a strong voice, and he walked outside the lines, raised his right fist and shouted, "Be excited about the labor movement taking on the production battle!"

We marched about four hundred yards, with everyone raising their right fist and shouting, "We are excited! Excited! Excited!"

We stopped at the farm. All the prisoners stood in one line, side by side, with two yards between us. In the middle of the farm was a command post. The flag and banner, the dragon head, drum, and costumes were placed there. A drum roll sounded. The Camp Political Officer made an announcement over the loudspeaker.

"Today, you will all participate in a hoeing contest. The person from each company who hoes the longest furrow will be named the 'Outstanding Man' and will be called `The Golden Hoe.' The best group in each company will be called 'The Golden Hoe Group.'"

A drum roll sounded again. All the reeducation prisoners held their hoes in a ready position. As soon as the drum roll stopped, we began hoeing. We all hoed as fast as we could. We hoed for forty-five minutes, then a drum roll sounded again. We took a break for fifteen minutes. While we rested, the cadre measured the length of each furrow.

The Camp Political Officer announced The Golden Hoes for the first hour. Everyone applauded them. The drum roll sounded again and when it stopped, we began the second hour.

I was excited by the competition and hoed quickly. The cadre continued this method for several hours. At noon, just before we left the farm, the Camp Political Officer announced The Golden Hoes for the last hour and The Golden Hoe Groups for the morning. We all applauded them.

We were in this program for three days. On the fourth day, we went to the conference hall. The Camp Political Officer reviewed the contest results and applauded the Outstanding Men and the Outstanding Groups. He said, "From now on, you will participate in The Labor Production. Many of you will leave here and will move to a new camp for The Production Battle."

I believed that we would move to a new camp, so I prepared my things. I cleaned my mosquito net, mat, and blanket. I dried them on ropes or on the barbed wire fences surrounding our camp. All the ropes and barbed wire fences were full of mosquito nets, mats, blankets, and kit bags. Many people used their sleeping time to repair their kit bags.

Early in the morning, we gathered in the conference hall. The Camp Political Officer announced that we would not go to work today, because many of us would be leaving here and moving to a new camp for The Labor Production. The cadre would kill a large pig to serve at the good-bye party.

When we heard this, we returned to our quarters and prepared our luggage. Cadre Nhi visited us in our quarters as we worked. We all sat down near him, smoked, and talked. While we were talking, he revealed that the Camp Commander and Camp Political Officer had gone to the new camp last week to prepare it for us. They said the new camp had many volunteer youths and military personnel who had used bulldozers and tractor plows to clear the forest. They had cleared over 2,500 acres of land, and they were still there, farming.

They had also built several houses and installed electric lighting in them. They had dug wells and prepared our beds and mats, too. We would work with the volunteers and military personnel for several months, then we would be released.

Cadre Nhi also revealed that our new camp would be near the road and our relatives would be allowed to visit us for as long as they wanted. We would be allowed to see our wives and children in the visiting house at any time of the day or night. In addition to this, we would be free to go to the market to buy anything we wanted. He told us that those who had their names on the departure list today were the lucky ones. He also said that anyone who left this camp after us would not be in as good a place as where we were going.

As soon as Cadre Nhi finished, someone asked, "Is our new place surrounded by barbed wire fences?"

The cadre answered, "No, it is not, because all the people who are leaving are progressive people. They were considered by the cadre to be good enough to be in the testing period of The Labor Production. If anyone does well, he will be released. If anyone does not do well, he will be imprisoned again."

Before Cadre Nhi left our quarters, he mentioned it would be best to keep what he had said a secret. If the other cadre knew he had revealed these things, he would be reported.

After we heard this news, we spread it throughout the camp. I thought that the new camp would be better than this one. And I hoped I would have my name on the departure list.

At lunch that same day, we ate some delicious pork. At 3:30, they announced the names of the people leaving. My name was on the list, and I returned to my quarters to collect my luggage. All of my friends came to congratulate me and say good-bye. They thought that whoever left our camp today was very lucky.

At 4:00, all who were leaving gathered together and were assigned to new groups consisting of 10 people each. The cadre led us to a parking lot. They wished us success at the new camp and hoped we would be released soon. Then they told us good-bye.

As we approached the parking lot, I saw about 25 Molotovas. This time, however, there were no cloth roofs over them.

Some people in my group said, "Probably because we are progressive, it is not necessary to cover us."

We were encouraged by the cadre's trust. Two soldiers guarded each vehicle as we boarded.

The convoy began to move at about 7:00. Six hours after we started, we came to the stadium of Phuoc Long City and parked. The soldiers told us to get out of the vehicles and sleep here. We put mats on the grass, lay down, pulled our blankets over ourselves, and went to sleep. While everyone was asleep, I woke up and looked for a place to urinate. I realized that all of the soldiers and drivers were asleep. No one was guarding us. I thought, "In a few hours we will be in a new camp." I believed what Cadre Nhi had told us about it. I imagined a beautiful scene of what it would look like, and I felt comfortable about going there. I did not think about escaping, and I went back to sleep.

In the morning, the soldiers woke us and we got back on the vehicles. Our convoy moved on. Six hundred sixty reeducation prisoners were moved from Long Giao Reeducation Center to the new camp, and no one escaped.

Eleven

MARCH 24, 1977 to APRIL 30, 1977

At mid-morning, the convoy pulled off the road to the right. We traveled on a narrow path about five yards wide that cut through the forest. After we went about 400 yards, the drivers parked the trucks.

One of the soldiers said, "Here is the place you've been waiting for."

We were in the middle of the jungle.

"Surely," I thought, "this could not be our new camp. Where are the houses, and the electricity? Where are the soldiers and the volunteers who are supposed to be preparing the camp for us and working with us? Where are the fields?"

Three cadre wearing military clothes mustered us. Their uniforms did not have any rank on the collars, but one of them introduced himself.

"I am Lieutenant Thau. I was stationed in this forest thirteen years ago, and now I am the Camp Political Officer here."

He introduced the other two cadre, "This is Lieutenant Uyen. He will be your Camp Commander. This is Aspirant Luan. He will be your Supply Cadre."

Lieutenant Thau informed us that we were in Camp D1, which belonged to Reeducation Regiment 16. The mail box number for our camp was 3136. Then he announced the camp rules. "You are here to learn about The Labor Production and to participate in The Production Battle. Even though there is no fence surrounding this camp, you are not allowed to go more than one hundred yards away from your quarters. You will be responsible for yourselves while you are in camp and when you go to work. The cadre and soldiers will only supervise your work. The cadre will choose a few reeducation prisoners from among you who will be assigned jobs as Block

Leaders, Deputy Block Leaders, Group Leaders, and Deputy Group Leaders.

"Every afternoon, all the Block Leaders will attend a meeting in the Camp Administration Section. These men will report what work has been accomplished for the day, then they will receive new orders to be given to the Group Leaders. Group Leaders will be responsible for announcing to their groups the work orders for the next day. The cadre will not count your numbers each day. Your Block Leaders and Group Leaders will be responsible for keeping track of your numbers, both in camp and while you work.

"You will be given a hoe and a bush knife to keep, maintain, and use at work. Those who obey the camp rules and work hard will soon be released.

"This camp will clear 250 acres of forest over the next month. There are no barracks for you and no houses for the cadre and soldiers. You will build them. You will build additional houses for our Camp Administration Section. This work will be finished by the end of April."

After the announcement, the cadres assigned us to new groups. Camp D1 held three blocks, with four groups to a block. Each group was made up of 55 reeducation prisoners. The cadre then picked Block Leaders, Deputy Block Leaders, Group Leaders, and Deputy Group Leaders. Finally, the cadre took us to a spot in the forest and told us this was our new camp.

They handed each of us a hoe and a long bush knife and instructed us to begin clearing out a place for our living quarters. I was still numb from the shock of realizing that the cadre from our previous camp had lied to us. I grabbed my tools and began working without thought.

I used my knife to cut down small trees. I lashed my hammock to larger trees nearby. Some people did not bring a hammock, so they made their bed out of small trees. I cut branches to make a roof over my bed and to provide shade from the afternoon sun.

I spent half an hour preparing my living area, then I walked around camp. A well stood in the middle of a valley that divided the camp into two zones. One zone was for reeducation prisoners. The other zone was for the cadre. In the cadre's zone was an old hut left behind by a group of minority natives living in South Vietnam near Cambodia, the Montagnards. The Montagnards often lived in forests, highlands, and mountains. They built temporary housing because they frequently moved from place to place.

At 1:00 PM, the cadre gave each group some rice and dried fish. We divided it equally, and we cooked our own food. I was surprised when we each received only 500 grams of uncooked rice and a small portion of dried fish. I had expected 700 grams of rice and more fish.

Some of my group members complained to Supply Cadre Luan about the rice. He told them that he was given orders to supply only 500 grams of rice, but he would talk to his supervisors about it. He promised to inform the prisoners of their answer as soon as possible. Still tired from our journey here, we all took a nap after lunch.

At 7:00 PM, the Block Leaders finished their meeting in the Camp Administration Section. They returned to our living zone and gave the Group Leaders orders for the next day's work. My Group Leader announced that we would clear forestland tomorrow. Some of the reeducation prisoners who knew about carpentry were put on a special crew. They were responsible for building our barracks and the houses for the Camp Administration Section. We slept in the forest that night. We burned dry wood and used it for light.

I was awakened early the next morning by shouting all around us. I was startled at first, then I realized it was only the birds and monkeys. At 7:30, my Group Leader called us to follow him and start work. As we passed through the Camp Administration area, I saw three cadre and six soldiers sitting on the ground in front of the cottage, eating breakfast. I thought, "These are not very many guards for six hundred and sixty prisoners."

Our Group Leader continued to lead us past the Camp Administration Area into a heavily forested area. I still expected to see bulldozers and tractor plows and youth volunteers. But when we reached the work area, all I saw were trees—no equipment, no volunteers.

I began to wonder why the cadre had lied to us. I knew I couldn't say anything. If I tried to rebel, I would surely be shot. I feared the cadre's power over us.

We stood in one line, six feet between us. We used knives and axes to clear the trees. We left them on the ground to dry so they could be burned at the end of the month. When we felt well, we worked. When we were tired, we took a break.

About a week later, the cadre chose two prisoners from each block to be cooks. We were no longer allowed to cook for ourselves. Now all our food was prepared in a designated area. Every day we went to work without breakfast, and hunger gnawed at my stomach. At noon we ate lunch and my hunger diminished a little.

I began to dwell on how the cadre from Camp 13 had lied. As my hunger increased, I thought about it more. In the evening, after dinner, I discussed it with my friends. They agreed that we had been tricked. My friend, Mr. Thang, commented, "It is stupid. The more we believed the cadre, the more we were tricked by them. They always lie and break their promises."

I became depressed about the Communist policies, and I lost my enthusiasm for our work.

In the morning, we went to work hungry again. When we reached the work area, we stood in one line. We used axes and bush knives to clear the forest.

I worked for half an hour, then I felt tired and hungry. I was not enthusiastic about this work, so I looked for a way out of working today. I quietly slipped into the forest, away from the rest of my group, and hid there.

About an hour later around 20 of my group joined me. We all hid in the forest and rested. By the third hour, there were 40 of us. By the fourth hour, there were only five prisoners still working.

Our Group Leader stayed in the field. He did not say anything, and he did not come looking for us. Sometimes he would work, and sometimes he would rest in the field.

At noon we returned to camp. We took a two-hour break, and I thought about how we had worked today. I thought, "Why should I work hard when the cadre just lie to us. None of my group members will turn me in, so the cadre will not know if I work hard or not."

At 2:00 o'clock, we went back to work. I worked with the rest of my group for half an hour. Around 2:30, I left my group and hid in the forest. I rested there for the remainder of our labor period and decided I would do so every day from now on.

The next day, the cadre requested 30 prisoners to follow one of the soldiers into a Montagnard hamlet and bring back cassava trees. I was curious about the Montagnards, so I volunteered and my Group Leader agreed to let me go. I grabbed my kit bag and reported to the Camp Administration Section.

One of the soldiers counted us, then walked ahead and told us to follow. We walked for about two miles.

When we reached the hamlet, I saw about 20 houses, all made of bamboo or thatch. Rice paddies surrounded each house, and each house sat near its own cassava tree garden. Also around each house were several banana trees and pawpaw trees and a few red pepper plants. These plants and fruit trees were quick-growing for short-term gardening. There were no mango trees or grapefruit trees or jack fruit trees.

I asked the soldier, "Do you know why the Montagnards don't build concrete houses or plant more permanent fruit trees?"

The soldier answered, "The Montagnards clear the

forest and plant rice for three years. After that, their farmland becomes unfertile, so they clear another area and move their families to a new location. Because they do not live in one location for very long, they do not build houses or plant fruit trees that require a long time to build or to grow."

"Do the Montagnards like to eat cassava?"

"No. They like rice more than cassava."

"Why, then," I asked, "does every family have a cassava tree garden near their house?"

"The Montagnards live in the jungle. Their rice paddies are easily destroyed by wild animals or insects. If this happens, they can still survive by eating cassava."

The soldier led us to a cottage inside the hamlet. He entered the cottage and asked the Montagnard for some cassava trees. He walked back out and told each of us to enter the garden and make a cassava tree bundle. After we finished, we had two hours to walk around the hamlet and buy a few things from the civilians.

I entered one of the cottages and saw a Montagnard family sitting on their beds, with their domestic animals (pigs, dogs, chickens) lying under the beds. I assumed the animals were allowed to live inside the cottage along with the family.

The walls and ceilings of their homes were blackened by smoke. In the middle of the dirt floor was a pile of burning firewood. During the day, they cooked their food over the fire. Since they did not have mosquito nets or blankets, they also burned firewood at night for heat, and used the smoke to keep mosquitos out.

I saw a man who looked like the husband and head of the family. He wore only a loincloth. A woman sat next to him, and I guessed she was his wife. Her chest was uncovered. She wore a piece of cloth wrapped around her waist, which hung down to her knees. Naked children sat near their parents. I was surprised by the openness of these people. They were almost naked, but they were not ashamed when they saw me enter their house.

I told them I was a reeducation prisoner, and that I came here today with a soldier and wanted to buy something from them. The husband said he would sell me some cassava. I told him I would buy one kit bag, so he led me to his garden. He uprooted several cassava trees, and put roots and all in my kit bag. He charged me one piastre.

I asked him, "Do you wish to sell anything else?"

"No," he answered.

Nevertheless, I wanted to be friendly to his family. I followed him back into his house and asked, "How many children do you have?"

He pointed towards his children and answered, "We have two boys. Here they are."

I looked at the smaller boy and asked, "How old is your younger son."

He told me he did not know, so I looked at the boy again. I estimated him to be about four years old. I asked, "How long has it been since your younger son was born?"

The man answered, "He was born on the day that some soldiers passed by my house."

I guessed the older boy to be about six. I asked the man's wife, "How long has it been since your oldest boy was born?"

She answered, "He was born on the day there was a battle taking place near the road."

I left that house and went into some others. All the Montagnards were dressed in the same fashion.

I walked through the hamlet, looking for someone to sell me a chicken. I met one family with many chickens and baby chicks inside their house. I asked them to sell me a chicken. They said they did not sell mature chickens, but only chicks. Each chick was as big as my fist and cost five piastres. I asked them how much they would sell a mature chicken for, if they were to sell one.

I showed them a rooster and asked, "How much does this rooster cost?"

They answered, "It costs five piastres."

"How much does this hen cost?"

They answered, "It costs five piastres."

I asked them, "A chick is smaller than a rooster or a hen. Why does it cost the same price as a rooster?"

They answered, "A chick is a chicken. A rooster is a chicken. A hen is a chicken. Each chicken costs five piastres, therefore a chick is the same price as a rooster. If you raised a chick for a few months, a chick will be as big as a rooster."

When I heard their reasoning I was amused and smiled. I did not buy the baby chick and left.

The soldier led a crew of 30 reeducation prisoners to a different hamlet each day. After a week, my friends and I knew the way to each hamlet. They were all from half a mile to three miles away from camp.

Sometimes I would work for half an hour in the morning, then invite a few friends to walk to a Montagnard hamlet with me. There, my friends would buy rice, chickens, and ducks. I did not have any money, but I went with them to relax for a few hours.

One evening in mid-April, I sat with several of my group members and discussed our food rations. Before we came here, we studied the Communist policies, which told us we would receive 700 grams of rice each day. We had waited three weeks and the cadre had not mentioned anything about why we received only 500 grams. I felt distrust towards all Communist cadre.

A week later I observed members of my group playing and singing songs from the Old Regime. No one sang the Communist Revolution songs anymore.

In the old camps, the cadre did not allow us to sing any Old Regime songs. We trusted them, so we followed their orders. Now, in this new camp, we had discerned their lies, and we did not care about their orders. During the fourth week of April, 10 prisoners escaped from our camp. Some prisoners from our Camp D1 and some from Camp D5 who were in Mr.

94

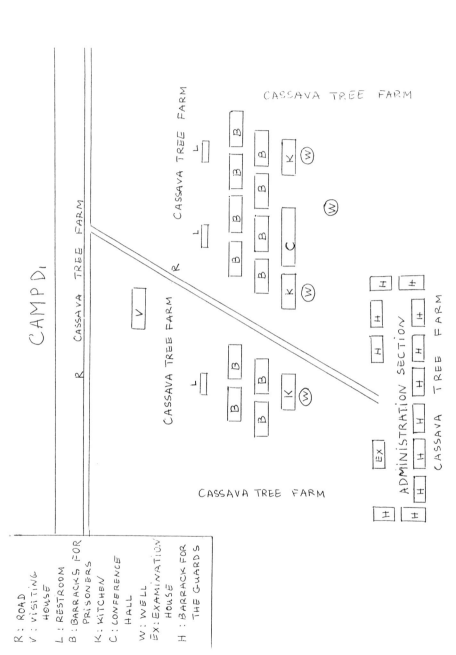

CAMP D₁

CASSAVA TREE FARM

ADMINISTRATION SECTION

R: ROAD
V: VISITING HOUSE
L: RESTROOM
B: BARRACKS FOR PRISONERS
K: KITCHEN
C: CONFERENCE HALL
W: WELL
Ex: EXAMINATION HOUSE
H: BARRACK FOR THE GUARDS

Bao's group had escaped together.

By the end of April we finished building the camp barracks and the Camp Administration Section. We had also accumulated a large pile of cassava trees. In May we would cut the cassava trees into four-inch pieces and bury them in the ground. They would grow into new cassava trees.

On the last day of the month, at a two-hour camp meeting, the Camp Political Officer reviewed our work for the month. As he spoke, my anger focused on him as though he was the one who had lied to us, and I did not pay much attention to what he was saying. I noticed that the other prisoners were talking privately to each other. It was noisy; no one cared about his message. Sometimes he stopped his speech and complained about the noise. Nevertheless, a few minutes later, the noise increased again.

Near the end of the meeting, he got our attention by saying, "Please, be polite and listen to me." He then concluded his speech and told us that we had done a great job clearing the forest and building the houses in our camp and the Camp Administration Section.

"Nevertheless, there are still some stubborn reeducation prisoners who have been lazy. While the other group members worked, they were absent and visited the Montagnard hamlets. There are some of you who continue to oppose the Communist government. These people intend to escape. Ten did escape last month. The cadre in this camp will deal with these stubborn prisoners."

Twelve

MAY through JULY 1977

The next day we did not go to work. We rested in our quarters and the cooks killed a large pig for our lunch in honor of Labor Day.

As I was resting, I saw six new soldiers arrive in camp. They carried kit bags and headed toward the Administration Section. The number of guards had just increased from nine to 15.

That afternoon at our camp meeting, the Political Officer announced, "Our camp will engage in a Production Battle over the next three months. You will tackle the work of seed sowing. Our plan is for you to finish by the end of July." He did not explain what "Production Battle" meant, but I could tell it had something to do with working. At the end of the meeting, he mentioned that we were not allowed to visit the Montagnard hamlets anymore. Then a truck carrying rice pulled up to our camp gate.

Ten reeducation prisoners were ordered to remove rice sacks from the truck and carry them into the storehouse. While they worked, one of them noticed that a sack had broken and some rice had spilled onto the truck bed. He picked up the loose rice and put it in his pocket. Four soldiers saw him. They brutally beat him as the other prisoners watched. Everyone talked about what had happened, and we all agreed to be more cautious in the future.

In the evening, three of the new soldiers assigned to our camp visited my barracks. They were very friendly and we all gathered around them and talked. They told us they had been civilians living in Saigon, and had been forced into the Communist Army a few months ago.

At 7:00 in the morning, a bell rang and woke us up. I was surprised at first, because it was the first time I had heard a bell ring in this camp. Then one of the cooks announced that we were to come to the kitchen to get our breakfast.

At 7:30, the bell rang again. Our Block and Group Leaders called us, and we followed them to the farms. When we got there, three soldiers were waiting. They had us muster, and then counted us. Then they told my block to plant cassava tree stalks today.

We stood side by side in one line and buried pieces of cassava in the ground with our hoes. The cassava would grow into trees in a week or two. The other two blocks sowed paddy seeds (rice still in its husk) in nearby farmland. The soldiers watched us and the Camp Commander and Camp Political Officer walked around the farms, inspecting us as we worked.

Because I had eaten breakfast, I was not hungry, so at first I held my hoe down and worked. But after 20 minutes, I became lazy and stopped working. I held my hoe by my side and rested. Five minutes later I saw Mr. Thin, one of the soldiers, walk toward me. He yelled, "Why are you being lazy! Why don't you work!"

I suddenly remembered the soldiers beating the prisoner last night. I was afraid they would beat me also, so I bowed my head and dug my hoe into the ground. I did not dare to be lazy again.

Two minutes later, I heard other prisoners from my block being yelled at. I looked around and saw that everyone was working hard.

At 10:00, we took a half-hour break. Then we mustered and the soldiers counted us. Then we began working again. At noon we stopped working and mustered again, and the soldiers counted us. Then we returned to camp.

We passed the Camp Administration Section. There I saw a prisoner I knew, Mr. Vinh, tied to a tree. His kit bag, filled with items he had bought from a Montagnard hamlet, sat next to him; a live chicken clucked beneath his feet. I overheard someone say that Mr. Vinh was being punished because he had returned to the Montagnard hamlet and bought food there. I also noticed some cadre supervising prisoners who were building a bamboo fence around the camp.

At 1:30, we headed toward the farms again. As we walked pass the Camp Administration Section, I saw that Mr. Vinh was still tied to the tree. When we reached the farms, three soldiers were waiting there. They counted us, then we went back to work.

At 4:00, we took a half-hour break. The soldiers counted us before we went back to work. At 6:00, they counted us again, then we headed back to camp.

On our way back, I witnessed four soldiers cruelly beating a prisoner, Mr. Tuan. They were yelling at Mr. Tuan for visiting the Montagnard hamlets. At the Camp Administration Section, Mr. Vinh was no longer tied to the tree.

That evening I heard a rumor that soldiers now guarded all the foot paths and would arrest any prisoner who went back to the Montagnard hamlets. I realized that if I continued to be lazy or left the farms, the soldiers would beat me also. I decided to stop visiting the Montagnard hamlets and start working hard again.

One evening, my Group Leader announced our new labor program. We each had to sow 200 square yards. Those who finished first could rest while they waited for the others, then we would all go home together.

The next morning, the bell did not ring. We got ourselves up and took enough food from the kitchen for our breakfast and lunch that day. When we entered the farm, the soldiers counted us. Then they walked to the foot of a big tree and sat down. Our Group Leader supervised us. We worked without a break until noon. We took a half-hour for lunch and went back to work.

By 2:00, everyone in my group had finished his quota. We mustered again, the soldiers counted us, and we returned to our quarters.

The cadre and soldiers were being easier on us today. I felt a little less nervous, but I still feared being beaten. I thought, "The soldiers did not bully us into working hard today. They still watched us and counted us twice, but today they stood farther back." I knew if I left during our labor period, I would surely be caught and beaten.

That evening, I overheard some prisoners from my group discussing a rumor. They said, "The United States is attacking Vietnam for the second time. The U.S.A.'s 7th Fleet has moved to the South China Sea. Hundreds of bombers have attacked Cam Ranh Harbor over the last week. Five thousand U.S. Marines have landed there, and the Cam Ranh battle is fierce." When I heard this I was surprised.

I asked, "How do we know this is true?"

One of the prisoners, Mr. Long, responded, "The three Saigon soldiers have a radio. They heard it from the BBC and told us. They also said to keep it a secret, because the cadre would reprimand them for revealing this important news."

I was very happy about the rumor. Whenever we were not working, my group gathered together and discussed it.

Two days later, the three Saigon soldiers told us that the BBC had announced the U.S.A.'s victory at Cam Ranh Harbor. They annihilated a Communist division and caused casualties all over Cam Ranh Base. B52 bombers were now attacking Nha Trang, and U.S. forces were moving from Cam Ranh to Nha Trang.

The cadre increased our food ration from 500 grams to 700 grams of rice per person per day. In addition, the food truck was delivering fresh fish, dried fish, vegetables, pumpkins, etc., twice a week, and we were given 2.4 piastres worth of extra supplies, such as soap, tobacco, and sugar. I overheard some of the other prisoners say that the increase in supplies was a Communist tradition. Since we were prisoners of war, the Communists were feeding us extra food to make us fat so they could exchange us for Communist prisoners captured by the U.S.

The Communists continued to keep us agitated. A prisoner disclosed to me that the three Saigon soldiers had visited his group and told them about another BBC broadcast. The station announced that U.S. forces now occupied Nha Trang. The Communist soldiers stationed there had lost their fighting spirit and had run away. In addition, hundreds of B52's were bombing Danang Harbor.

The cadre reinforced the rumors by ordering 20 prisoners to the Camp Administration Section to dig foxholes and connecting trenches.

That same evening, I overheard another rumor that the cadre were worried about U.S. bombers attacking our camp. One prisoner commented, "This is why they need the foxholes and connecting trenches—so they can fight, if necessary."

The rumors made me happy. Smiling, I turned to my friends and repeated what I had heard, "The cadre are worried about U.S. bombers attacking our camp."

A couple of days later, the three Saigon soldiers told another group of prisoners about a BBC broadcast reporting a half-day battle over Danang between the United States and the Communists. The air battle resulted in the U.S. shooting down more than 100 Communist fighters. None of them escaped. They also told us that the U.S. Marines had landed at Danang Harbor, and the fighting was fierce.

The next day, the cadre supplied us with 2.4 piastres worth of extra supplies again.

On May 18, the three Saigon soldiers told us, the BBC announced that U.S. armies had taken over Danang.

One afternoon soon afterward, I was in the Camp Administration Section with about 20 other prisoners. We were helping a carpentry crew build a new house. I became aware of the cadre and soldiers attending a meeting in the conference hall when the Camp Political Officer shouted, "Are you determined to fight against the U.S.A. again?"

I heard the cadre and soldiers shout in response, "We are determined! Determined! Determined!"

They did this three times. As I listened to them, I

became convinced that the rumors were true. When my work crew returned to camp, we told everyone what we had heard.

Later I overheard some other prisoners talking. They had been in a work party picking up food at the storehouse at the Regiment Administration Section to bring back to camp.

At the storehouse, they heard Cadre Luan say to another cadre, "It is crazy. How foolish the U.S.A. is! They failed and ran away two years ago. Now they dare attack Vietnam again?"

The other cadre answered, "Yes, the U.S.A. is foolish to attack us these last few weeks. Even though they have more troops than the first time, and we have had more casualties, I still doubt they will win."

All the prisoners who heard this returned to camp and repeated it to us. We all believed that the cadre spoke honestly, which convinced us even more that the rumors were true.

The three Saigon soldiers told us of another BBC report of hundreds of U.S. bombers attacking Vung Tau. At the same time, U.S. warships were firing heavy guns at the harbor. They also said U.S. Marines were prepared to land at Vung Tau very soon.

A few days later, the cadre reinforced their previous rumors by spreading an additional one. Some prisoners from my group said, "A few nights ago, a prisoner was sleeping, and woke up to urinate. While he was outside, he saw a United States airplane overhead, flashing a light several times."

I thought about his story and told myself that the plane was probably taking pictures of our zone.

The following day, the cadre announced that we would receive another 2.4 piastres of extra supplies. When we went to the storehouse to pick them up, Supply Cadre Luan informed us that his supervisor had ordered him to give us extra food before the Communists exchanged prisoners of war with the U.S.

A day later, the cadre gave us fresh pork. They told us that the cadre at the Regiment Administration Section had been awakened from their sleep the night before by a roaring tiger. At first, they thought the tiger had caught a man, so they scared it away by shooting their guns in the air. When they investigated, they found out that the tiger had killed a pig and eaten it's head. Today, we would eat the rest of the pig, which the tiger had left behind. The cadre's story discouraged me from trying to escape, because I was now afraid of being attacked by a tiger.

At the end of May, I heard a rumor about Mr. Bao's crew who had escaped about a month ago. They had traveled to the border of Vietnam and Cambodia, but had been killed by Cambodian soldiers (whom the Communists called Red Khmer). One man escaped. He was hurt and pretended to be dead. He lay motionless until the Cambodian soldiers left, then he crawled into the forest and hid for three days. He returned to Vietnam and met some Vietnamese soldiers. They took him to the hospital where he told his story. I did not want to be killed by the Cambodian soldiers, so that was another reason why I did not to try to escape or leave camp.

When my friends and I had any leisure time, we gathered in small groups and discussed the rumors. I was excited about the U.S. attacking Vietnam again and about the stories of people who escaped. We all believed the U.S. was winning many battles. We were convinced that we would be exchanged as prisoners of war soon. I was very hopeful. I also felt sorry for the people who had escaped. My friend, Mr. Cuong, commented, "Because they escaped, they were killed by tigers or Cambodian soldiers. If they had not tried to escape, they would have been released in a few more months on the Glorious Day."

Thinking about the Glorious Day, I designed a plan for myself. When I am exchanged, I thought, I will farm. I spent much time thinking about my future, and I forgot about my weariness from the hard labor.

My friends designed plans for their futures as well. Mr. Cuong intended to go into business. Mr. Liet intended to join the Army again and said he would kill all the Communists he could find.

We also agreed that we had to stay here for a short while, and we repaired and built tables and chairs for ourselves. A few prisoners planted new vegetable gardens. No one attempted to escape. The bamboo fence completely surrounded our camp now. It had three gates but no guard posts. No one guarded the gate, and we were free to enter and leave at will.

On the evening of May 31, all our Block and Group Leaders attended a meeting at the Camp Administration Section. The cadre reviewed our work for the month. Afterward, the Group and Block Leaders returned to their barracks and announced that we would begin our new labor plan tomorrow. Our labor quota would increase from 200 square yards to 300 square yards per person per day.

The next morning, we started working toward our new labor quota. The soldiers no longer mustered us or inspected us. Instead, they stayed in their quarters.

Our Group Leaders supervised us and measured each group member's area. Because I had to finish my labor quota within the day, I worked hard without taking a break. I worked continuously from 8:00 until noon. I took a half-hour lunch, then worked until 4:30 when my area was finished. Thirty minutes later all of my group were finished. At 5:00 our Group Leaders led us back to camp.

In the evening, I ate dinner and participated in a small discussion group. We talked about the U.S. attacking Vietnam again. Focusing on this, I forgot about my weariness.

After working three days on our new labor quota, I realized that none of us were complaining about it. No one showed any weariness. Whenever we had any leisure time, we sat around and discussed the U.S. attack on Vietnam.

During the first week of June, our Block and Group Leaders attended a meeting where Supply Cadre Luan made an announcement. He told them that the rich people in our country were hoarding all their cash. Since they were not spending their money, the government did not have any cash, and the cadre did not have money to buy us food. Consequently we would not have much to eat until the government printed more money. They were buying paper and ink now, and would probably have the printing done in a few months.

For the rest of June and all of July we no longer received fresh fish, dried fish, or vegetables. We were apportioned only 700 grams of rice per person per day.

The day after we were told that the government had no money, the three Saigon soldiers divulged to us that the cadre had collected their radio. The cadre worried about the soldiers losing their fighting spirit if they heard that the U.S. was attacking us. They did not want the soldiers to be afraid to fight. Nevertheless, these soldiers confided to us that the U.S. had probably already taken Vung Tau and Saigon would be next.

We all regretted the radio being confiscated, and no one discussed the food decrease. Everyone was excited about the rumors and did not pay attention to the decrease in food, so no one opposed it.

Two days later all the Block and Group Leaders attended another meeting. Supply Cadre Luan made another announcement. He said, "Water is flooding Thanh Hoa Province and Nghe An and Ha Tinh. The people there are hungry. Everyone in our country has to help them. Therefore we will save a little rice to help the hungry people."

The next day our rice allotment decreased from 700 grams to 400 grams per day, but no one complained.

That evening, several soldiers came to our quarters. They talked to us in a friendly manner and asked us to sponsor them. One of the soldiers, Mr. Trung, confided in us that the civilians hated the Communists very much now. His family was in northern Vietnam, which was very far from here. If the Americans attacked our camp, he was afraid they would kill him, and he did not know where to hide. He needed us to help him by sponsoring him when the Americans arrived.

Mr. Trung said, "Because of this situation, all the cadre are afraid. They are worried that they will be killed. None of the cadre dare make any trouble for you, and none of the soldiers dare guard you. You can even go to the Montagnard hamlets again."

We believed this soldier, so we went to the Montagnard hamlet on the next Sunday. No one got into any trouble, so we continued to go.

I did not feel that the food shortage or labor was hard on me, because I believed it would not last long. I was sure that the Communists would exchange all of their prisoners soon, and then I could return home. I decided to stay in camp and wait for the Glorious Day. I accepted all the difficulties occurring at this time without question.

I worked hard and did not have enough food for my body, but I stayed hopeful for about a month. By the first week of July, I had had a high fever and a cold for two weeks. Several of my group were also sick. Mr. Ha was in the same condition as I. Mr. Hop was worse and had to be taken out of camp to the clinic.

Mr. Yen and Mr. Vinh, from another group in my block, were healthy in May, but were now partially paralyzed and had to walk with a cane. I became worried about my own health. I feared that if I continued to live without enough food, I too would become paralyzed. I hoped that the exchange day would come soon, so I could get out of this situation.

On the morning of July 31, we all attended a camp meeting. The Camp Political Officer reviewed our work for the last three months. We had finished sowing all the farm land our camp was responsible for. We all had worked hard and obeyed the camp rules well, and no one had tried to escape. The Camp Political Officer and the other cadre applauded us for accomplishing our goal, and a large pig was killed to celebrate.

Thirteen

AUGUST through NOVEMBER 1977

At a camp meeting on the afternoon of August 1, the Camp Political Officer informed us that for the next four months we would weed grass on the farms. He also told us our relatives would be allowed to visit. The visiting policy was:

> —A prisoner who received a visiting permit would mail it to his family.
>
> —Each reeducation prisoner was allowed three visitors at a time. We were allowed to sleep with our visiting relatives in the visiting house for one night.
>
> —We were allowed to accept supplies from our families. The cadre would not check these items.

After the meeting, I heard several prisoners discussing the new policy. They were excited about seeing their relatives and receiving supplies. The married prisoners were especially excited, because they would get to spend a night with their wives.

I didn't share the others' excitement, because I was single. My parents, younger brothers, and sisters had left Saigon in 1975 and moved to Kien Giang Province to farm. Their income was low; they earned barely enough to live on. They had spent the family savings in January of this year to buy supplies and pay for their trip to see me. I planned to cancel my visiting permit when my turn came up. I had only one hope. I believed the rumors that the U.S. was attacking Vietnam, and I waited for the Glorious Day when I would be exchanged as a prisoner of war. I eagerly waited for the other prisoners' relatives to visit, so I could ask them how the war was going.

The following day a crew of prisoners was assigned to

build a visiting house about 200 yards away from camp, between us and the main road. My group continued to work on the farms.

We stood in one line, side by side. We weeded the grass with our hoes. We supervised ourselves.

Inspecting our work, the Camp Political Officer noticed Mr. Thanh digging up the root of a young cassava tree and eating it. The next day, during our group meeting, the Camp Political Officer discussed this incident with us. He cited Mr. Thanh for taking the young cassava and eating it. Mr. Thanh disobeyed the labor rules and destroyed the production; therefore, he was sentenced to three more years of imprisonment in the reeducation camps. (Five months later, Mr. Thanh had his name on the release list. We realized then that the Camp Political Officer had only been trying to scare him.)

In early August, Camp Political Officer Thau, Camp Commander Uyen, Supply Cadre Luan, and several soldiers went on vacation to visit their families in north Vietnam. Four new cadre arrived. Captain Boi replaced the Camp Political Officer. Captain Hon replaced the Camp Commander. The other two, Lt. Bong and Aspirant Thao were regular cadre. There were fewer than 10 guards now, not many for 650 prisoners.

At the end of the first week in August, the prisoners finished building our visiting house, and all our Block and Group Leaders attended a meeting in the Camp Administration Section. The Camp Political Officer announced that the cadre would be issuing visiting permits in batches. Every two weeks, 20 percent of the prisoners from each group would receive permits. Our Group Leaders would recommend to the cadre those group members who should receive permits.

The Camp Political Officer also advised us that our food rations would increase from two meals a day to three. Furthermore, once a week, trucks would deliver dried fish, vegetables, pumpkins, soy sauce, and fish sauce. When our relatives arrived, the kitchen would supply us with enough food for three people. Our relatives would receive the same food rations we received each meal. I thought the cadre would specially prepare our food for us so that when our relatives tasted it they would think it was good.

The next day, 20 percent of my group received visiting permits and mailed them to their families. In the evening, many of the prisoners sat around discussing plans for their relatives' visits. Those who were to be visited called upon their friends to help them with chores such as cooking or cleaning up the visiting house afterwards.

Relatives began showing up in mid-August. One of my group, Mr. Dien, was the first to have visitors. I was anxious to hear about the U.S. attacking Vietnam, so when Mr. Dien came back from the visiting house, I asked him what his relatives had said about it. He answered, "There is nothing! All these rumors are false."

I stood motionless as the shock enveloped me. A blanket of numbness covered my body, as though I were falling into a dark abyss, and there was nothing I could do about it. My hopes of being released on the Glorious Day and being united with my family again had been dashed against the sharp rocks of reality.

I saw some of my friends later that day and told them the bad news. They confirmed Mr. Dien's report.

That evening I sat with several friends. No one discussed the rumors of an American invasion anymore. They only discussed their visiting relatives and how they could get supplies from them. My friends were so excited about the visiting policy that they did not care if the rumors we heard three months ago were false or not.

That night I lay in bed, depressed about my future. I was angry at the three Saigon soldiers who gave us the false news. I wanted to find them and ask them why they had lied to us.

The next day I looked for the three soldiers, but could not find them. They had been quietly transferred to another camp.

Visiting relatives often arrived at around 3:00 PM. The prisoner being visited greeted his relatives at the visiting house, then returned to his quarters and told his friends all the good news. He then took drinking water and mats to the visiting house. He put the mats on the beds and sat and talked to his relatives. His friends carried bathing water for his relatives from camp to the visiting house. The friends then returned to camp and cooked dinner for them.

At 7:00, his friends served them dinner in the visiting house, and the prisoner often invited his friends to join them. Afterwards, his friends took the bowls, dishes, and food containers back to camp and washed them, but he stayed in the visiting house for the rest of the night.

At 7:00 the next morning, his friends brought breakfast to the visiting house, then they returned to camp and went to work. The man being visited had breakfast with his relatives, then they said their good-byes to him and left and he brought the supplies his family had given him back to camp.

The cadre did not check the supplies anyone received from his family. He was allowed to keep everything he received, even live chickens or ducks.

One of my group, Mr. Thang, wrote to his relatives asking them to bring a big dog and a few liters of alcohol. When his relatives left, he invited his friends to join our group in our barracks. We killed the dog and had a party. We ate dog meat, drank the alcohol, and had fun. I saw prisoners in other groups do the same.

At first, everyone adhered to the visiting policy. But after a couple of weeks several prisoners designed schemes to allow their wives to stay longer.

According to the policy, three relatives were allowed to visit one reeducation prisoner, but many men would ask a prisoner with a visiting permit to give their wives one of his positions. Even the men who had already been visited were eager to see their wives again, so they would ask, too. So the prisoner who had a visiting permit would give one position to his wife and would allow two of his friends' wives to use the other two positions. In this way, three men would be visited on each permit.

Since wives were allowed to visit for only one night, they had to leave the next morning. The men wanted their wives to stay a few more days, so they told the cadre that their wives were very sick and could not travel right away. Their wives were then allowed to stay in the visiting house a few more days. Every time I came back from work, I walked past the visiting house and saw at least five women who had reported being sick.

By the beginning of September, the visiting house was full of relatives and there was no place for them to sleep. The Camp Political Officer solved this problem by ordering the female relatives to stay in the visiting house, and the male relatives to sleep in the conference hall. In addition, prisoners were no longer allowed to sleep in the visiting house. In practice, none of my group took their male relatives to the conference hall to sleep. Instead, they took them to our quarters, and they stayed with us.

Despite the fact that the cadre did not allow prisoners to sleep in the visiting house, the men still desired to sleep with their wives and they looked for ways to get around the new policy.

By 8:00 PM, many of them had returned to camp after eating dinner with their relatives. At 10:00, they would go into the cassava farm near the visiting house and hide there until they were sure the cadre were not inside, then they entered the visiting house and went to sleep. The cadre sometimes checked the visiting house at night. If the cadre ran a surprise check, the prisoners would launch themselves out of the house and run into the cassava farm and then return to camp.

In early September, Mr. Hoang and Mr. Khanh went to the visiting house to see their wives. Mr. Hoang had a scheme for when his wife came. He asked another prisoner, Mr. Liem, to take his place in camp, in case the cadre came by to check on him. Mr. Hoang then went to the visiting house and slept with his wife.

Unfortunately for them, the cadre checked the visiting house that night. All the prisoners who were sleeping with their wives ran out of the house into the cassava farm, and then to camp.

Mr. Khanh ran back to camp in a panic. That night it rained and was very dark. Mr. Khanh could not see well, and he fell into a large cesspool. His clothes were covered with filth, but he was lucky enough to return to camp without being caught.

Mr. Hoang, however, was caught and arrested by the Camp Political Officer. He was kept in the visiting house while the Camp Political Officer checked the rest of the prisoners being visited to see if they were still in their quarters. The Political Officer returned to camp and ordered all of those prisoners to gather outside.

Mr. Liem did not know that Mr. Hoang had already been arrested, so he took his place in line. While the Camp Political Officer called each prisoner's name, Mr. Liem listened and waited. When the Camp Political Officer called Mr. Hoang, Mr. Liem raised his hand and answered. The Camp Political Officer's eyes widened with surprise. He looked at Mr. Liem and asked, "What is your wife's name and address?"

Mr. Liem was embarrassed and could not answer and he and Mr. Hoang were caught.

The next day, my group and the Camp Political Officer rebuked Mr. Hoang and Mr. Liem at our group meeting. The Camp Political Officer scared them by saying, "Mr. Liem and Mr. Hoang tricked us. This behavior means that they intended to trick The Revolutionary Organization and the people of our country; therefore, their punishment will be three more years of imprisonment."

The following week, Mr. Liem revealed to me that the Communists came to his family and announced that he would be released soon. His family had to fill out sponsoring documents. Many of my group whose relatives visited disclosed that their family had also filled out sponsoring documents for them.

During this period, the cadre reinforced the notion of our being released soon. Many prisoners were abruptly called to the Camp Administration Section and told to declare where they would like to be released.

Frequently, we would be asleep at night and the Camp Political Officer would burst into our quarters with a lamp and order one or two prisoners to report to the Camp Administration Section. The first few times we worried that these people were in trouble and when they returned, we gathered around them and asked them what had happened. They said, "The cadre received orders from their superiors to add the release location to our documents, since we were to be discharged soon."

One day I was working on the farms when the Camp Political Officer suddenly came up and told me and several other prisoners to report to the Camp Administration Section. When we arrived, he told us that his superiors intended to release us soon, but they needed a release location.

Often the Camp Political Officer would unexpectedly call five prisoners to the Camp Administration Section. He would then explain that they all had their names on the release list, and he would have three of them report their release location. The other two he would not allow to report because he did not consider them ready to be released yet. He was postponing their release until they learned to work well in the camp. Mr. Hung had this happen to him, so we voted him the outstanding man for two consecutive turns. Mr. Hung was then called again and allowed to report his release location.

We discussed with one another the news from our families and the goings-on in camp and concluded that we would be released soon. We were hopeful about it and waited, and no one tried to escape.

By the end of September, many prisoners had been visited and given food and money by their relatives. When we finished our labor, we were free to go anywhere in the forest. Afternoons, I saw prisoners visiting Duc Hanh Village or Montagnard hamlets to buy rice, vegetables, live poultry, alcohol, and tobacco.

To get out of camp, we had to pass through a bamboo fence that had been built four months earlier. There were many gates through which we could exit, but instead we began pulling pieces of bamboo out of the fence to make new openings. They were about four yards long and tied together with ropes. Eventually the ropes broke, especially near the big holes. Some of the bamboo began to separate from the fence. When we noticed the loose bamboo, we took it to burn in our cooking stoves.

We did not get in trouble the first time, so we continued doing it. After a while, other group members noticed that we were taking the loose bamboo, and they began imitating us. The number of people taking bamboo increased until at last everyone in the camp was doing it. They even took parts of the fence where the rope had not broken.

In less than a month, the bamboo fence had completely disappeared into the prisoners' stoves. There was no longer a fence around our camp. I suspected that the cadre knew this but did not say anything because none of the prisoners tried to escape anymore and the fence was no longer necessary.

When our labor was over, we were free to use our time any way we wanted. Some prisoners chose to read a book. Some visited their friends in nearby camps. Some cultivated vegetables in their gardens, raised chickens, played chess, or played music. Some prisoners gambled at cards. Some gathered to eat and drink together. Many times I was startled awake at midnight by drunken prisoners shouting outside my quarters.

By the end of October, most of us had been given enough food by our families to bring our bodies back to health and the symptoms of paralysis had disappeared. Then the cadre changed the visiting policy. If our relatives came without a visiting permit, they were allowed to stay in the visiting house for one night. The kitchen no longer provided food for them, and we were responsible for feeding them ourselves.

Our food rations were also cut back. Our old ration had consisted of three meals a day. Our new ration consisted of two meals each day. Each meal consisted of 200 grams of uncooked rice. I figured the cadre did this because they realized we already had an abundance of supplies from our relatives.

At the end of November, the number of guards were increased to 20. Some of the cadre had finished their vacations and were now returning to camp. Among them were Cadre Boi, Cadre Hon, Cadre Thau, Cadre Uyen, Cadre Bong, Cadre Luan, and Cadre Thao.

On the last day of November, the Camp Political Officer reviewed our work for the last four months. He said we had done a good job of cultivation and most of us had been visited. We were comfortable and stayed in camp, waiting for the release day. Even though there was no fence around our camp and the soldiers did not guard us and we were allowed to go to civilian zones, still, no one had tried to escape. He added that the cadre from our camp applauded us on our progress.

Fourteen

DECEMBER 1, 1977 to JANUARY 15, 1978

In early December, all of the Block Leaders and Group Leaders attended a meeting in the Camp Administration Section. That evening, our Group Leader told us what Camp Political Officer Boi had announced at that meeting: "Our Camp will begin a `Production Battle.' We will attack the harvest work, and the cadre in our camp plan on having all the rice paddies harvested in one and a half months." He added that the Camp Political Officer did not think we would finish, because he had orders to prepare all prisoners for transportation to a new camp very soon. Therefore, all the cadre were preparing to leave this camp.

I was surprised by the news of our leaving. All of my group members reacted with surprise also, and we discussed this exciting topic right away. We were worried that if we moved to a new camp now, we would be short of supplies again.

I thought of ways to deal with this situation, and I wrote a letter to my mother's friend, who lived in Ho Chi Minh City (formerly Saigon; I had only recently become accustomed to the new name). I asked her to loan me some money and medicine. I explained that since my family lived so far away, they would visit her later to repay my debt. I wrote a second letter to my family and told them my plan.

When I finished my letters, I ran to the visiting house and asked a young woman there to mail my letters for me when she arrived back in Ho Chi Minh.

Other group members also wrote letters that evening and took them to the visiting house. No one said anything about the harvest work. We were so concerned about being short of supplies that no one paid attention to our impending labor.

The next morning we went to work. None of the cadre

or soldiers came to the farms or inspected us.

We worked until noon, took an hour break for lunch, then continued to work until 4:00. We carried rice paddy from the farm to the storehouse. It took two men to carry one basket of paddy.

At 5:00 we returned to our quarters. Several of my group began to prepare for our move. Some of them killed the chickens they had raised. Some of them harvested all the vegetables from their private gardens. Some tore down their garden fences and hen houses and burned the wood in their stoves. The trash pits were filled with chicken feathers.

I began harvesting the vegetables out of my private garden, too. I wanted to eat them all before we left. I didn't plant more because I believed we would soon leave.

Every afternoon when we returned home, most of my group ran to the visiting house to see if their relatives had brought them supplies yet. I also hoped my mother's friend would come as soon as possible.

Three days after we mailed our letters to Ho Chi Minh, relatives started crowding into the visiting house, bringing fresh supplies. I began to worry that my mother's friend would not show up. One of my friends, Mr. Cuong, told me that he feared his wife would come too late, after we had already left this camp.

On Sunday we did not work. I continued to prepare for leaving. I washed and dried my blanket, mosquito net and mat. My kit bag was broken, so I repaired it.

One week after I had mailed my letters, my mother's friend sent her daughter with medicine and money. I was relieved and very glad.

One day I felt sick, so I reported to the examination house. Several other patients were there. We sat and talked until it was time to be examined. The soldier who did this was the kitchen cook. The examination was simple. He asked for our names and symptoms, then he wrote them in his notebook.

He did not give us any medicine. Instead, his prescription was for each of us to go into the forest and make four dried-bamboo bundles. The bundles had to have seven bamboo pieces, each four yards long, and we had to bring them back to the kitchen to be used for firewood.

After I received my prescription, I returned to my quarters and found my knife. I went into the forest and made two bamboo bundles. Each bundle consisted of only five bamboo pieces. I intended to make more, but I saw other patients with only two bamboo bundles returning to their quarters. So I carried my bamboo bundles back to my quarters also and lay on my bed and rested.

At noon I saw the other patients carry their bundles to the kitchen and I followed them. I told the soldier that I had tried my best, but was too sick and tired to make any more than two bamboo bundles. I asked him to decrease my work, but he refused. I told him I would do it in the afternoon, but in the afternoon I noticed that none of the other patients worked. Instead, we all rested.

The next day, I claimed to be sick again. The soldier examined us and gave us the same prescription as the day before. Each patient had to make four bamboo bundles. However, he told me I had to make six bundles. I had to make four bundles for today plus two more to repay my debt for yesterday. I still made only two bundles.

I felt much better by the third day and was healthy enough to work, but I still felt lazy and did not want to. I realized that I could avoid the hard labor and take advantage of this opportunity by pretending to be sick a few more days.

I continued to make only two bundles on the third, fourth, and fifth days. On the sixth day, the soldier told me to make a total of 14 dried bamboo bundles. I had to make four for the sixth day and 10 more to repay the debt over the last five days. Again, I made only two bundles.

I reported my illness six days in a row, and my debt was now up to 12 bamboo bundles. I realized that my debt was great, and I wanted to rub it out, so I quit pretending to be sick and went to work for two weeks. I hoped the soldier would forget my debt by then so I could pretend to be sick again for another week.

At this time, the number of prisoners reporting sick was very low. I figured it was because they were excited about moving to a new camp and had forgotten about their weariness. Our camp held 650 prisoners, but there were only three to seven patients reporting sick each day. Because of this low number, the cadre were easy on those of us who did report being sick.

In the third week of December, I heard a rumor from some of my group that civilians were dissatisfied with Communists policies. They were participating in the Phuc Quoc organization, a political organization secretly opposed to the Communists. (The word "Phuc Quoc" means "take over the country again").

When I heard this rumor, I was not sure if it was true. I discussed it with my friends and my group members. We did not know the actual situation in the civilian zones since we had been in reeducation camps for more than two years. The best way to find out would be to ask our relatives. We went to the visiting house and asked the people there about this political organization. They told us that the government had arrested several people over the last two years who were involved with this secret organization. Because of this rumor and the news from our relatives, we gathered every evening and discussed the Phuc Quoc.

In the last week of December, the cadre spread a second rumor. I overheard two of my group talking about a woman who visited one of the prisoners in our camp. They said the woman told them she had heard, over the Manila radio station, an announcement from the Phuc Quoc. She said the announcement was in Vietnamese and contained 10 points. She could remember only the following three:

1. From now on, if the Phuc Quoc organization took over any area, they would defend that area. They would stop their old guerilla strategy of taking over and withdrawing.

2. The Old Government employees would have to report to and would be employed by the Phuc Quoc organization. They would receive reparation money for the time they spent in Communist prisons.

3. They asked the reeducation prisoners to stay in the camps, obey the camp rules, and not try to escape. Escaped prisoners would be dangerous, so the Phuc Quoc organization would make arrangements with the Communists to have us released instead.

I considered all the rumors and news I had heard during the last two weeks. I was encouraged and discussed them with anticipation. I hoped the Phuc Quoc political organization, would succeed and bring about the fall of the Communist government. Mr. Vinh said, "If we continue to stay in the reeducation camps for a short while, we will return home on the Glorious Day and have some compensation money."

By the end of December, while we were distracted by the rumors of impending freedom, without saying anything, the cadre decreased our food ration. Our old food ration consisted of two meals a day, each meal being 200 grams of uncooked rice. Our new food ration was still two meals a day, but the cadre replaced the rice with millet. No one said anything about the decrease in food.

Most of the prisoners received food from their families. My family could not afford to give me food, but I was not hungry. Fortunately for me, there were many cassava farms around our camp. The cassava roots were very big now. When I got hungry, I just pulled up roots and cooked them. The cadre did not say we could take them, but they did not stop us either.

I received a letter from my family informing me that my father had died. My mother and younger brothers wanted to visit me, but they could not afford it. The family's savings had to go for my father's funeral. My mother told me she would repay her friend for the money she had given me when she could.

I was very sad. Many nights I lay in bed, unable to sleep, tears running down my cheeks. I missed my father very much. I didn't get to say good-bye, and I worried about my family, since I could not be there to help them.

On January 1, the cadre broadcast an announcement from Hanoi over the loudspeakers. The announcement reported on a border war between Vietnam and Cambodia. The Vietnamese government claimed that the Cambodians were shelling Vietnamese villages and military units with artillery.

I discussed the rumors and news we had heard with my friends and we agreed that the Communists must be having a lot of problems. We thought they were not able to get a good grip on the country and their empire would soon fall. My friends and I hoped this was true, and we stayed in camp and waited for the Communist government to fall. No one tried to escape and we all forgot about our weariness.

Thirteen days later, we finished harvesting all the rice. we did not go to work the next day. We rested in our quarters and attended a camp meeting. The Camp Political Officer reviewed our work over the last month and a half and told us that the cadre applauded us and that they had killed a pig today to congratulate us for accomplishing our camp's goal.

Fifteen

JANUARY 15, 1978 to FEBRUARY 28, 1978

That afternoon all Block and Group Leaders attended a meeting. In the evening, my Group Leader relayed the cadre's orders. Over the next month and a half our camp would clear 200 acres of forest; each of us had a quota of 60 square yards per day.

At 7:00 the next morning my group arrived at our work site. We used axes and bush knives to cut down all the trees and left them lying on the ground. They would be dried and burned before the rainy season started. Our Group Leader supervised us.

We completed our quota around noon, then rested in our quarters for the rest of the afternoon and were free to pursue our own interests.

In the evening, my group sat and talked about the Phuc Quoc and their opposition to the Communists.

The next morning, the cadre released 10 prisoners. My group and I wondered why these particular men had been released. Some of us suspected that the released prisoners had been sponsored by Communist relatives. That afternoon we heard a rumor that more prisoners would be released soon.

Three days later, a second group of 10 left. Then we heard another rumor that most of us would be released. Some people thought this rumor was true and some thought it was false. Nevertheless, we all paid attention to the people being released and we began to forget about the Phuc Quoc which we had been so concerned with last month.

On January 24, the cadre revealed the names of the third group of prisoners to be released, and they announced the projected release of 60 more. They said it was because these prisoners had families who were currently living in the farm areas. The cadre also said they would issue one-month furloughs to 120 prisoners so they could return to their families and prepare their documents. After they returned to camp, the cadre would issue their release permits, which would allow them to live as civilians again. Then they were supposed to move out into a farm area.

That evening, Cadre Thao came to our quarters. He said, "All the people who are on leave will prepare their documents. When they return, some will not have their documents ready and some will. They will all be released anyway, because our superiors have already decided to release them. This is the case not only in our camp, but in all the other reeducation camps as well. After the third group is released, the cadre will continue to release all of you in groups, until no one is left. This camp will then be closed. The cadre will be assigned new jobs at new places." I went to sleep that night feeling very happy.

The next afternoon, just as Cadre Thao had told us, the cadre began to leave for new jobs elsewhere. The number of guards decreased. I watched 14 of them pass through our camp, carrying luggage.

A day later, the guards in the Camp Administration Section had been reduced to a mere six in number. Among them were Cadre Bong and Cadre Thao; the rest were soldiers. These six guards controlled 630 prisoners.

The other prisoners and I all agreed that the Communists would release us soon. I intended to obey the camp rules and work hard. I hoped I would be considered one of the good people, so the cadre would release me. No one escaped during this time.

The next day, I did not feel well, so I reported to the camp nurse, who was also a reeducation prisoner. He told me, "You are the only one sick today. If you want to rest, you can." I rested for that day, but everyone else went to work.

I later asked the other prisoners who often reported being sick, "Why don't you report being sick anymore?"

One of them, Mr. Long, answered, "It is foolish to

report being sick now, because the Communists have begun to implement the release policies. I do not feel well, but if I report being sick now, I am afraid they will consider me unworthy and not release me."

He advised me, "Please, try to work well. Don't report being sick anymore, so the cadre will think that you are deserving and release you, too."

Mr. Ha and Mr. Lich gave me similar answers. I decided that, starting tomorrow, even if I did not feel well, I would not report my illness anymore. Instead, I would try my best to go to work and show the cadre I was a competent worker, worthy of being released.

While we were concentrating on being released, the cadre quietly decreased our food ration again, from two meals of millet a day to five meals every two and a half days. One meal would be millet and the other four would be boiled cassava. The millet tasted good compared to the boiled cassava. Few of us ate the cassava. We threw almost all of it into the trash pits.

We all hoped to be released soon, so no one complained about our food rations. Besides, many prisoners still had food and money from their families, and they used the money to buy food from local civilians.

At 8:00 PM on January 27, 60 prisoners received release permits and 120 received furloughs. The cadre told them that they would be given bus money tomorrow morning. Still, the prisoners were very anxious to return to their families as soon as possible.

I heard Mr. Liet say to someone, "These cadre often change their minds. Besides, we do not need the money for a bus ticket. What if we wait and sleep here tonight, and tomorrow morning the cadre change their minds and take back our release permits and furloughs? How horrible that would be! It is better to leave here as soon as possible."

Mr. Liet and most of the others gathered their kitbags that night. They walked fifteen miles down the road from our camp to Phuoc Long City and returned to their families.

An hour after they left, the cadre discovered they were gone. They came to our quarters and seized the release permits and passes of those remaining. They said they did not want anyone leaving at night.

The prisoners who had had their documents confiscated sat together. One man said, "If I had known this was going to happen, I would have left with the others. It will be unfortunate for us if the cadre change their minds and do not let us leave tomorrow morning."

These people worried so much they did not sleep that night. But the cadre did not change their minds and returned their release permits and passes. The cadre also gave them money for bus tickets. After they left, there were still 450 reeducation prisoners left in the camp.

On the afternoon of the following day, all the Group and Block Leaders attended a meeting at the Camp Administration Section. They came back and told us that Cadre Bong had said we would all be released soon. Since the Lunar New Year Festival, or Tet, was coming, we would be allowed to have our relatives visit so they could celebrate with us. We could build small huts for them at the edge of the forest or in the cassava farm.

We were glad to hear this, and my friends all wrote letters to their families that night. I did not write because I knew my family could not afford the trip. Mr. Cuong knew that they were poor. He wanted to help me, so he offered to share the food his wife had brought him. I accepted his offer and thanked him.

After we finished our labor quota the next day, several prisoners entered the forest to gather bamboo. Some built bamboo huts on the edge of the forest or on the cassava farm where they had been told they could. Others built their huts in the camp, near their barracks. Many intended to have their wives and children stay in the huts during Tet, and they built them together in a group so their families could stay close and have a picnic. Some went to the civilian sector and bought live ducks or chickens, alcohol, beans, and uncooked rice. They brought these back and prepared them for Tet.

Three days before Tet, Cadre Bong announced to us, "Four divisions of the Red Khmer are deployed on the border of Vietnam and Cambodia. They intend to attack Phuoc Long Province during Tet and take over all the reeducation centers in this zone. Our camp will be one of the targets, so the cadre have devised a plan to deal with this situation.

"If the Red Khmer attack our camp, your relatives will follow Cadre Thao. All of you will follow me. We will lead you and your relatives to safe places."

Cadre Bong continued, "The Reeducation Administration Division will deploy several patrols during Tet who will police the roads or be stationed at key locations. They have orders to arrest all cadre, soldiers, and reeducation prisoners they come across."

We all agreed that this could happen. We made sure our kit bags were prepared with essential items. We also made our own plans, should our camp be attacked. If the Communists withdrew, we would follow them; but along the way, we would escape. Because of our having been part of the Old Regime, we knew that it would not be safe to follow the Communists. If they failed, they would surely kill us, because they saw us as their enemies.

In the days just before Tet, large numbers of relatives arrived at our camp. The prisoners took their wives and children to the huts that they had prepared. Some prisoners had not built themselves a hut, so they put their relatives in the barracks. Since many prisoners were on leave, we who remained packed ourselves into one half of our barracks and left the other half for our relatives to stay in. There were a lot of women and children in camp and they walked around in large crowds. It reminded me of the military family sections I saw when I served in the Old Regime.

We prepared a dragon head and costumes for Tet. On

the evening before, the Chinese dragon crew began dancing its way through camp, stopping at each barracks. They beat on drums as they danced. Excited by the dance, about 100 prisoners with their wives and children followed them in a swarm. They held torches that flickered against the dancers like fireflies illuminating an open field.

When the Chinese dragon came to one of the barracks, the people there hung a gift on the door, then went outside and enjoyed the dance. After the dragon passed through all the barracks, it moved to the Camp Administration Section where it danced as the dragon crew wished the cadre and soldiers a happy New Year.

Just then I realized that Cadre Thao was the only one there. He watched the dragon dance and wished us a happy New Year on behalf of all the guards. The other Communists had disappeared, though their houses were still lit by petroleum lamps. I wondered where they had gone, and why.

When I returned to camp I heard my friend, Mr. Dai, say, "Because there were only six guards, they were afraid of us. They probably worried that we would kill them and escape. So tonight, when such a big crowd came up to the Administration Section and danced the dragon dance, it must have startled them. They panicked and ran, and hid on the cassava farm. They left only Cadre Thao to watch us on their behalf. Because they were in such a panic, they probably forgot to turn off the petroleum lamps in their houses."

We all agreed with Mr. Dai, then gathered into large groups and ate and drank. I saw the women and children eating cakes and candies and drinking tea. I also noticed some prisoners who were very poor and could not be supplied by their families. They were lying inside their mosquito nets, looking bored and lonely. Mr. Cuong's wife did not visit him during this Tet, but stayed with her family in Ho Chi Minh city, so he and I cooked sweet soup and ate together.

On the first morning of Tet, the Chinese dragon crew played again, but this time they played in front of the visitors' houses only. A few firecrackers were set off by those celebrating.

On the second morning of Tet, my friend Mr. Vinh suddenly became seriously ill. A guard and some prisoners took him to an emergency clinic about half a mile away, near the Regiment Administration Section.

While Mr. Vinh was in the clinic, I asked Mr. Cuong to visit him with me. Mr. Cuong hesitated. He said he wanted to go, but was afraid. He worried that the roads would be patrolled and that the soldiers would arrest anyone they saw.

I suggested we could watch for patrols on the road to the clinic. If we saw one, we could jump into the bushes. Since both sides of the road were lined with trees, it would be easy for us to hide.

Mr. Cuong agreed and we left camp together. We walked about 400 yards before we reached the road. At that point, we hid behind a bush and observed the road for half an hour. We didn't see anyone, so we went back out on the road and turned left. We walked another 600 yards to the clinic.

Two prisoners named Mr. Ket and Mr. Ngoc were nurses at the clinic. They told us that their medicine was very poor, and they could not treat Mr. Vinh. I asked them what kind of medicine they needed. They wrote the prescription on a piece of paper and handed it to me.

We visited with Mr. Vinh for an hour and left. When we returned to the road, we saw that it was still clear. Mr. Cuong told me he had friends in Camp D5. He wanted to go there and ask if they had the medicine Mr. Vinh needed. He said he would borrow it and Mr. Vinh's family could repay him for it later. I agreed, so we continued on to Camp D5.

It was about 400 yards. On the right side of the road stood about 20 small houses (the Administration Section for Reeducation Regiment 16). To our surprise, we did not see any soldiers or cadre at the gate.

We went another 400 yards and came to the camp. Two bamboo fences enclosed it. The guard post was vacant. We entered the gate and walked to the quarters of one of Mr. Cuong's friends. The prisoners were surprised to see us.

Mr. Cuong's friend blurted out, "How did you get here?"

We both answered, "We walked on the road."

The prisoners told us that yesterday morning at 7:00, three prisoners from this camp went to visit friends in other camps. When they walked out the gate, they were caught by soldiers hiding in the cassava tree farm across the road. The soldiers arrested them and beat them.

All the prisoners in Camp D5 were aware of this incident, so no one else dared leave that day. However, two more prisoners did attempt to leave camp at 7:00 this morning, but they were caught and beaten as well.

I asked, "Do you have any visitors?"

They answered, "We haven't had any visitors for the past three days, because of the Tet festival."

Mr. Cuong then visited all his friends, but none of them had the medicine Mr. Vinh needed. At noon, Mr. Cuong and I walked back on the road and returned to our camp.

That afternoon I thought about what Mr. Cuong and I had discovered. The Communists had told us that four Red Khmer divisions were attacking this zone and Communist soldiers were patrolling vital locations and roads. But in reality the soldiers did nothing, and the roads were empty. Also, the policies at Camp D5 were very different from what they were in our camp. In D5 the soldiers beat the prisoners and did not allow visitors. In contrast, our camp was crowded with visitors, and no one was beaten.

I discussed these things with Mr. Cuong. We rationalized that because the Tet festival was the most important one of the year, everybody celebrated it. However, the Reeducation Administration Division did not want the cadre and soldiers to enjoy the festival and shirk their responsibility to guard the camps, so they made up the story about the Red Khmer divisions to keep the cadre, soldiers, and prisoners off the roads and in the camps.

We also figured that Camp D5 was easier to keep the prisoners in, because it was surrounded by fences. The soldiers were at the gate only once a day, around 7:00 AM. That is why when Mr. Cuong and I arrived there around noon we were not beaten. Our Camp D1 did not have a fence around it, so the cadre kept us in by allowing us to have our visitors stay throughout the Tet festival. Since we would be busy with our relatives, we would not try to leave.

These were guesses only, so on the third day of Tet, Mr. Cuong and I decided to test our theories. We left our camp and turned right at the road. We walked for about two miles and left Reeducation Regiment 16, entering a different regimental zone. We walked into Camp D4B, which was on our way. We noticed a bridge and a hill, but the Communists did not deploy any troops there. This was a strategic point, because it was only one mile away from the Reeducation Administration Division section. It would have made sense to defend this position, if they were really expecting to be attacked. Since the road was vacant, we figured that our theories were valid.

Mr. Cuong and I visited a friend, Mr. Lai, in Camp D4B. Unfortunately, we still did not find the medicine Mr. Vinh needed, and we returned to our camp. As soon as we reached our quarters, we heard that Mr. Vinh had died. We felt very sad and helpless. We had tried our best, but were unable to help our friend.

The Tet festival lasted for three days, but our relatives stayed for a week. When they left, they felt at ease about our conditions here.

At the end of February, 120 reeducation prisoners were on a one-month leave of absence. Only 119 prisoners returned. Those who did return carried documents showing that they would move to a farm upon their release.

Because they thought the cadre would prepare their release permits a few days after they returned to camp, none of them brought many supplies. Each had only a small bag with some clothes and money in it. A few of my friends were on leave. Before they left, they said that they would look for a boat by which to leave the country.

Now they were returning to camp, so I asked one of them, Mr. Liet, "Why didn't you escape?"

He answered, "I don't think it is necessary to escape. The Communists have released many reeducation prisoners and soon they will release us all."

I also asked Mr. Huu about the rumors of a Phuc Quoc organization. He told me what had happened to his cousins, who lived under the Communist regime in North Vietnam from 1954 to 1975. Many people there did not like the Communists, so the Communists spread stories about political organizations that were revolting against them in many of the provinces. His cousins waited, hoping the Communists would fall. While they waited, the Communists quietly strengthened their government.

Mr. Huu revealed that while he was on leave he checked into the rumors we had heard last December. He discovered that the rumors concerning the Phuc Quoc were false. There had been a Phuc Quoc to begin with, and they began working in the civilian zones. However, the Communists infiltrated them. They compiled a list of the people in the organization, then arrested them. The Communists then spread stories about this organization in order to create hope in other people who did not like the Communist regime.

On the last day of February, our Group Leaders told us that Cadre Bong had told them that we had accomplished the camp's goal of clearing 200 acres of forest, and everyone had obeyed the camp rules. None of us had escaped during this period, except for one prisoner who did not return to camp after his furlough. He and Cadre Thao applauded us for these things and said that tomorrow we would rest in our quarters and relax for the entire day.

Sixteen

March and April 1978

In March, my group was ordered to harvest 80 kilograms of cassava per prisoner per day. We would carry it about two miles from the harvest area to our camp. Another group from my camp would then peel, slice, and dry it in the sun.

On March 2, we walked to the harvest area and uprooted cassava trees. We put the cassava into sacks, then walked back to camp. Our first cassava sacks weighed about 25 kilograms.

After I filled my first sack, I decided I did not want to walk two miles back to the harvest area. Instead, I entered the middle of the cassava farm near our camp and secretly filled my second and third sacks of cassava. I carried them back to camp and weighed them. I observed several of my group doing the same and we all finished our labor quota before noon.

When we carried our sacks from the cassava farms to the road, we had to avoid being spotted by cadre or soldiers. If they caught us taking cassava from the farms near our camp, they would punish us. We knew we were not allowed to harvest cassava there, but we did it anyway.

One evening a couple of days later, our Group Leader told us that the 119 prisoners who had been on leave were returning. The cadre would continue to allow our relatives to visit us and stay as long as they wanted, but they were confined to the visiting house. We were no longer allowed to put our relatives in the huts near the edge of the forest or on the cassava farms or in camp.

A few days later some of my friends who had been on leave returned. They waited a week for the cadre to issue their release permits, but did not hear anything about it. They were worried; I saw them sitting together, talking about when they might be released.

During the second week in March, I heard that these prisoners had to have documents showing they would live in the rural areas, and that it would take the cadre a month to prepare them.

Mr. Liet, who had returned from leave, said, "Never mind. I will wait for one month."

He wrote a letter to his family, explaining that he would not be released right away. Other prisoners who had returned from leave wrote letters to their families, too. Within 10 days some of their families brought them fresh supplies.

A week later we stopped harvesting cassava and were issued orders to clear the old farms. The next day we worked in the rice paddies that we had planted the year before. We cut down the small trees and the stems of the old rice plants, then we laid them on the ground to dry. We worked without supervision. We did not take a break, but worked continuously until noon. We stopped then, whether we had completed our quota or not, and rested for the remainder of the day.

One afternoon, all the Block and Group Leaders were called to a meeting. Cadre Bong complained that we were incorrectly reporting our work in the rice paddies. For example, our crew worked in a 25-acre paddy for one week and reported having cleared 30 acres. The cadre were suspicious of these numbers and came to the paddies to check for themselves. They discovered that we had cleared only 20 acres. From then on, we had to work an additional hour, not leaving the rice paddies until 1:00 PM.

At the end of the month, many people were uneasy. Mr. Liet said, "Why is it taking so long? I have been patient. I have waited a whole month, yet the cadre have not mentioned anything about my release permit."

On April 4, unrest filled the camp. One of my group said he had heard that the cadre had completed the release permits, but could not release any prisoners yet. Supposedly, the camp supplier owed us all money for our food because the

Communists had not given us enough food while we were imprisoned. The camp supplier did not have enough money to pay his debt, but was working on it. He intended to have the money by April 10. At that time, the cadre would release 119 prisoners. My friends responded to this rumor by saying they would wait one more week for their release permits.

On April 8, I heard that the camp supplier left our camp and went to the Reeducation Division Administration Section to ask for money. He would return in a few days. Then the prisoners would be released. During this time, I did not see the camp supplier in our camp. I was convinced that we would all be released soon. For the next two days, I waited.

Every few hours I heard my friends ask each other, "When will the camp supplier return?" In the evening, people lay on their beds and tried to sleep. They asked, "Does anyone see the camp supplier returning?"

Eventually, the rumor circulated that the camp supplier had returned, but the Reeducation Division Administration did not have enough money to pay the camp's debt to us. They owed each of us 150 piastres. The amount was too much, and they did not have it. They promised to repay the amount owed on April 20. The prisoners would be released on that date. We waited again.

Later, another rumor circulated that the camp supplier was preparing to go to the Reeducation Division Administration Section the next day to collect our money and release permits.

The following morning, while we ate breakfast, the camp supplier walked past our quarters with a satchel in his hand.

Some people shouted as they saw him pass, "The camp supplier is leaving for the Reeducation Division Administration Section! He is going to bring back our money! There he is!"

Most of us were eating. We grabbed our rice bowls and ran to the doors. We stood in the doorway, our eyes sparkling with hope, as we watched him leave. Until now we had never cared about him, a Communist soldier. Now he was the most important man in our lives and we paid close attention to him. If he was absent for one day, we would ask each other, "Where is he?"

That afternoon many of us asked, "Has he returned yet?"

Some people responded, "We've been waiting since this morning, but we haven't seen him return yet."

At night, before going to sleep, they asked, "Has the camp supplier returned yet?"

At 5:00 PM on April 20, someone shouted, "He is returning! Here he comes!"

I ran outside. I stood motionless, watching him. We all were eager to see if he had brought the money back.

Mr. Liet said, "His satchel is still flat."

A man standing near me said, "Never mind. There are only 119 of us. The amount of money is not much, only 18,000 piastres. It is a small amount." After that we waited.

The next day we heard that the Reeducation Division Administration still did not have enough money to pay their debt. They had only half of the amount, so they suggested the camp supplier take half now and the other half later. He refused because he worried that if he took half of the money now, it would be too easily stolen. He decided to wait until the Reeducation Division Administration had all the money; then he would take it all at the same time. We waited.

In the fourth week of April, the number of guards suddenly increased from six to 25. Among the guards were Cadre Boi, Cadre Hon, Cadre Uyen, Cadre Bong, and Cadre Thao. The rest were noncommissioned officers and soldiers.

On the last day of the month, all the Block and Group Leaders attended a meeting in the Camp Administration section. Cadre Bong reviewed our work. He said we had done a good job and had cleared all of the rice paddies. He said we had obeyed the camp rules and had worked hard.

That evening, the cadre burned all the dried plants and trees. The next morning, the surface of the ground would be covered by ash. The ash would fertilize the ground, so we could sow the fields.

Seventeen

MAY and JUNE 1978

May 1, 1978, was a Labor Day festival, so we did not work. Instead, we rested and attended a meeting. The Camp Political Officer announced a new plan for the next two months. Our camp would fight a "Production Battle" and attack the job of seed sowing. The cadre wanted us to finish by June.

To accomplish this task, the cadre needed as large a number of prisoners working on the farms as possible. They reassigned all the prisoners who had been barbers or carpenters or blacksmiths to work on the farms.

To save time, we would pick up our breakfast and lunch in the kitchen every morning at 7:00. For breakfast, we would eat boiled cassava in our quarters. For lunch, we would take rice and dried fish to work with us. By eating on the farm, we would not waste time walking back and forth to camp. We would not return to camp until late afternoon, when we would be finished working for the day. At that time, we were to pick up our dinner from the kitchen, which would be rice, dried fish, and vegetable soup.

The cadre did not want us to waste time visiting our relatives. We would be allowed to sleep in the visiting house for one night only, and all the relatives had to leave camp by the next morning.

The following morning, a cadre and two soldiers walked into the visiting house. Armed with rifles, they ordered the visitors to leave immediately.

A half hour later, all the prisoners left camp and went to the farms we had cleared last February. We gathered the wood which had not been completely burned and put it in piles, then burned it again. One cadre and four soldiers watched us work, their rifles preventing us from being lazy.

That morning, I saw two prisoners from my block, Mr.

Hung and Mr. Chau, brutally beaten because they had stopped to rest. My other group members and I did not want to be beaten and we all worked hard.

We did not have a labor quota, so we worked until noon, took an hour's break for lunch, then went back to work. We returned to camp one hour before the sky darkened. By the time we reached our quarters it was dark outside.

On the morning of May 4, 1978, I felt especially tired and wanted to avoid the hard labor on the farms, so I reported sick. When I reached the examination area, I saw 40 other patients there. When it was time for our examination, a soldier came by and wrote our names in a notebook. Then he said, "Today, all the other people are working hard in the farms, and all of you are here resting, so we will look for some easy work for you to do. Please try your best to do these easy tasks."

He handed the patient list to Soldier Tong and Soldier Phan. I knew that these two soldiers were cruel and often cursed at us.

Soldier Tong and Soldier Phan led us to their house, then ordered us to cut all the saplings and weed the grass in their yard. While I worked, I began a light conversation with the patient next to me.

Fifteen minutes after we started working, the two soldiers walked towards me. They pointed their hands at me and the man I was talking to and shouted angrily, "Why do you talk to each other while you are working! Leave your bush knives there! Stand up and follow us!"

It quickly became obvious that these soldiers intended to beat us. I knew that if I wanted to avoid this beating, I would have to think fast and choose my words carefully.

We stood up and followed the two soldiers to their house. As soon as I stepped into the doorway I said, "Excuse me, I would like to tell you something."

I stood there and politely looked at them. When the

soldiers saw my calm manner, their eyes softened and their anger subsided. I felt fairly confident then that I would avoid being beaten. One of them asked, "While you were working, you were talking to each other. Why were you talking?"

Quickly, I thought up an answer, "I am sick today and did not have any medicine. I asked this man if he had some medicine I could borrow, to help this cold. I just asked him for some pills. Please, sir, forgive us for talking."

One of them answered, "Very well, but don't talk anymore. Return to your places and grab your bush knives. We will take you to a different place to work."

They told us to dig up and remove a large tree stump near their house. They handed me a shovel. I looked at the shovel and realized that the blade was cracked from the left side to the middle. I did not say anything, but I figured that this was a trap. These soldiers had not forgiven me and had not given up. They were looking for a reason to beat me, so they gave me a cracked shovel. If I used it, the blade would break. Then they would say that I did not want to work and broke the shovel on purpose. That would be their excuse to beat me.

Trying to avoid this trap, I dug the ground up with my bush knife. I carefully used the shovel to pick up the soil. Sometimes the soldiers came by and inspected my work. I tried very hard to get on their good side and exchanged a few words with them.

At noon the soldiers told us to stop working and take the tools to their house so we could return to camp and take a break. When I turned my shovel in, the two soldiers looked at it. Then they looked at each other, but did not say anything. Even though they did not speak, I understood what they meant to say. They wanted to say to each other, "The blade of the shovel is not broken in half yet."

I pretended not to know their intention. Before I left there I talked with them. I tried to get sympathy from them because I still had to see them that afternoon.

When I returned to camp many of the other patients gathered around me. They congratulated me and said that yesterday the number of patients suddenly went up to 60. One of the patients, Mr. Lan, was beaten by these same two soldiers. Today, the number of patients was down to 40.

Everyone thought I would be beaten, but I had avoided it. I learned that the cadre had increased the labor quota and were forcing us to work by taking away such ways out as reporting sick. I worked until dark that afternoon along with all the other patients.

The next day I did not report sick, but I asked two patients, Mr. Ha and Mr. Lich, how many people had reported being sick that day. They said the number of patients had decreased to four. All were allowed to rest in their quarters and none had to work.

During the second week of May, the labor program changed: the Camp Political Officer announced we would begin sowing. The quota for each of us was to sow 200 square yards per day.

The number of guards had been reduced from five to two. Now there were only two soldiers inspecting my block, and when they came to the farm they looked for a tree to rest under. Our Group Leaders supervised us, but I was still uneasy. I thought if I was lazy or left the farm I would be beaten, so I stayed and worked hard.

Because we had to complete our labor quota within the day, I did my best to finish as soon as possible. I worked without taking any breaks, and I used only half an hour for lunch. All of my group did the same, and we completed our quota by 3:00 PM. Our Block Leaders reported our work to the soldiers and we returned to camp. We were back at our quarters by 4:00.

In the morning, the cadre released the first set of prisoners, 40 of those who had been on leave the previous February. That afternoon I heard that the cadre would release many more of us, in small sets like this. In the evening, we sat and talked, paying close attention to the news of the releases.

Two days later, the cadre released a second set of 40 prisoners who had been on leave in February. That afternoon I heard the rumor again that the cadre planned to release prisoners in several small sets, but this time we were convinced that the cadre were ready to release all of us. That evening I sat with my group, discussing the topic of release. We were so excited that we ignored our weariness from the hard labor and didn't go to sleep until almost 10:30.

The next day the cadre ordered each block to kill the pig it had been given last month. My group and I were surprised, because when the cadre gave us our pig it weighed only 25 kilograms. At that time they told us, "Raise this pig until the Lunar New Year Festival; by then it will be big enough to kill and eat at our party."

Our pig was still small, so we asked the cadre, "It is small. Why kill it now?"

They answered, "Our superiors told us to kill the pig and eat it, because all the reeducation prisoners will be released soon, and there will be no food for the pig to eat."

That evening, we ate pork and excitedly discussed the anticipated release.

It rained heavily the next day. Strong winds blew against our quarters, shaking the walls. We worried that our barracks would fall down. Our Block Leader asked the cadre to allow some of us to go into the forest and bring back some wooden poles to support the roof. The cadre would not allow this, saying, "It would be a waste of time to repair the barracks, because you will all be released soon."

The following morning, the cadre told 30 prisoners who had not been on leave to report to the Camp Administration Section. The cadre prepared the documents for their release and told them to get ready to leave. They also ordered those who had jobs such as Block Leader, Deputy Block Leader, etc., to let someone else take over their position.

The cadre called two prisoners from my group, Mr.

Hien and Mr. Khanh, to the Camp Administration Section. They had not been on leave like the others, but the cadre prepared their documents anyway. Since Mr. Khanh was our Block Deputy Leader, the cadre told him to choose another prisoner to take his place.

The next day, the cadre ordered 20 prisoners to work at the Reeducation Regiment Administration Section. While they worked, they heard the Regiment Commander tell the Supply Cadre, "Even though we are having a lot of difficulties, we still only have from now till the end of June to repay our debt to the prisoners. In 1977, the government announced that this program would last for only three years. By the end of June 1978, these men will have been imprisoned for three years, and it will be time for us to release them. Therefore, our superiors have ordered the food rations of the cadre and soldiers to be decreased to the lowest level possible. We will use the money saved to repay our debt to the prisoners."

When the prisoners who heard this returned to camp, they shared the good news with everyone else.

Thirty-nine prisoners who had been on leave during February were released the next day.

My friends and I were convinced that we would be released soon. I intended to work hard so the cadre would consider me a good worker and release me sooner. We forgot our weariness and stayed up late every night, discussing our release.

The cadre took advantage of our excitement. In mid-May the Camp Political Officer announced that our labor quota would increase from 200 to 300 square yards per day per person. My group talked only about being released; none of us said anything about the increased quota. We were so excited about being released that we did not care about the quota.

The next day, I did not see any guards on the farms. I worked hard without taking a break. I took half an hour for lunch, then worked until I finished my quota.

It was dark by the time we returned to camp. We got our food from the kitchen. The cooks told us that tomorrow our ration would be decreased from three meals a day to two. Our food had been boiled cassava for breakfast, then rice and dried fish for lunch and dinner. Now we ate rice for breakfast, boiled cassava for dinner, and nothing for lunch.

To deal with the food decrease, I ate with my friend, Mr. Cuong. For breakfast, we harvested cassava roots from the farms around the camp. For lunch, we ate the rice that the kitchen provided every morning. For dinner, we cooked the food that Mr. Cuong's wife supplied him. I noticed others of our group doing the same. I still thought the cadre would release me soon, and I wanted them to consider me worthy, so I did not complain. I did not hear anyone else complain about the decrease in our rations either. I only heard talk about being released soon.

One day I did not feel well, so I reported sick. Only two other patients were there. The soldier responsible for the examinations allowed all three of us to return to our quarters and rest. I realized then that it was easy to rest at home, so I decided to report sick for one week straight. After four days I noticed the number of patients ranged from two to four people, and we all were allowed to rest in our quarters.

I asked Mr. Lich and Mr. Ha, who had often claimed to be sick, "Why don't you report sick anymore?"

They looked at me in surprise. "It is foolish to report being sick now, because the cadre are considering who they will release. If we report sick a lot, they will not think we are good workers and may not release us." Because of their advice, I changed my mind and went back to work the next day.

At the end of June 1978, we finished sowing. We waited, but the cadre did not release any more of us.

Two of my group, Mr. Hien and Mr. Khanh, became very angry, and I heard one of them say, "We have been tricked once more by the cadre."

I also knew that the cadre had lied to us, but I did not

want to say anything. If I got mad or spoke out against the cadre's policies, it would not solve anything, and I would get punished for it.

On the last day of June, Camp Political Officer Boi reviewed our work for the last two months. He said we had done a good job and had finished sowing on all the farms. All the cadre applauded us for accomplishing the camp goal. To congratulate us, they ordered the cooks to kill a pig.

Eighteen

JULY 1978

That evening, our Group Leaders announced the cadre's new four-month-plan. We would weed grass on the farms we had already sowed. Our labor quota was 300 square yards per person per day.

At 7:30 AM on July 1, we entered the farms and began to weed with our hoes. No one supervised us and we completed our quota by noon. We rested for the remainder of the day.

In the evening, I sat with several other reeducation prisoners and talked about the rumor of our being released by the end of June. We had all believed it. Everything the cadre had done had supported this promise. But we had not been released. We were dumbfounded over the unfulfilled promises of the cadre, and their deception angered several of us.

Mr. Khanh, who had been issued his release documents last May, spoke out in anger, "It was stupid to believe the Communists. We've already spent three years in the reeducation camps. The policies were clearly explained on paper, but the cadre did not honor them. The more we believed them, the more they tricked us."

Two days after this discussion one of the cadre came to our barracks while we were all still asleep. He told Mr. Hung to gather his luggage and prepare to leave right away. When we got up, we were all surprised and uneasy about what had happened to Mr. Hung.

We said to each other, "Why does he leave alone? Before, we always moved to a new camp in a vehicle convoy. The cadre never moved one man alone before. What kind of trouble is he in?"

That afternoon, I heard a rumor from one of my group: "Mr. Hung made a mistake while at work last May and had been one of the prisoners beaten that month. The cadre watched to see if he made any more mistakes. Today, they took him to a secret place to beat him again."

We worried about Mr. Hung. We wondered where they took him, and how badly he might be treated.

The next day, we listened in fear as one of my group narrated a rumor he had heard.

"The Communists have been following all the reeducation prisoners for three years now and have singled out the stubborn ones. Without warning, they will take each one to a secret place to kill him. If the cadre take one prisoner away alone, like Mr. Hung, it means he is in grave danger.

"In other camps this has happened. The cadre took prisoners, one at a time, away at night. Their relatives have been waiting for a year now and still have not received any news from them.

"If we do not want to be taken away and killed, we should be careful about what we say and not express any more disagreeable thoughts."

We all agreed that we were in a dangerous situation. We believed we would be killed if we said anything that showed dissatisfaction with Communist policy. No one even mentioned the Communists' promise of a three-year reeducation period. Mr. Khanh, who had spoken out earlier, was especially afraid and regretted what he had said. He did not say anything else about his discontent.

While we worried that the Communists would kill us, the cadre announced that a typhoon and flood had taken place in northern Vietnam. We therefore had to save our rice to help the hungry population. Our new food ration was two meals of boiled cassava per day. We lost one meal of rice per day, but no one dared to say anything about the decrease.

On July 8 the cadre took advantage of an actual conflict between China and Vietnam. They gave an old newspaper to each of several groups of prisoners and let us read about it. The Chinese government was protesting the Vietnamese government's poor treatment of Chinese living in Vietnam. (At this time, there were about 2,000,000 Chinese living in Vietnam, with Vietnamese citizenship. They had been in Vietnam for several generations and most of them lived in the cities and worked in business trades.) The Chinese government had announced that they would bring ships to Vietnam and repatriate the ethnic Chinese.

I was surprised because China and Vietnam were two brother Communist nations. Why were they having this problem now? I discussed it with some of my group. One of them said, "A war will probably break out between them." That evening no one mentioned the reeducation policies. The cadre had successfully used an actual event to distract us from thinking about their broken promises.

A couple of days later, one of my group told me about a BBC announcement that Chinese warships had moved in close to Vung Tau, about 75 miles from Ho Chi Minh City. The ships sat three miles offshore and tried to provoke the Vietnamese, but the Vietnamese army did not respond. He also said the BBC claimed that local authorities in Vung Tau were forcing civilians to build anti-tank traps and ditches along the seashore, to defend the shoreline in case the Chinese attacked.

I lay in bed that night and imagined the Chinese warships provoking the Vietnamese army at Vung Tau. I was anxious about this and decided to ask some of the visiting relatives tomorrow.

When I came back from work the next day, I walked to the visiting house and talked to three women staying there. I asked them about the rumor regarding Chinese warships attacking Vung Tau. They said they did not pay any attention to politics and did not know whether it was true or not because they were too busy just trying to survive and provide for their families.

They did mention, though, that Camp Political Officer Boi had come to the visiting house and talked to them. He explained that the cadre had intended to release all of the reeducation prisoners, but now that they were having a conflict with China, they had to delay the release for a short while. He promised that the cadre would release the prisoners later, when it was safe.

The next morning, the cadre ordered us to repair our barracks. We weatherproofed them from wind and rain. That afternoon, they gave a small pig to each block of prisoners and told us, "Raise this pig until the Lunar New Year Festival. We will eat it then."

My group members and I believed the rumors about the Chinese conflict were true. We all believed we would not be released now, but would only have to stay in the reeducation camps for a while longer.

Soon we began to clear the land around our barracks, and to sow seeds for individual vegetable gardens.

In mid-July, the cook for my block announced that our food ration had been changed from two meals of boiled cassava to two meals of millet per day. Millet tasted better than cassava. The cadre also supplied us with 2.4 piastres of extra supplies such as soap, sugar and tobacco. We were a little more relaxed because of the increase in our food and supplies.

Then the cadre created hope for us again. One of my group told me he had heard that the BBC had announced the introduction of a government in exile in Australia. They were led by Vinh Xuan Nguyen, a former Colonel in the South Vietnamese Air Force (under President Diem Dinh Ngo). Nguyen had previously resigned his position in the Old Government in order to study at an American university. When he graduated, he worked for NASA. He quit this job and now led this new government. I was glad to hear this rumor and discussed it with my group.

A few days later, the cadre reinforced it with another. One of my group said he had heard that a boat had escaped from Vietnam last week. When it came to Truong Sa Island the refugees saw a lot of navy ships flying flags from the Old Regime. The sailors supplied the refugees with water and food and told them, "The political situation of Vietnam will be changed very soon, so please return there. Don't escape again. It would be a waste to do so."

The cadre continued to reinforce the rumor of a government in exile. I heard about a lady who had visited one of the prisoners in my camp. She claimed that she had received a letter from a relative in the U.S.A. that said, "If you want to know about the situation in Vietnam, please read the stamp and you will understand."

Everyone in her family was surprised. They looked at the stamp and saw nothing on it. Then they peeled the stamp off the envelop and the words, "Vietnam will be changed soon" appeared on the back of the stamp.

My group and I were happy about these rumors. We talked about them and thought that the political situation in Vietnam would soon change, which was why a government in exile had appeared in Australia.

We heard other stories. A member of my group told me that he had heard of an Army Ranger unit from the Old Regime appearing on National Road Number One (in the Rung La Forest 90 miles north of Ho Chi Minh City). The Rangers stopped some buses and told its passengers to get off. They then gathered the civilians together and told them, "Be patient a while longer. A government in exile is leading the Vietnamese people and army units from the Old Regime. We will fight the Communist government and it will soon fall."

Yet another rumor concerned civilians living in Long Khanh Forest. When they went to work on their farms, they encountered numerous soldiers from the Old Regime. These soldiers, who were in hiding, said to the civilians, "When you return home, please do not reveal that we are here."

My group believed that the political situation of Vietnam would soon change, so we stayed in camp and waited. No one tried to escape and we entirely forgot about the Three Year Reeducation Policies Study Program.

Late in July, I stopped at the visiting house on my

way back from work. One of the visitors was an old man. I walked over and began talking with him. I said I had heard many rumors and I wanted to know if they were true or not.

I asked him about the conflict between China and Vietnam. He revealed that a few months ago the Vietnamese Government had succeeded in implementing its policies throughout Vietnam. They inspected the homes of the rich and confiscated all their property, claiming they were acting in the public interest. Among these rich people were several Chinese with Vietnamese citizenship. The Chinese Government protested this seizure of personal property, and the Vietnamese newspapers reported it. However, the newspapers had not written anything about Chinese warships at Vung Tau Harbor, and he had not heard anyone else talk about it. I realized that this rumor had been spread in our camp only.

I asked him about the government in exile. He said he had listened to the BBC and had read the newspapers every day, but he did not know anything about a government in exile. He said that no one from any exiled government or Old Government Army units worked in Vietnam anymore. Now I knew that all these rumors were false.

That afternoon, a friend of Mr. Hung's asked his relatives if they knew what had happened to him. They revealed that Mr. Hung had been taken to Ham Tan Reeducation Center. He was safe and sound.

Nineteen

AUGUST and SEPTEMBER 1978

I was sitting in my barracks talking with some of the other reeducation prisoners. Mr. Tuan had recently visited some of his friends in Camps D3 and D5. They told him of some prisoners from those camps who escaped last week. The escaped prisoners told their friends they could no longer believe the cadre. The cadre had told too many lies and broken too many promises over the last three years. They could not be patient anymore. They thought if they continued to wait they would spend the rest of their lives in camps and die from malnutrition.

We discussed Mr. Tuan's story and realized that no one from our camp had escaped over the last month.

Early in August, Camp Political Officer Boi announced that from now on, we would get our breakfast of millet in the kitchen by 6:30 AM. We would continue to weed on the farms, but our labor quota had been increased from 300 square yards to 800 square yards per day per person. We would receive a second meal of millet for dinner in the evening.

Mr. Cuong and I gathered some cassava root from the farm near camp and cooked it that night: we would eat it for breakfast the next day. We also boiled our drinking water. We planned on eating the millet provided by the kitchen for lunch while we were at the farms.

The next morning at 6:30, a bell woke me up. I had not heard it before, and the sound startled me. As soon as the bell stopped, the cooks called us to the kitchen for breakfast.

I took the millet back to my barracks and began eating the cassava that I had cooked the night before. I had just started eating when the bell rang again. It was 7:00 sharp. Soldiers and cadre rushed into our barracks, pointing their guns at us and yelling, forcing everyone outside for muster.

I was afraid of being beaten, so I dropped my bowl, seized my hoe, and ran outside. One of the soldiers counted the number of prisoners in my block. Then four soldiers and a cadre guarded us as we walked to the corn fields three miles away. When we reached the fields, we mustered again. The soldier counted us again and we started working. One soldier stood behind each group, and we were all closely watched.

As I looked at the corn fields, I realized that I could not finish my quota of 800 square yards in one day. It had been a while since the fields were harvested, and the grass grew thick over the ground. I worked at my regular speed, until the labor time was over. I did not try to work harder or faster because I knew I would not be able to leave any sooner. I saw that my group members worked at their regular speed also.

At 10:00, we took a 15-minute break. At 12:00 we took a half-hour lunch break and at 4:00 we took another 15-minute break. The soldiers counted us before and after each break. Because we were so closely guarded, I was forced to stay and work and did not dare leave the fields.

After dinner that evening, I prepared for the next day by heating some drinking water and cooking cassava root. I finished at 9:00 and was exhausted. I went immediately to sleep, as did all my group members.

The next day, the cadre ordered all the relatives to leave the visiting house. I thought this was because the cadre wanted all of the prisoners to go to work on time and not be preoccupied with their relatives.

After a week of increased labor, I concluded that the cadre were probably trying to keep us from escaping by increasing security and ordering a labor quota that we could not fulfill. This kept us from leaving the fields. We worked all day and did not have any free time. By the time we returned to camp, it was night. We were very tired and went to sleep early.

By mid-August, I was physically exhausted. I wanted to avoid hard labor in the fields, so I intended to fake being sick the next day. Mr. Lich and Mr. Ha had pretended to be sick today, so I asked them how it went. They told me that the number of patients had increased to 40. I figured that a large number of prisoners had decided to avoid the work by pretending to be sick and that the cadre would probably deal with this soon. I decided to go to work instead.

The next day when I returned from work, I learned that the number of patients was still 40, and that Camp Political Officer Boi had examined them and prescribed a special medicine. All patients would be under his care for three days. They were to stay in the Camp Administration Section and were not allowed to return to camp. During the day, they sat in the conference hall and were not allowed to do anything. The cooks brought each of them two small bowls of millet soup twice a day. At night, they all slept in the storehouse. The door was locked and no one was allowed to leave. Armed soldiers patrolled outside the storehouse.

On the following day the patients felt worse than before their first day of treatment. They were hungry and wanted to take a bath. Earlier that morning, the Camp Political Officer ordered one of the prisoners to act as a nurse and stay in the conference hall to take care of the patients. He then went to the farms and inspected our work. The patients saw this as an opportunity to return to camp. First Mr. Chau pretended to be seriously sick and fainted. The nurse reported Mr. Chau's condition to the soldier in charge. The nurse suggested to the soldier that the "unconscious" patient be taken back to camp and treated there. The soldier agreed. Four strong patients took Mr. Chau back to camp. As soon as they reached camp, they looked at each other and laughed. All five patients removed their shirts and proceeded to take a bath at the well. They returned to their quarters, cooked some food, and ate. They remained naked to their waists, while they lay sleeping in their hammocks or sitting on their beds playing chess. The other patients in the conference hall followed Mr. Chau's example and started fainting and had to be carried back to camp by other patients.

At 5:00 the Camp Political Officer returned. He came to the conference hall to check on the patients, but was surprised to find that all 40 patients were gone and the conference hall was vacant. He called all the patients back to finish their treatment. Then he added that from now on anyone fainting would be treated in the Camp Administration Section and would not be allowed to return to camp.

The second night, all the patients slept in the storehouse again, and the soldiers beat three of them. Mr. Can and Mr. Anh were caught talking to each other and laughing out loud. Soldiers heard them, dragged them outside, beat them, then put them in the discipline cell for two hours. The discipline cell was a square hole measuring two yards by two yards, and was three yards deep. The hole had a foot and a half of water in it. There were a lot of mosquitoes. Mr. Ha was also beaten that night, but he was not put in the discipline cell afterwards.

All 40 patients were forced to continue Camp Political Officer Boi's prescription on the third day, but no one else was beaten.

On the morning of the fourth day, "Physician" Boi announced that all the patients had recovered from their illness and ordered them to get out of his "hospital" and return to work.

No one dared pretend to be sick anymore. I'm sure some people felt sick, but when they thought about the Camp Political Officer's prescription, they became afraid and their illness disappeared.

Near the end of August, Mr. Ninh escaped. He was the first to escape from this camp in more than a year.

At 5:00 AM on September 1, the cadre came into our barracks and roused us from our sleep. They ordered us to muster outside. All the prisoners stood outside, and 150 were ordered to pack up immediately. They were taken to other reeducation centers that morning. I guessed the cadre were moving them to higher security camps to keep anyone else from trying to escape. There were now 300 prisoners in my camp.

Later that week I realized some things about the re-education camps. In February, one of my group, Mr. Huu, told me he had a cousin who lived in northern Vietnam. His cousin said the Communists used rumors to deal with the civilian population and to accomplish their goals.

When Mr. Huu told me this, I became uneasy. I tried to remember everything that had happened over the past three years. Whenever I had a free moment, I sat alone and silently reviewed it all in my mind. I had been doing this for six months now, and Mr. Huu's story finally made me realize what the Communists were doing. They had manipulated us with rumors and selected news items and had acted in a way that supported the rumors.

The other prisoners and I heard the rumors and observed the show of behavior that the cadre put on to reinforce them. We discussed them with excitement and believed them. We had acted just as the cadre wanted us to.

I realized, too, that the cadre had accomplished many of their goals in the camps. Some took a few weeks to accomplish and some took a few months. In my mind, I sectioned each set of goals, or plan, into a chapter and memorized it.

After I figured out the cadre's plans, I looked for a way to determine their goals for each succeeding period. I thought a lot about this, and by the fourth week of September, I had developed a method for understanding what the cadre were trying to accomplish.

First, I determined the cadre's intent. What did they intend to accomplish in this period?

Second, I determined the cadre's action plan. What camp rules did they enforce? What type of work did they have us do? What news and information did they provide us or allow us to overhear? What rumors did they spread? What action did they take to reinforce camp rules, rumors, and information?

Third, I determined the prisoners' reaction. What did I and the other prisoners think? What did we say? How did we behave?

Fourth, I determined the results of the cadre's action plan. Did I and the other prisoners react the way the cadre intended us to?

I recalled everything I'd experienced in the camps. I identified all the points in the cadre's action plan and in the prisoners' reactions. I guessed the cadre's intentions and deduced whether or not we had reacted the way they intended us to.

When I finished developing this method, I decided to write this book when the opportunity arose. I tried to remember these incidents by reviewing them in my mind, a few chapters each night, before I went to sleep.

Twenty

OCTOBER 1, 1978 to OCTOBER 20, 1978

At the beginning of October, the cadre announced that Camp D1 was closing. That day, 200 prisoners from Camp D1 were transferred to Camp D4B. I was in this group. The remainder of the prisoners from D1 were transferred to Camp D3.

We carried our own luggage and walked about a mile to Camp D4B. When we arrived, our quarters were ready. I spent an hour preparing my sleeping area, then walked around the camp.

The camp was divided into two areas. One area was the Camp Administration Section, where the guards stayed. The other was the reeducation camp, where the prisoners stayed. The prisoners' section had 12 barracks which housed 50 people each. Cassava trees surrounded the camp and there were no fences.

A stream flowed between the Camp Administration Section and the reeducation camp, and a road stretched along both areas. An iron bridge hung above the spring, and any vehicle driving on the road had to pass over it. A guard post sat at the roadside near the Administration Section and about 50 yards from the visiting house. Soldiers were posted there all night, but not during the day. When we had visitors, we walked 300 yards from camp to the road, over the iron bridge, past the guard post, and on to the visiting house.

The prisoners were in three blocks. Each block had four barracks and one kitchen, and consisted of 200 reeducation prisoners. I was in a block of prisoners who had transferred with me from Camp D1. Another block was made up of prisoners who had transferred from Camp D5B. Prisoners who had been here for a while were in the third block.

I talked to some of the prisoners from D5B. They told

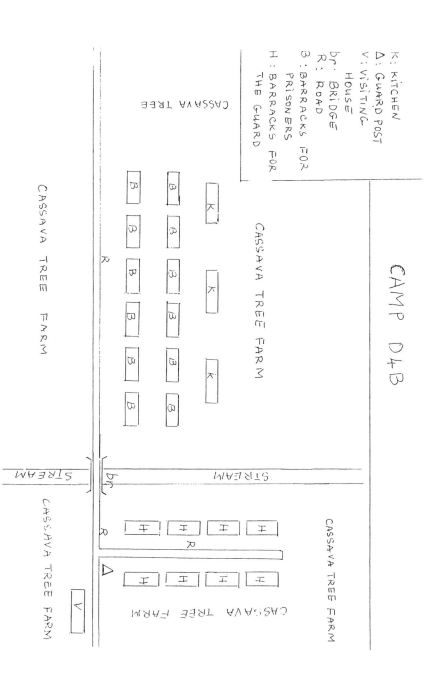

CAMP D4B

K: KITCHEN
△: GUARD POST
V: VISITING HOUSE
br: BRIDGE
R: ROAD
B: BARRACKS FOR PRISONERS
H: BARRACKS FOR THE GUARD

me that in 1977 Camp D5B held about 600 prisoners, but in the spring and summer of 1978, the cadre released several of them. In September, they also transferred many prisoners from Camp D5B to other reeducation centers. Then they closed D5B and moved the remaining 200 prisoners here.

Several of the prisoners who had been in this camp for a long time told me a similar story. The cadre had released some prisoners from this camp in the spring and summer of 1978 too, and in September they transferred others from D4B to different reeducation centers. The remaining 200 were still here.

After talking to them, I realized that our old Camp D1 was in the same situation as Camps D4B and D5B. Many prisoners from these three camps had been released or transferred. Those remaining were so few that the cadre gathered us all into one camp. This made it easier for them to guard us and to supervise our work. I figured that the cadre would eventually take us out of this zone.

Our Block Leader, Mr. Trieu, attended a meeting in the Camp Administration Section. When he returned, he told us that tomorrow my block would go into the forest. Each prisoner would cut eight bamboo pieces, each eight yards long, and carry them back to the Camp Administration Section. A carpentry crew would use the bamboo to build new houses for the cadre.

At 9:00 PM, all the prisoners mustered on the road. The cadre counted us, then Camp Political Officer Chuong announced that from now on, each night at 9:00 PM our camp would collect here and the cadre would count us again.

The next morning, I walked to the forest with my group. I cut down a bamboo tree and measured off an eight-yard piece. I carried it about 500 yards back to the Camp Administration Section. It was heavy, and I could carry only one piece at a time.

At noon, we stopped working and took a two-hour break for lunch. We walked back to camp, ate, and took a nap.

At 2:00 we went back to work, and at 5:00 we stopped working. I did not complete my labor quota, cutting seven bamboo pieces. I checked with my group members. Several of them had achieved their quota, but several had not.

At 5:15 we returned to our barracks. Unfortunately, a few minutes after our return, our Block Leader announced that we needed to muster so the cadre could check our hair. I was surprised because I had been in the camps for more than three years and I never saw the cadre check hair before.

We mustered, then waited several minutes. Finally, one of the cadre came to our block. We sat in several lines. He came to each of us, looked at our hair and said, "Your hair is too long. Cut it. If your hair is not cut the next time we check, we will punish you."

He paused, then looked at us, "All of you have hair that is too long. Next week, we will check again. Anyone whose hair is too long then will be punished."

He paced up and down our line, then continued, "Because many people in your block did not finish their labor quota today, we will punish your whole block tonight. All of you will have to come to the Camp Administration Section and work from seven o'clock to nine o'clock."

After he left, I looked at my watch. It was 6:00 PM. I had only one hour to cook and eat dinner, take a bath, and boil my drinking water for tomorrow. I hurried as fast as I could.

At 7:00, the cadre announced that several prisoners had relatives visiting. These prisoners were excused from the extra labor and went to the visiting house instead. They had to return to camp before 9:00 PM, however, and were not allowed to sleep in the visiting house that night.

I finished eating at 7:00, then our Block Leader called us to go to work at the Camp Administration Section. We dug up dirt, carried it away, then laid the foundation for the new houses that would be built.

We stopped working at 8:45. At 9:00 we mustered outside our quarters and the cadre counted us. Afterward I was so weary that I went straight to bed and fell asleep. We all fell asleep early that night.

The following morning, our Block Leader led us to some cassava farms near the Camp Administration Section. Each of us had to clear 200 square yards. The farms had been harvested a while ago and the forest grew four yards high everywhere. I thought it would be impossible to complete our quota.

We cut down all the trees, then heaped them into several piles. At noon, we returned to camp. After lunch, my group and I sat and waited for the barber to cut our hair. By the time he finished, it was time to go back to work.

We continued cutting trees and piling them up. We stopped working at 5:00. No one in my group had completed his quota.

At 5:15, we returned to camp. As soon as we reached our barracks, our Block Leader announced we would have a barracks inspection in fifteen minutes. We spent that time cleaning our sleeping areas.

At 5:30, one of the cadre came to our quarters. He ordered our block to sit in rows in front of our barracks. Once we were all outside, he went in to inspect. When he finished, he stood in front of us and lectured us on what parts of our quarters were or were not clean enough. Then he told us that our block was being punished for not finishing our labor quota. We had to work in the Camp Administration Section that evening from 7:00 to 9:00.

He finished his speech at 6:00. We had to hurry. In one hour, I took a bath, boiled my drinking water for tomorrow, and ate dinner.

At 7:00, my block went to the Camp Administration Section to work. We again removed dirt and laid foundations for the new houses.

At 9:00, we quit working and the cadre counted us. Afterward, I went straight to bed.

The next day, many of us did not finish our quota, so

we all had to work in the Camp Administration section again.

It was the same the following day. Two other blocks suffered the same punishment.

Reeducation prisoners who reported being sick had to work in the Camp Administration Section for eight hours each day. The soldiers watched them closely as they worked.

I realized that the cadre wanted to keep us in the camp, so they gave us a labor quota that we could not finish. Then they punished us for not finishing and had us work in the evenings. They kept us busy all the time. We did not have any free time and could not go anywhere. At night we were too tired to do anything but sleep.

There were 20 guards, and they were all military personnel. Among them was Camp Political Officer Chuong, who was a captain, and Camp Political Officer Boi (from our previous camp), who was now the Assistant Camp Political Officer.

On October 6, two prisoners from my block, Mr. Son and Mr. Thach, escaped.

A day later, two prisoners from another block escaped.

That evening, our Block Leader, Mr. Trieu, returned from a meeting at the Camp Administration Section and complained about the four men who had escaped.

The prisoners escaped when their wives came to visit them. They came to camp and visited in the evening and when they left the next morning, the prisoners went with them. Our Block Leader criticized these men for not waiting until a few days after their wives left before escaping. It was not good for the rest us.

I thought about Mr. Trieu's words and knew that the cadre would do something to keep anyone else from escaping, but I did not know what they would do.

A couple of days later, I was working on the cassava farms. While on break, some of my group told me about a story they had heard. They said that during the last week, the fiance of one of the prisoners came to our camp to bring supplies and visit. The next morning when he came to the visiting house to say good-bye, he found her crying, so he asked her what was wrong.

Tears rolled down her face as she spoke, "Last night while I was sleeping, a stranger came into my room, pressed me down to the bed, tore my clothes off and raped me. I fought him, but he was too strong and I could not do anything. I shouted for help, but no one came. The most valuable thing, my virginity, I had kept and intended to serve you with it on our wedding night, but last night it was destroyed. How miserable I am!"

My group and I paid much attention to this story and frequently discussed it. The next day I heard another story that a prisoner's sister had come to visit her brother a few days ago. The next morning when he came to the visiting house to say good-bye, he saw his sister crying. He asked her what was wrong, and she told him that the night before a stranger came in and raped her while she was sleeping. She had also called for help, but no one came.

The cadre reinforced the effect of these stories. Five prisoners had relatives in the visiting house. We all worried about them. We suggested the prisoners tell their relatives about the two women who were raped, so they could take precautions that night.

All of the visitors were women. At night each slept in a separate room. Because of the stories, they were afraid. At midnight a stranger in a T-shirt and shorts entered one of the rooms. He lifted up the mosquito net, put his hands on the woman sleeping there, and scared her into thinking he was going to rape her. The woman shouted for help and the stranger ran out of the house. An hour later he returned and did it again. The woman shouted and he ran away again. The visitors were all afraid, so they gathered in one room to sleep for the rest of the night; but the stranger returned three or four more times throughout the night.

The next afternoon, our Block Leaders reported these

terrible incidents to the cadre. Camp Political Officer Chuong told them, "We will investigate them and deal with them."

But that night the same thing happened. The women in the visiting house were terrified and we all worried about their safety.

Again, we prisoners discussed this. We knew that the cadre had not done anything and were not protecting the visitors from the intruder. The guard post was only 50 yards away from the visiting house, and soldiers were there all night. We couldn't understand why the soldiers did not come when the women called for help. The married men worried: What if their wives came to the visiting house and were raped? That afternoon many of my group wrote to their wives, telling them not to visit now.

The rumors interested me and I looked for the two prisoners, the one who had a fiance and the other who had a sister. I tried my best, but I could not find either of them.

An intruder continued to scare the women in the visiting house over the next three days. From October 16 to October 20, the visiting house was vacant. No one had any visitors, and no one else escaped.

On October 20, the Camp Political Officer said, "We investigated the rumors of raped visitors, and we are sure that none of the women were raped in the visiting house. Your relatives who slept there at night were probably afraid of ghosts."

I was certain that the cadre wanted to stop anyone from escaping with his wife, so they spread stories of women being raped in the visiting house. One of the soldiers probably broke into the visiting house and scared the women, pretending that he was going to rape them. Because the men were afraid that their wives would be raped, they all wrote to them and told them not to visit anymore.

I believed that the rumors had been started by the cadre, but I could not figure out how they spread them.

Twenty-one

OCTOBER 21, 1978 to NOVEMBER 4, 1978

On the morning of October 21, the cadre ordered us to gather our luggage and muster in front of our barracks. They then assigned all of us to one of three groups, with 200 prisoners in each group. Camp Political Officer Chuong announced that Camp D4B would be closing today.

Trucks moved one group to another reeducation center. A second group walked to Camp D5, the third to Camp D3. I was assigned to Camp D3.

In 1977, Reeducation Regiment 16 consisted of five camps: D1, D2, D3, D4 and D5. Camp D4B, which we were now leaving, originally belonged to another regiment. It had been added to Regiment 16 a few months ago, making a total of six camps. Four camps: D1, D2, D4 and D4B had recently been closed. Now only D3 and D5 were left.

I figured that because several prisoners had escaped from these camps over the last few months, the Communists probably realized that their methods of information disclosure, rumors, and reinforcement were no longer working on us. They must have decided to close these camps and move us to more secure reeducation centers.

My group reached Camp D3 around noon. There were not enough barracks for all of us, so we were crammed together in the few existing barracks. I spent half an hour preparing my living area, then I walked around camp to see what it was like.

Cassava trees surrounded the camp. There were no fences or guard posts. A large soccer field occupied the center of camp, and barracks lined both sides of the field. There was only one well, but it was seldom used. Instead, I noticed the prisoners walking to a stream about 100 yards away. That would be where we would take our baths, clean our clothes, and

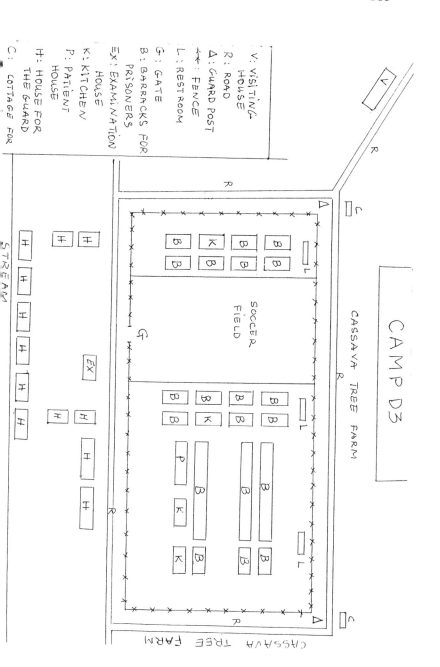

CAMP D3

Legend:

V: VISITING HOUSE
R: ROAD
Δ: GUARD POST
↔ : FENCE
L: RESTROOM
G: GATE
B: BARRACKS FOR PRISONERS
EX: EXAMINATION HOUSE
K: KITCHEN
P: PATIENT HOUSE
H: HOUSE FOR THE GUARD
C: COTTAGE FOR

SOCCER FIELD

CASSAVA TREE FARM

CASSAVA TREE FARM

STREAM

draw our drinking water. A forest lined the far bank, and the Camp Administration Section sat on the near bank.

That afternoon, everyone attended a camp meeting on the soccer field. Camp Political Officer Ngo said, "This morning, many prisoners from our camp were taken to other reeducation centers, and 200 prisoners from Camp D4B were moved here. The number of reeducation prisoners in our camp is now 650. There are several barracks which are old and not safe for you to stay in. Therefore, you will build new barracks and rebuild several of the old barracks over the next two weeks."

In the morning, my Group Leader announced our labor quotas. Each of us had to go into the forest and cut 10 bamboo pieces eight yards long and bring them back to camp. We would give them to a carpentry crew who would build the new barracks. The forest edge was only 100 yards away from our camp, so we were able to finish our labor quota in the morning and rest in the afternoon.

While my crew gathered bamboo, and the carpenters built barracks, I noticed some work quietly going on that the Camp Political Officer had not mentioned in our meeting. A crew of about 30 prisoners were building two bamboo fences, half a yard apart, around our camp. Another crew of 10 was on the other side of the fences, laying a road around our camp. Still another crew of 10 were building guard posts along the outside fence. A soldier could stand at the guard post and easily observe the entire camp. This same group was also building a small cottage next to each guard post so the soldiers would have a place to stay while on duty.

There were 20 guards in Camp D3. Among them were five cadre: Captain Quy, Captain Thuy, Captain Tu, Lieutenant Ngo, and Lieutenant Bong. The others were soldiers.

Captain Thuy was the Camp Commander. Captain Quy, who had previously been the Camp Political Officer, became the new Deputy Camp Political Officer, and Lieutenant Ngo became the new Camp Political Officer. The other prisoners and I wondered why Lieutenant Ngo was given a higher position than Captain Quy, given that his military rank was lower. We concluded that Lieutenant Ngo had probably been in the Communist Party longer.

That evening, I lay in bed and reviewed my experiences of the past two days. Questions popped into my mind: Why are the cadre ordering prisoners to build fences and guard posts around our camp? Why didn't the Camp Political Officer announce this work, during our camp meeting? Why are the cadre being so quiet about it?

I thought about this until I fell asleep. I suspected that because several prisoners from this and other camps had escaped during the last few months, the cadre decided to secure our camp. If the Camp Political Officer had openly revealed this to us, the number of prisoners trying to escape would have increased. Therefore, the cadre needed to accomplish this task quietly, so we would not take notice of it.

The next afternoon I heard from one of my group members that the cadre would inspect our luggage and collect all of our rice, sugar, medicine and cotton. The cadre would confiscate any items we could possibly use in an escape.

That evening some soldiers came to our barracks. They told us that the cadre would check our luggage and collect our supplies sometime within the next few days.

When they left, we discussed what the soldiers had said. We all agreed that these supplies were necessary for our survival and decided to conceal them from the cadre.

Afterward, I went to the barracks of my friend, Mr. Cuong. Mr. Cuong and I cooked and ate our food, then he informed me that one of the soldiers had just come to his group and warned them that the cadre would inspect their luggage. He intended to put his supplies in an iron box and bury it in the ground.

The other prisoners in Mr. Cuong's group told me they intended to hide their supplies also. Mr. So said he would hide his medicine in the roof of his barracks. Mr. Dai said he would put his rice in the hollow middle of a piece of bamboo, then tie it to the wall.

The following afternoon soldiers came to our barracks and told us that the cadre would check our luggage and collect our supplies the next day. When we heard this, my group members, Mr. Cuong and I discussed our plans. We put our sugar, medicine, rice, etc. in iron boxes, dug a hole in the ground, and buried the boxes there.

We waited all the next day, but the cadre did not come. In the evening, we dug up our supply boxes, took out some rice, and cooked and ate it. We put our supplies back in our bags when we finished. A few hours later, some soldiers came by. They had just left a meeting with the cadre. They explained that the cadre had planned to collect our supplies, but they did not have time today and intended to do so in the next day or two. The soldiers also said that they would be in a lot of trouble if the cadre found out that they had leaked this information to us.

Regardless of the soldiers' request, we spread the rumor throughout camp. We all buried our supplies. Two days later the cadre still had not checked anything.

On the evening of October 27, we dug up our supplies, cooked our rice, and ate it. A few hours later, the soldiers came to our quarters again and said that the cadre had intended to collect our supplies today. Instead, they held another meeting and decided it was necessary to build our barracks first. Therefore, they would not collect our supplies until tomorrow. After we heard this, we discussed it and excitedly passed the information to other prisoners. Everyone buried his supplies again. Then we waited.

In the morning, the cadre ordered us to take our luggage to the soccer field so they could check it. As soon as we heard this, Mr. Cuong said, "These soldiers are very good, they told us the truth."

All the people who hid their supplies were glad. We grabbed our luggage and gathered on the soccer field. Some people, however, had not hidden their supplies. They did not know what to do so they threw their supply boxes in one of the trash pits along the way.

The cadre did not take anything from us. They walked through our quarters and when the soldiers saw the supply boxes in the trash pits, they picked them up and brought them to the soccer field. In the places where we buried our supplies, the color of dirt was different from the ground around it. I thought they could easily see it, but they pretended not to notice and did not disturb any of these places.

After they checked our quarters, they came to the soccer field. They stood next to where we all sat and held a meeting. During their meeting, we clearly heard one of them say, "How smart the prisoners are! They guessed that we would check their luggage and collect their supplies, so they hid everything. We found only a few boxes. I think if we want to find their supplies, we should hold a surprise inspection sometime next week." They returned all the confiscated supply boxes to us.

Two days later, we were prepared for them to check our luggage; we kept our supplies buried. We waited all day, but the cadre did nothing. In the evening, we dug our supplies up, took out the rice, then cooked and ate it. A few hours later, the soldiers came to our quarters again and told us that the cadre would check our luggage in the next day or two. We quickly buried our supplies again.

The next day, we waited, but the cadre did not check our luggage.

The day after was the same. In the evening we dug our supplies up, took the food, cooked and ate it. A few hours later, the soldiers came to our quarters and told us that the cadre had just finished meeting and intended to check our luggage tomorrow or the next day. We spread the news to the other prisoners and buried our supplies again.

The following day the cadre still did not check our luggage. Nor the day after. In the evening, we dug up our supplies, cooked and ate. Then the soldiers came and told us that the cadre would surely check our luggage tomorrow or the next day. We buried our supplies again.

On the morning of November 4, the cadre announced that they would check our luggage. We were all glad that we had hidden our supplies. Mr. Cuong said, "The last time we buried our supplies in the ground, and the cadre could not find it. This time I think that even the ghosts could not discover where our supplies are, let alone the cadre or soldiers."

When we gathered on the soccer field, the cadre did not check the luggage we brought with us. Instead, they went to our quarters and looked for places where the color of the dirt was different from that of the ground around it. We watched helplessly as the cadre pushed iron rods into the ground to look for our supply boxes. They found everything, and we lost it all.

In the evening we attended a camp meeting on the soccer field. Political Officer Ngo reviewed our work. He said, "You did a great job. You rebuilt all the old barracks and constructed four new barracks over the last two weeks. Now all the barracks are in good condition, and the cadre applaud you for this. Nevertheless, the cadre have complained that there are a few prisoners who continue to oppose Communist policies, and two prisoners have escaped." One of the escaped prisoners was Mr. Lac, from my block. I did not know who the other prisoner was.

As I listened to Officer Ngo, I realized that while we had all focused on hiding our supplies from the cadre, no one had paid attention to the fences and guard posts being built. Now they were finished. Our camp was about 200 by 400 yards and we were completely enclosed by fencing. Once again we were under tight control.

Twenty-two

NOVEMBER 5, 1978 to NOVEMBER 30, 1978

On November 5, Political Officer Ngo announced that from now on we had to stay inside the bamboo fences when our labor period was over. If anyone wanted to go outside the gate, he had to ask permission from the soldier at the guard post. Also, we would finish harvesting all the rice paddies that our camp was responsible for by the end of November. Our individual labor quotas were 45 kilograms of paddy per day.

I woke up at 6:00 AM. I had one hour to eat and prepare for our labor. Today we ate boiled cassava and dried shrimp for breakfast.

At 7:00 the bell rang, and we gathered at the gate. The cadre and soldiers inspected our bags, paying close attention to any that appeared overstuffed. One prisoner, Mr. Hung, had put two coats in his, so the cadre pulled him out of line and did not allow him to go to work with the rest of us.

After our inspection, we walked to the farms in two lines. Soldiers walked on both sides and guarded us with loaded AK-47's. When we reached the farms, we mustered. The cadre counted us, then announced that the soldiers had orders to kill any prisoner who walked 50 yards or more beyond our work area. As we worked, the soldiers kept their rifles trained on us.

At noon, we took a half-hour lunch break. The cadre gave each of us a loaf of bread. Both before and after our break, we mustered so the cadre could count us.

At 5:00 a truck arrived and we loaded it with sacks of paddy. Then it drove on to the storehouse. The cadre did not weigh the sacks before the truck left.

We finished at 5:30. The cadre counted us again and we left the farm.

We returned to camp at 6:00. Before we went through the gate the cadre counted us again. As we went inside, I saw a small hut that had been built while we were at work. It stood near the gate, just inside the fence. Mr. Hung was there, his legs chained to this hut. (The cadre kept him there for two weeks.)

Looking at Mr. Hung, I decided I would not put very much in my bag when I went to work tomorrow. I would bring only a water pot and a little food. No one put much in their bags after seeing Mr. Hung.

When I returned to my barracks, Mr. Cuong told me that the cadre had started a camp patient house. All the patients in the clinic received orders to return to camp to stay in the new patient house.

Mr. Cuong said that the prisoners assigned to special crews had received orders to return to camp at night, as well. These prisoners worked in the vegetable gardens, pig sty, storehouse, or forge and had houses near their work places outside of our camp. The cadre trusted them, so they were put on special crews and allowed to go alone to their work places and back to camp again unguarded. I guessed that the cadre now decided to keep all the reeducation prisoners in camp whenever we were not working, so they could more easily guard everyone.

At 6:30, I brought my dinner back from the kitchen. We ate rice, dried fish, and vegetable soup. The food ration was almost enough to satisfy our hunger.

After dinner, Some reeducation prisoners who had relatives visiting them gathered at the camp gate. A soldier led them to the visiting house. They stayed for two hours, then returned to camp for the night. They would be allowed to come back for 15 minutes the next morning to say good bye.

At 9:00, we mustered on the soccer field, and the cadre counted us. After that, Camp Political Officer Ngo gave recognition for our first harvest day. He said, "Please try your best to work better. Your friends in Camp D5 work better than you do. They all finished their labor quotas. Each of them harvested 45 kilograms today. You harvested a mere 20 kilograms each today, and we do not feel good about reporting these low numbers to our supervisors."

I felt uneasy about his statement because I did not see the cadre weigh the paddy sacks today. I wondered how they knew the weight of our sacks. Nevertheless, I overheard some of my group say, "Camp D5 did very well."

In the afternoon of the following day, the paddy truck broke down and we had to carry our paddy sacks from the farms to the storehouse by foot. At the storehouse I saw friends from Camp D5. They praised us on how well we harvested.

I was surprised and asked them how they knew we did so well. They said that their Camp Political Officer had told them that everyone in our camp had harvested 45 kilograms of paddy per day, and they had only harvested 20 kilograms pounds of paddy per person per day.

When I explained to them that our Camp Political Officer had told us just the opposite, we understood that both Camp Political Officers had lied.

Later that afternoon, I was weary and wanted to avoid the hard work. I intended to act sick the next day. But that night I noticed 30 patients who were still working and I realized that this was not a good time to feign sickness.

The following day, while we were harvesting, I saw a soldier escort 13 patients from camp to the farms. There they were forced to work like other, healthier people.

Soon one patient fainted and four others carried him back to camp. Fifteen minutes later another fainted, and after that every 15 minutes a patient fainted and was carried back to camp. By mid-morning all of the patients had returned to camp.

That night we gathered for an announcement from the Political Officer. He said that from now on, the reeducation prisoners who were assigned to be camp nurses had to come to the farms and treat the patients there. The cadre would not allow any more unconscious patients to return to camp. If a prisoner fainted and other prisoners carried him back to camp, the cadre would confine all of them to a discipline cell.

The next morning I reluctantly went to work and no one reported being sick. A friend told me that six prisoners escaped last night through a hole they had made in the bamboo fence.

That evening, the cadre began spreading more rumors. Some people in my group said that we would be leaving this camp and moving to a new camp soon. We would start harvesting rice, but would probably not finish. Soldiers would come here to replace us and finish the harvest. The cadre would bring the soldiers by vehicle convoy, then those same vehicles would take us to a new camp. The cadre were preparing for this now and intended to accomplish it by the 15th or the 25th of this month. I anxiously discussed all of this with my friends.

One day later the cadre ordered us to complete an information sheet with our names and old military ranks noted on the upper right hand corner of the first page. We were told to finish quickly and take it to the cadre that evening. I heard from members of my group that the new place would divide us into camps according to our rank. That was why the cadre needed this information, so they would know what camp to put us in.

Mr. Cuong related another rumor he had heard. Two of our cadre, Captain Quy and Captain Tu, had left to bring the soldiers to our camp. Mr. Cuong was the camp barber, and he had received an order to report to the Camp Administration Section today to cut the cadre's hair. When he arrived, Captain Quy and Captain Tu were the only ones absent, so my friend was sure they had left to get the new soldiers.

The next morning a crew of reeducation prisoners who worked in the rice storehouse saw a banner hanging up at the Regiment Administration gate. The banner read, "Welcome to the New Comrade Warriors joining our Unit." The prisoners told everyone of this as soon as they returned to camp.

One evening Mr. Cuong told me about an incident that had happened earlier that morning. Some reeducation prisoners were working inside our camp at the patient house when they saw six cadre captains from the Regiment Administration Section examining our quarters. The cadre entered the patient house and reported to Political Officer Ngo who was inspecting the prisoner work crew. The prisoners heard one of the cadre say in a loud voice, "All of the houses are still in good condition. When our soldiers come here, they will not have to repair anything."

As soon as Lieutenant Ngo heard these words, he said with a straight face, "You, Comrade, are careless. You have revealed important plans. If the prisoners know about it, how will we achieve it?"

When Lieutenant Ngo finished speaking, the cadre knew that they had made a mistake, and they bowed their heads and went away. The prisoners working there at the time saw this happen, and they told everyone in camp about it.

The rumors and the events that the cadre created to reinforce the rumors inspired excitement throughout our camp. My friends and group members sat up late talking about our leaving.

On November 14, one of the cadre called the bakery crew to report to the Camp Administration Section immediately. Normally this crew made bread in the morning and we ate it at noon. Today, the cadre ordered them to bake bread that evening. While the bakers worked, soldiers came to my quarters and told us that we would all be moving to a new camp tomorrow.

Later, observing other groups, I realized that all the reeducation prisoners were preparing to leave. Some of them cooked sweet soup or sticky rice. Some killed their chickens or cooked food for a good-bye party. Many were packing their personal belongings in whatever bags they could find or make.

I went to the barracks of my friend, Mr. Cuong. He had cooked sweet soup and was waiting for me to eat it with him. The soup was to say good-bye for tomorrow, in case we did not have time to say it then.

While we ate, I told Mr. Cuong, "During the last harvest period the Political Officer in Camp D1 also told us we would move. In fact, we did not. I believe the Communists will do this again and we will not move."

Mr. Cuong thought about this for a few minutes and responded, "These cadre are very smart. Sometimes they do what they say, and sometimes they do not. The best way would be for us to be prepared, just in case."

Mr. Cuong and I finished talking and I returned to my barracks. On the way, I saw several people holding petroleum lamps waiting in line at the latrine. I thought these people waited now because they worried they might not have time tomorrow morning.

In bed, I reviewed all that had taken place that night. All of the reeducation prisoners were excited about moving. We had been going to sleep around 11:00 the last few nights, but now many of us were still up at 2:30 in the morning, preparing to move tomorrow.

We got some sleep, but got up again at 6:00. I watched everyone hastily put their possessions in their bags, then tie them with string. They ran to the kitchen and got their breakfast. I did not pack anything yet. Instead, I waited for the cadre's orders.

At 7:00 the work bell rang. Everyone looked confused and asked, "Are we leaving or not?" Cadre and soldiers burst into our quarters, yelling at us to go to work. We all ran to the gate to muster. Many prisoners did not take their water pots because they had put them in their bags and forgot to take them out again. When they reached the farms, they would not have any drinking water.

I heard my group members curse and say to each other, "This was stupid. They spread false news. I did all this preparation for the move, but nothing happened."

The next day, one of my group told me that we were supposed to move yesterday, but there were some problems with the vehicle convoy and they could not bring the new soldiers. It was certain, though, that everything would go as planned on November 25th instead.

That evening my group agreed that we might move on November 25th, but no one was sure. Someone said, "This time, we will wait until the cadre announce the list of people leaving before we prepare."

By the end of November, we finished harvesting all the rice. We did not move to a new camp. Nevertheless, we discussed moving in anticipation of it throughout this period. We prepared for it and it kept us busy, and we forgot about our weariness from the hard labor.

On the last day of November, Political Officer Ngo said we had done a great job because we had finished harvesting all the rice that our camp was responsible for. The cadre applauded us for achieving the camp goal.

Still, Lieutenant Ngo complained that there were many reeducation prisoners who were stubborn or who had escaped. Each special crew of prisoners working in the vegetable garden, forge, and storehouse had at least one person escape. The number of escaped prisoners had gone up to 20 during the 25 days of the harvest. Lieutenant Ngo advised us not to escape because Public Security would arrest anyone who returned to his family neighborhood.

Twenty-three

DECEMBER 1, 1978 to MARCH 14, 1979

On December 1, we rested for the day. I was glad to relax, but I grew concerned when the cooks did not call us for breakfast. I was hungry, so I went to the kitchen and asked about breakfast. I was told that from now on the kitchen would serve only two meals of millet each day. I guessed the cadre had decreased our rations because we would not be working as hard now, and because most of the prisoners' families provided them with extra food and supplies.

That afternoon, our Block Leaders were told that we would yoke rice straw at the farms and carry it back to camp.

The next morning we mustered at the gate. The special crews who worked in the vegetable gardens or forge mustered with the rest of us. However, when they went to work each crew was guarded by only one soldier.

A cadre and two soldiers counted us and led us to work. We walked in two lines, with armed soldiers guarding each side of the formation.

When we reached the farms, the cadre counted us again. We made two bundles of rice straw. Before we left, we mustered and the cadre counted us another time. We yoked our bundles and walked back to camp. The cadre and the soldiers guarding us kept their fingers on the triggers of their rifles. Near camp, we stopped and put our bundles in large holes in the ground. In a few months, the decaying rice straw would make good fertilizer.

When we finished dumping our straw, we mustered again. The cadre counted us, then he and the two soldiers led us back to the farms. We each yoked two more bundles of rice straw and returned to camp at noon.

We rested the remainder of the day. We could not go outside the fences, and soldiers stood at the guard posts around camp. Because we were so closely guarded, I felt that it was useless to look for an opportunity to escape.

At 9:00, we mustered and the cadre counted us. Afterwards, one of the cadre walked around our camp every 15 minutes, checking the bamboo fences with a flashlight. He kept checking all night.

I smiled as I told some of my group, "No one is foolish enough to try to escape while the cadre are checking the fences. If anyone wanted to pass through the fence, he would wait until they stopped checking." We all thought it was a waste of time.

One morning some prisoners from my block told me a story about Mr. Chin, who had decided to irritate the cadre. Mr. Chin and some of his group members had woken up around midnight and had gone outside to urinate when they noticed the cadre inspecting the fences. Mr. Chin threw a piece of dirt at the fence. The dirt hit the bamboo fence about 20 yards in front of the cadre and made a resonating sound— "Katch!" As soon as the cadre heard it he pulled his gun out of its holster and ran to where he heard the noise. He pointed his flashlight towards the sound and shouted, "Stop! Stop! Don't move!"

When the prisoners saw that the cadre had been tricked, each of them threw dirt at the fence. The dirt hit the bamboo and resounded "Katch! Katch! Katch!" The prisoners ran back inside the barracks, laughing. The cadre realized that he had been tricked and turned his flashlight on the barracks. He did not see anything, so he walked away and continued checking the fences.

At the end of the first week of December, one block of prisoners was led outside the gate to repair the fences. Since the prisoners worked near the camp, the cadre must have reasoned that it was not necessary to guard them. This was a mistake, because nine prisoners escaped.

The next week, I heard that several prisoners who were in the special crews had escaped also. Some of them escaped when they asked to move their bowels. A few prisoners from the buck-saw crew escaped when the soldier guarding them fell asleep under a tree. Some prisoners from the vegetable garden crew escaped when their guard left to move his bowels. Each special crew had a few prisoners escape. Every time my group and I heard about a man escaping, we were glad for him.

On the evening of December 15, our entire camp mustered on the soccer field to be counted. Then Political Officer Ngo addressed us. "There are several reeducation prisoners in our camp who remain stubborn. They continue to oppose Communist policies. Thirty prisoners have escaped over the last two weeks. The cadre realize that many prisoners still here intend to escape. If these stubborn people do not correct themselves and forget about escaping, they will be severely punished. The cadre will deal with them."

In the morning we mustered at the gate. Six soldiers also lined up at the gate. One wore a military coat, civilian shorts and a military hat, but his feet were bare. Another had on a military coat, military pants, and military shoes, but nothing on his head. A third had on a military coat, civilian pants, a military hat, but rubber sandals on his feet. The fourth wore a civilian coat and civilian pants, but his head and feet were bare. The fifth soldier held an AK-47 and the sixth held an M-16. These soldiers were not in uniform.

Captain Tu commanded this crew. He wore military clothes, military shoes, and his insignia of rank on his collar. The soldiers were waiting to leave, and one of them was smoking, another had his hands in his pants pockets, and another stood with his arms folded.

When it was time for them to depart, the commander looked at his watch and ordered, "Attention!" He stood straight and put his feet together. But the soldiers did not respond. The one smoking continued to do so. The one with his hands in his pockets did not move, and so on.

After the commander gave his order, he said, "Dear

comrades, today our superiors have favored us and provided us with training. Please do as the instructor says and study hard."

He gave his next order. "Attention! Let's go! Hurry, or we'll be late!"

He bowed his head and walked forward. The six soldiers followed about 20 yards behind him, walking in a single line. Two minutes later, the line had disappeared. Soon two other soldiers ran by us in the direction the first soldiers had gone. They were late. One had on a military coat, black civilian shorts, and a military hat. In one hand, he held an AK-47 and in the other a boiled cassava which he ate as he ran. The other soldier wore a white T-shirt, red shorts, and a military hat. He held an M-16 in one hand and a boiled cassava in the other. He also ate as he ran to catch up with his crew.

These soldiers were very different from those in our former, professional, armies. My group smiled in amusement as we watched them.

One man said, "How strange this army is! They are not in uniform. Their commander says only 'Attention' and not 'At ease.' When he orders them to move, they ignore him. I just don't understand how they could have beaten us."

When these soldiers had gone a cadre and a soldier counted us and led us to work. As I walked, I thought about the soldiers who had just left and decided that they had been in the guerilla armies (what we called bush fighters).

Bush fighters usually lived with their families and farmed. Their appearance and the way they fought were completely different from those of a professional army. When the cadre planned to attack a military base, they would build a base similar to it and have the bush fighters practice their attack several times. This way they knew what to do and were successful when the real battle occurred. When the battle was over, the bush fighters returned to their families.

Since today only one soldier and one cadre guarded our block, I figured that half of the soldiers in our camp were participating in the training. They were practicing ways to deal with prisoners attempting to escape.

Four days in a row, the cadre and soldiers mustered at the gate to leave for the training sessions. On the fifth day I did not see them, and we had two soldiers guarding us again.

That evening I heard a rumor that the Reeducation Division Administration had issued a warning to our Camp Administration to take care in case some units from the Old Government attacked. These military units were supposedly at the border of Vietnam and Cambodia, in Cambodian territory.

The following evening I heard that six reeducation prisoners who had escaped two months ago had walked through Cambodia to Thailand and were now in a refugee camp. They wrote to their families in Vietnam, reporting the news of their escape.

The next day a member of my group said that while working on the farms, some prisoners had picked up fliers. On them were the flag of the Old Government and the words, "Dear warriors of the Republic of Vietnam imprisoned in Communist jails: Please, be brave, stand up, break the Communist chains, then come to the border of Vietnam and Cambodia. We are military units from the Old Government and are supported by the Free Side. We will receive you with open arms and will pay you back wages to compensate for the suffering you have endured under Communist rule."

We were encouraged and discussed the possibility of escaping. We estimated that it would take only three days to walk to the border of Vietnam and Cambodia.

Mr. Thong asked me to collaborate with him in trying to escape. Others had already organized themselves into groups of three to seven, intending to escape and join the Old Government forces. We were all optimistic, but I told my friend I did not think we should try right now. The soldiers were watchful and I could not think of any time during the day when we would have an opportunity to escape.

We could have concealed ourselves in the darkness of

night and cut holes in the fences to escape through, but I guessed the cadre had already thought about this. That is why they sent their soldiers away for training. I was sure that if we tried to escape now, we would fall into a trap.

Mr. Thong agreed with me, so we planned our escape for February. We figured by then the cadre would be less likely to expect it, and our chances would be better.

This evening many people were sitting together on the soccer field. I guessed everyone was discussing their escape plans. This was a good place to do it, because it was quiet at night. It was also between our barracks, so the cadre did not guard here. There were other groups gathered on the roads inside the camp.

Many prisoners spent the following afternoon drying slices of bread and cooking rice, millet, and cassava in the sun, to eat during their escape. The cadre must have realized what all these discussions and preparations were about, but they did not say anything. I was sure they were preparing for actual escape attempts.

On December 24, 1978, I fell asleep at 10:00 PM. At 11:00, I awoke to the sounds of gunshots ringing through the night air. Soldiers were shouting.

We launched ourselves out of our mosquito nets and ran to the doors. I saw soldiers standing near the stream, flashlights illuminating the bushes as they fired into them relentlessly. The soldiers rummaged around the area for 15 minutes, then returned to camp.

We were ordered to muster outside where the cadre counted us. Seven prisoners had escaped. We were ordered to return to our barracks. The cadre and soldiers returned to the stream. One escapee was captured and taken to the Camp Administration Section.

I heard a voice cut through the night air, "Oh my God! I'm hurt! Oh, it hurts!"

A cadre said, "Don't beat him anymore."

Other soldiers searched the area around the stream for

another half hour before giving up. We returned to our beds around midnight and tried to go back to sleep, but I had trouble sleeping. My thoughts were with the unlucky prisoners who had fallen into the cadre's trap.

I thought about all that had happened between December 15 and the present: the Camp Political Officer first warning us about escaping, the cadre devising a plan to prevent us from escaping, the cadre enticing us to try to escape, how we were deceived into preparing supplies and planning an escape, and how the cadre ambushed the first group to try.

In the morning we gathered on the soccer field. Political Officer Ngo addressed the camp. He was extremely humble and courteous today.

He clasped his hands and said, "Gentlemen, today we are very sorry. We regret the incident that happened last night. We did not want to do this. But put yourselves in our position. We had a difficult time explaining to our superiors how 30 people escaped in December. There are others who do not want to accept the reeducation program. They escaped. We had to stop them. Please consider our difficult situation."

He asked all the block and group leaders to go with him to the stream to identify the dead prisoners. The rest of us returned to our barracks.

As we watched them walk towards the stream, we came out of our barracks again. We crowded into the open area between our barracks and the fence. From there, we could look through gaps in the bamboo fence and see the area around the stream.

The sound of gun shots jolted me as the bullets flew over my head. Soldiers were standing outside the fences, firing repeatedly at us, shouting, "Enter your barracks! Enter your barracks!" Frightened and disoriented, I ran back into my barracks with everyone else. I realized later that the cadre themselves were frightened by our anger over our friends being killed, and, so, used their weapons to disperse us.

The block and group leaders returned to camp and

gave us an update. Among the seven people who escaped, Mr. Tung, Mr. Toi, and Mr. Duc had been killed. Mr. Yen, Mr. Minh, and Mr. Giao had gotten away. The other man (whose name I can no longer remember) was arrested.

That day the cadre ordered us to stay in our barracks. We did not work and quietly mourned our dead friends. No one discussed escaping anymore.

In the afternoon, 10 prisoners carried mats to the stream and wrapped the bodies in them. The mats were donated by some of us. Because these people were killed trying to escape, the cadre would not give us wooden coffins to bury them in. The mortuary crew buried the bodies in the prisoners' graveyard.

When they returned to camp, they told the rest of us that each of the three dead men had one bullet in his body or his leg and several bullets in his head. This indicated that the soldiers had wounded the escaped prisoners so they could not run away. Then, when the prisoners were helpless, they did not try to capture them, but simply killed them. I thought to myself that the cadre wanted to evoke fear in us, to prevent anyone else from escaping.

That night we gathered on the soccer field and the Political Officer announced new camp rules:

From now on we had to go to bed after we mustered at 9:00 PM.

We were not allowed to come within three yards of the fence at night. If anyone did, he would be shot.

If we used the rest room at night, we had to hold up a lamp.

We were not allowed to raise dogs.

In the morning, the cadre ordered us to grab our hoes and go to work. At the gate I noticed that the number of guards had increased. A few days before, two soldiers and one cadre guarded my block. Today there were four soldiers and a cadre.

The cadre counted us, then the soldiers loaded their rifles. We walked in four lines. As the soldiers walked alongside, they kept their guns pointed at us.

When we reached the rubber tree plantations the cadre counted us again. We worked without a break, weeding grass until 12:30. Then we stopped for the day and returned to camp. Some prisoners obeyed the new rules: they killed their dogs which they would eat later that day.

In the evening, a cadre patrolled the fence every 15 minutes. At 9:00 PM we mustered. The cadre counted us and everyone went to bed.

Since all the dogs in our camp had been eaten, there were none left to warn us against strangers entering the barracks. Mr. Cuong told me the next day that when some of his group woke up to urinate they were startled to see an image of a man sitting at their table. At first, they thought it was a ghost, but a few minutes later, they realized it was the Camp Political Officer.

Some of my friends in other barracks recounted similar incidents of a dark image sitting at a table or squatting in a corner. The image always turned out to be a cadre or a soldier and we came to the conclusion that the guards were watching for prisoners attempting to escape.

Early the next morning, I was abruptly awakened by a prisoner yelling, "This is stupid! Just yesterday someone went here and I cleaned it up once already! Today, they did it again! If I catch anyone doing that, I'll beat him!"

The prisoners whose beds were near the door smelled stool just outside the doorway of our barracks. I got out of bed and walked to the doorway. Someone had stepped in the stool and tracked it all over the entranceway.

I guessed that some people were afraid of the "ghosts" of the dead prisoners and didn't want to walk to the latrine at night. Instead, they moved their bowels at the doorway. Then someone else must have passed through the doorway when they got up to urinate. They did not see the stool in the darkness and stepped in it.

On the evening of January 1, I sat with several members of my group. We we were living in a tense situation. The guards were very watchful, especially at night. There were no opportunities to escape. We discussed the seven prisoners who had escaped a week earlier. We believed that if we tried to escape now, the guards would kill us. We decided it was better to wait for an opportunity later.

Over the next few days some of my group begin to hoe the ground and plant vegetable seeds for their individual gardens again. I saw some eat the dried slices of bread, rice, and cassava that they had prepared for their escape. No one sat and discussed plans to escape anymore. The soccer field was vacant at night.

The cadre increased security in our camp for 10 days. Then I noticed a change in policy. When we mustered at the gate and reported for work, the cadre was not present.

The day before, four soldiers and a cadre had held loaded guns pointed at us as they counted and escorted us to the farms. They walked at our flanks, closing any gap through which we might escape. They stood behind us and watched us as we worked.

Now the four soldiers told our block leader to count us. The soldiers casually hung their unloaded rifles on their shoulders. They walked behind us and guarded us more leisurely. When we reached the farms, they sat down together about a hundred yards away and talked to each other.

When we returned to our barracks, the cooks announced that from now on our food rations would increase from two to three meals a day. We were also given a little dried fish, vegetable soup, and 2.4 piastres of extra supplies such as sugar, tobacco, and soap, things we had not received for a while. The increase in food and supplies made me feel a little more comfortable with my situation.

At the end of the first week of January, the soldiers started to become friendly with us. After work some came to our area and invited us to play soccer with them. Some of my group were angry.

One said, "Two weeks ago, these soldiers killed our friends! Now they dare to come here and invite us to play soccer with them! Whoever wants to play with them can, but as for me I'll never play anything with them."

The soldiers waited on the soccer field for 15 minutes, but none of us joined them. They asked us to play again, but nobody responded the second time either.

They asked a third time. This time they said they would write down the names of anyone who played soccer with them, and if these prisoners were tired afterwards, they would be allowed to rest in their quarters tomorrow. I looked out my barracks door and saw 10 prisoners walk out onto the soccer field.

I watched them play. During the game, the soldiers often resigned the ball to the prisoners and the prisoners won the match. Before the soldiers left, they praised the prisoners for playing well and asked them to play again tomorrow.

The soldiers continued to play soccer with the prisoners every afternoon. In every match, the Communist teams often resigned the ball to the prisoners. The soldiers always lost, and they always praised the prisoners for how well they had played. Soon more people began to participate.

During the second week in January, I heard that the soldiers regretted having killed the three prisoners. Also, some of them were dissatisfied with the Camp Political Officer's policies. Two soldiers known for their cruelty, Mr. Mac and Mr. Trung, seemed especially angry. Mr. Trung had tried to shoot Political Officer Ngo, but other soldiers had stopped him. Now Mr. Trung was in the discipline cell.

All the soldiers were humble and courteous to us. They did not shout at us or beat us anymore. We believed that the soldiers really did regret killing our friends.

Mr. Cuong said, "If the soldiers did wrong, and they regret it, it would be better to forgive them. They are the tools of the cadre, because they were only following their orders. I think it would be wrong to hold that against them."

We began to show friendliness towards the soldiers as we gradually began to forgive them.

About the middle of the month our block leaders told us that Cadre Quy would be the new Camp Political Officer. Political Officer Ngo had been assigned another job in a different camp. He had already left.

That evening, I heard that Political Officer Ngo had not followed Communist policy and had been punished for killing the prisoners. Consequently, he lost his job as Camp Political Officer. When I heard this rumor, I was glad.

One of my group said, "Mr. Ngo went too far. If we escape, the cadre will only catch and imprison us. Communist policy does not allow them to kill us."

That evening, I sat with several of my group, discussing the soldiers' new manner and the recent rumors. We concluded that the soldiers regretted their mistake. Political Officer Ngo was the one who ordered them to kill the prisoners, and he had been punished for it, so we decided it was no longer necessary to be angry.

I realized that no one thought about escaping anymore, so I said to Mr. Thong, "We had planned to escape this February, so should we start preparing the supplies for it now? Will we do this next month?"

Mr. Thong's eyes widened with surprise, "It is foolish to try now. We would be killed. Please be patient and look for another opportunity. We will do it later." Many people thought like this, and no one tried to escape.

Soon the cadre devised a new way to motivate us. We gathered on the soccer field to hear a speech from the new Camp Political Officer, Captain Quy. He announced that Vietnamese armies had invaded Cambodia and won many battles. I was surprised to hear this, and that evening my friends and I wondered aloud how far into Cambodia the Vietnamese would go.

A few days later, the cadre gave us a newspaper. In it, we read that the Red Khmer had withdrawn to Thailand. The

Vietnamese had taken Cambodia.

Soon there was a rumor that said Chinese armies had moved to Thailand to reinforce the Red Khmer. Toward the end of January we heard that the United Nations was protesting Vietnam's invasion of Cambodia.

Then there was a rumor that all the countries of Southeast Asia were preparing to attack the Vietnamese in Cambodia.

Because we heard so many rumors in just a few days, and because we had read the newspaper which confirmed some of them, we were all excited about the situation in Cambodia. The cadre took advantage of our excitement.

On the first day of February, our Group and Block leaders told us we were free to take a bath at the stream. We could go anywhere we wanted, in fact, and we were free to enter and exit the camp gate, but we had to be back in camp before 6:00 PM.

The next day, when we went to work, I noticed that there were no soldiers on guard at the gate. The guard posts around camp were also vacant. Only two soldiers waited at the gate for us to muster. Our block leader counted us, then we followed the soldiers.

We walked about three miles to the edge of Duc Hanh Village where one of the soldiers told us to make two thatch bundles apiece and to return here at 1:00 PM.

I walked to some houses and asked the people there if they had anything to sell, like tobacco or alcohol, or some rice or vegetables, or even a live duck, chicken, or pig.

At 1:00 PM, we reported back to the two soldiers. Each of us carried a yoke of two thatch bundles and one bag of food. Some prisoners were carrying a whole quarter of a pig. I asked, "Why do you buy so much pork?"

One of them answered, "Four of us went to the Montagnard hamlet and bought a pig weighing about 45 kilograms. We killed it and divided it up. We will each take one quarter to camp and sell the pork to the other prisoners for a profit."

I saw some other prisoners with a gallon bottle of alcohol and asked, "Will you drink a gallon of alcohol tonight?"

One answered, "No, I bought this so I could sell it in camp."

At Duc Hanh, the people sometimes killed a pig and sold the pork. I decided that the next time I had the opportunity, I would buy eight kilograms. I would take the pork back to camp, eat one kilogram and sell the rest to the other prisoners.

The soldiers did not check our bags when we entered the gate. I felt comfortable with the cadre's new policies. I walked out the gate and took a bath at the stream. I saw several prisoners standing on the bank with fishing poles. Other prisoners were making fish traps nearby.

That afternoon the cooks announced, "From now on, you will be served only two meals instead of three, and each meal will be millet only."

The extra supplies such as sugar, tobacco, and soap had also stopped, but none of the prisoners complained. I figured that the cadre realized we were being supplied food and money from our visiting relatives, and since several of us went to the civilian zones and bought more food there, they could decrease our food ration and no one would mind.

At 9:00 PM, I waited to see if the cadre would count us, but they didn't. I did not see them walk around and check the fences anymore at night. The gate to the camp was locked and chained, but left unguarded.

The next day several of my group built new hen houses and many began to plant individual vegetable gardens. Mr. Cuong and I planted a small vegetable garden together.

That evening, several prisoners sat down and ate and drank alcoholic spirits. Some gambled at cards. Mr. Cuong had two decks of cards, so every night he rented both decks for five piastres each. Other prisoners rented out their cards also. At that time, it costs two piastres to buy one quart of uncooked rice, and ten piastres for one kilogram of pork. Mr. Cuong used his rent money to buy more food for himself and me.

By February 8, we had been working and living under the new policies for one week. During this time, the other prisoners relaxed by spending their spare time at hobbies like chess or dominos or gambling.

At the beginning of the second week, some soldiers bought a pig in the civilian zone, killed it, and carried the meat to camp where they sold it to some prisoners.

Then they bought tobacco and a five-gallon container of alcohol. They sold these also to the prisoners.

The next time the soldiers came, they chose some prisoners to buy these items from them and then resell them to the other prisoners. By mid-February we were buying various goods from them once a week and we were becoming friendly towards them, because of the extra food and supplies they provided us with.

One evening some off-duty soldiers cut a hole in the fence and entered our camp. They came to our barracks and ate and drank with some of the prisoners. When everyone was drunk, these soldiers invited us to go out through the hole in the fence and come to their hut just outside camp. They played music there until 1:00 in the morning, then the prisoners came back to camp.

In the third week of February, the cadre broadcast news from Hanoi over the loudspeaker. The news report said China was attacking Vietnam. We paid close attention to this.

A few days later, one of my group told me the BBC had reported that the Chinese had taken over six Vietnamese provinces near the Chinese border. The Chinese were moving to Hanoi. Chinese navy and marine forces had attacked Hai Phong Harbor in the north, and Vinh in central Vietnam.

At the end of the month there was still another rumor that the BBC had reported that the Vietnamese army had broken and run from the Chinese. The Chinese now controlled

14 provinces in northern Vietnam and four provinces in the center. At the same time, the Chinese were within three miles of Hanoi.

The following week another rumor had it that the United Nations had intervened. Vietnam had stopped following Communism and had released all of its political prisoners. As a result, the Chinese had withdrawn from Vietnam.

These rumors made the rounds continuously and we discussed them every day. We thought the political situation in Vietnam would be changed soon. We thought this would change our fates, and we would be released also, so we did not try to escape during this time.

In the second week of March, Mr. Cuong's wife came to the visiting house. Because we were free to come and go, I walked to the visiting house and talked to her also. I was anxious to know more about the rumors we had heard concerning the United Nations' involvement in the China-Vietnam conflict.

When I asked her about this, she said she was very busy working to support her family and did not pay attention to political events. All she knew was that Vietnam took over Cambodia, and that the Chinese had attacked Vietnam. She did not know any of the details.

Luckily, I met an old man while I was there. He told me he followed the political events very closely and listened to the BBC every night. I asked him about all the rumors I had heard. I asked especially about the rumors I had heard in December, encouraging us all to escape. He told me these rumors were false. There was no military unit from the Old Government working in Vietnam now.

When I heard this, I realized that I and many others had gotten excited over false rumors. We had been encouraged to escape. I felt sorry for the first three people who had tried and were killed. I also felt my friends and I had been lucky. If we had tried then, we too would be dead.

About the Vietnam-Cambodia conflict, the old man

said Vietnam had conquered Cambodia, and the United Nations did oppose this invasion. However, the rumors about the Chinese reinforcing the Red Khmer and about Southeast Asian countries preparing to attack Vietnam were all false.

Finally, I asked about the Chinese attacking 18 Vietnamese Provinces. He said the Chinese had attacked only six northern Vietnamese Provinces near the Chinese border.

When the old man had finished, I saw again that many of us had been tricked into believing false rumors once again. I felt I had been careless in allowing this, and I regretted that I had not recognized the cadre's deceit sooner.

That evening I thought over the old man's words. I realized the cadre knew we did not like the Communist regime, and by creating hope in us, they kept us from trying to escape.

On the afternoon of March 14, everyone attended a camp meeting on the soccer field during which Political Officer Quy reviewed our work. At the end of the meeting, he concluded, "There were a small number of reeducation prisoners who were stubborn and opposed Communist policy. Thirty of them escaped during the first two weeks of December. The cadre had warned these stubborn people, but they did not improve. On the night of December 24, three prisoners who tried to escape were killed. After that night, the others corrected themselves and stopped trying to escape. The cadre are very pleased with these progressive prisoners."

Twenty-four

MARCH 15, 1979 to APRIL 30, 1979

The next day my block and another were ordered to clear and prepare the farms for planting in May. Our daily labor quota was 200 square yards per person. A third block was assigned to cut bamboo and wood and carry them back to camp. They would also help the carpentry crew build two barracks and another kitchen.

In the morning my block mustered at the gate. Our Block Leader counted us, then we walked to the farms. The Block and Group Leaders supervised us as we worked. We cut saplings and small stems from the old rice plants. We stopped working at 1:00 PM, even though our labor quota was not completed.

That afternoon, when we returned to camp, I watched the carpentry crew for a few minutes building the new barracks and kitchen in an open area in front of my barracks. Then I ate lunch and took a nap.

At about 4:00 I walked to the stream and took a bath with several other prisoners. There were no soldiers around, and we were free to walk out the gate, so I walked to the cassava farm near camp. We were given only two meals a day, lunch and dinner. As this was not enough food, I pulled up some cassava roots. Mr. Cuong and I would cook and eat them in the morning. Some of my group fished in the stream or walked to the Montagnard hamlets to buy food.

That evening we did not have to muster, so my friends and I spent our time talking. We were all uneasy about the new barracks being built. We did not understand why the cadre were building them.

The next day some of my group said the cadre were building more barracks to prepare for a block of new prisoners from Regiment 2 whose camp had been closed. I hoped

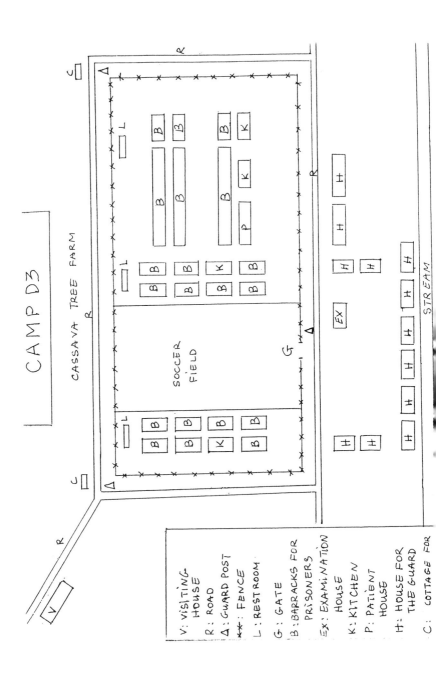

CAMP D3

CASSAVA TREE FARM

SOCCER FIELD

STREAM

V: VISITING HOUSE
R: ROAD
△: GUARD POST
××: FENCE
L: RESTROOM
G: GATE
B: BARRACKS FOR PRISONERS
Ex: EXAMINATION HOUSE
K: KITCHEN
P: PATIENT HOUSE
H: HOUSE FOR THE GUARD
C: COTTAGE FOR

some of my old friends who were in Regiment 2 would be transferred to my camp.

In the morning, one of the cadre came to the farm where I was working and told us that the cadre had killed a pig and would be selling the meat at the Regiment Administration Section. We could go there after we finished our labor quota. I was very glad to hear this and intended to buy some on my way back to camp.

We completed our work quota at noon and walked to the Regiment Administration Section. One of the cadre there said they would be selling pork twice a week.

I asked him what days he would be selling it.

"I'm not sure," he said. "If you want some, you will just have to check every day."

When I returned to camp, the soldiers who had been selling us pork over the last few weeks said that they would no longer be selling it. If we wanted to buy some, we would have to pick it up from the Regiment Administration Section on the days we went to work. I realized that if I reported being sick and stayed in camp, I might miss out, so I decided I would go to work every day.

At noon the next day we had our money ready, hoping to buy some pork. However, when we checked with the cadre in the Regiment Administration Section, we found that they were not selling pork today. We checked every day. Finally, after a week had gone by, the cadre sold us pork twice, just as they had said.

At the end of the month, 200 more reeducation prisoners were trucked into our camp. I thought they were from Regiment 2, so I anticipated seeing my old friends as I watched the prisoners disembark from the trucks. My anticipation turned to disappointment when I talked to some of the new prisoners and realized they were not from Regiment 2 but had come from Thanh-Ong-Nam Reeducation Center near Ho Chi Minh City. There they did not have hard labor like we did here.

Our camp now held 800 prisoners divided into four blocks of 200 each. Each block consisted of four groups of 50 prisoners. All of the new prisoners were assigned to the same block.

That evening, I settled down on my mat and wondered why the cadre had spread the rumors about the new prisoners. I guessed it was to keep them from trying to escape when they learned they were going to be moved so far from Ho Chi Minh. Also, when we began to build the new barracks for the prisoners, the cadre sensed our apprehension. The rumors distracted us by encouraging us to believe we would see some of our old friends.

On the first day of April, soldiers told us that some cadre from the Division Administration Section had come to the Camp Administration Section that morning to look at our documents. They had decided to release us in two groups. One would be released in the middle of April, the other at the end of the month. Because so many people would be released, the cadre worried that they would not have enough prisoners to work on the farms. This is why the prisoners from Thanh-Ong-Nam Reeducation Center were transferred here, to take the place of those being released.

We discussed this. Every one of us hoped our name would be on the release list but some of my friends wondered if this rumor was true, so they asked some prisoners who practiced fortune-telling. These fortune tellers used cards to predict the future. They said we would be released in large numbers, in two groups, during the month of April. Half of my friends believed them and half did not. The two sides debated the issue, but could not come to an agreement. They finally wagered that the losing side would have to pay the other side 50 piastres. If the cadre released anyone in the middle of April, the side that believed the rumor would win the 50 piastres. If no one was released by the middle of April, then they would have to pay the 50 piastres to the other side.

On April 10, the cadre released seven prisoners. The

people who bet that the rumor was true won and they collected their money. Now we all paid attention. We waited and hoped that the next group would be released at the end of April. But the month passed and no one else was released.

On the night of April 29, the cadre burned the dried plants we had cleared from the farms. The next morning, the farms were covered with ash. Now they were fertile and ready for cultivation.

The next day we did not go to work, but rested. That afternoon, we all attended a meeting on the soccer field. Camp Political Officer Quy said, "The majority of you have obeyed the camp rules and worked hard. The number of people pretending to be sick has been very low. Our camp built two new barracks and a new kitchen for 200 new prisoners, and you cleared all the farmland. The cadre applaud you for this. Nevertheless, there are still a few of you who are stubborn and do not obey the rules. Seven of these prisoners escaped during this period."

Among the seven were three from my block: Mr. Ha, Mr. Nghia, and Mr. Hanh. I did not know the other four.

Twenty-five

MAY through AUGUST 1979

On May 1, our block leaders told us we would be sowing the rice paddies. Our individual labor quota was 200 square yards a day.

Early the following day, we received one meal of millet from the kitchen. The rainy season was approaching, so after we ate we grabbed our raincoats and mustered at the camp gate.

At 7:30, my block leader counted us, then led us to the paddies. Two soldiers followed. When we reached the paddies, we mustered again. This time the soldiers counted us, then they went to sit under a nearby shade tree. They did not inspect our work. Our Block and Group Leaders supervised us.

We took a half-hour break at noon. Around 3:00, our block leader reported to the soldiers that everyone had finished his labor quota. We mustered, the soldiers counted us, and we returned to camp.

In camp, we were free to do as we wished. I walked outside the gate and dug up some cassava roots on a nearby farm. I prepared these for my breakfast the next day. After that, I grabbed my fishing pole and headed to the stream. I caught some fish and then I took a bath.

At 5:30, we received our second meal of millet. When I finished eating, I sat with friends and talked. Some had relatives visiting. They got to see their relatives in the visiting house for two hours, then had to return to camp to sleep in the barracks.

The next day, our block leader told us, "The cadre are going to choose one reeducation prisoner with medical training to be the nurse for each block. The nurse will keep the medicine and take care of everyone in his block. When someone reports being sick, the nurse will examine him and decide if he can stay in camp and rest or go to work."

The following morning, I felt weary. I did not want to go to work, so I pretended to be sick. The nurse said, "Your symptoms are not serious, so you cannot rest today."

When I heard this, I became angry. I tried my best to hold my anger in and remain calm and polite. I did not want the nurse to get angry at me, because he decided who could stay back and who could not.

For the next two days I reported to the nurse, but each time the nurse told me I had to go to work. Then I did become ill. The nurse agreed, but before I could return to my barracks, I had to be examined by one of the soldiers. When I went to the Camp Administration Section for my examination, I was surprised to see only 24 patients. This was not very many for a camp with 800 prisoners.

The next day, I wanted to report being sick again, but the nurse did not agree. "You were sick yesterday and rested at home. So please allow one of the other patients to rest today."

Hearing these words, I got angry and said, "If I work or rest, it does not hurt you. Why don't you let me rest?"

He responded, "The cadre only allow a limited number of patients each day and I cannot abuse this. Please consider my position."

Later that morning, before I went to work, I heard some of my group talking. They had pretended to be sick, but the nurse wouldn't let them stay back. As they walked, they cursed the nurse.

One of them said, "It is stupid. If I go to work or rest, it does not hurt the nurse. I have reported my sickness for five days, but he will not let me stay back. Why is he like that?"

As I walked to the paddies, I realized again how smart the cadre were. They chose a nurse to take care of the patients, but also to hear the complaints of those prisoners he turned away each morning. This way, everyone blamed the nurse instead of the cadre.

During the second week of May, two prisoners from my block escaped together. One was Mr. Hy, my Block Leader.

The other one was Mr. Trang, one of our Group Leaders.

One afternoon the cadre gave us some newspapers. There was a picture of the Secretary General of the United Nations. The newspaper said he had visited Vietnam.

Rumors started again. Some of my group said that the Communists planned to deport all the reeducation prisoners who had worked for the Old Government, and the Secretary General of the United Nations had come to Vietnam to discuss this with the government.

A few days later, another rumor reinforced this one: The government was having financial difficulties and would be given money to deport the reeducation prisoners.

I discussed these rumors with my friends. Some of the single prisoners were excited, but some of the married prisoners were worried. If they were made to leave Vietnam, how long would it be before they saw their wives and children again? Some of my friends reasoned that if the United Nations took us out of Vietnam, they would have a plan for our families to join us.

Nevertheless, we all agreed that it was best for us to study English and be prepared to leave. Some of my friends wrote letters to their relatives, asking them to bring English books and dictionaries.

In mid-May my friend, Mr. Cuong, joined a group of about 10 other prisoners and started taking English lessons. Other prisoners who spoke English well taught them.

In the evening, many people in my barracks sat on their mats with English books and dictionaries illuminated by the light of petroleum lamps. It was the same in other barracks as well.

The cadre continued to feed us rumors. A high-level meeting between the free side and the Communist side would take place between the fifth and tenth of June. President Carter and Mr. Brezhnev would attend. The main topic would be the Communists' deportation of all reeducation prisoners.

On June 11, I heard that a meeting of top officials

from the free side and the Communist side had taken place in Geneva. Secretary General Brezhnev had agreed to the deportation of all prisoners who had worked for the Old Government. My friends and I were excited and thought we would be free soon.

Late in June, some of my group told us that 70 nations would meet in Geneva on July 20 to discuss a plan for refugees. The first to leave Vietnam would be reeducation prisoners. The next to be deported would be American-Vietnamese (half American and half Vietnamese) and anyone who needed to be reunited with his or her family.

Because my friends and I expected to be deported soon, we decided to stay in camp and study English.

We forgot our weariness from the hard labor because we were paying such close attention to the topic of deportation and studying English. By the end of June, we had finished the sowing in all of the paddies our camp was responsible for.

On June 30, we rested in camp. That afternoon, our block leaders informed us that we would be weeding grass in the rice paddies and harvesting cassava during July and August. We would rotate the two types of work between four blocks. Two blocks would weed while the other two harvested. Every three days, we would switch jobs.

The next day we mustered at the gate, then walked to the paddies, carrying our hoes. We weeded the grass, standing in one line, side by side, two yards apart. Our daily labor quota was 300 square yards per person. No one supervised us and none of the soldiers inspected our work. Since the ground had been burnt near the end of April, there was little grass to be weeded. At 1:00 we finished work and returned to camp. At 2:00 we were in our quarters and free to do as we wanted.

Three days later we harvested cassava. We each took a sack and a bush knife to the cassava farms. At the farms there were two scales, one for each block. A soldier and a block leader stood beside each scale. We dug the cassava trees up, put the roots in our sacks, then brought them to the scales where the soldier weighed it and the block leader noted the amount for each prisoner in his block. Each sack weighed between 20 and 25 kilograms, so it took four or five trips to achieve our daily labor quota of 110 kilograms of cassava each.

We did not want to work this hard and looked for a way to trick the soldiers. At the farms, we waited until we had a group of about 50 prisoners, then we all carried our sacks to the scales at the same time and crowded around them. We shoved each other and tried to be the first to have our sacks weighed. We were supposed to pour the cassava into a big pile after weighing it, but instead, we took the sacks back to the center of our group, waited for a few minutes, then took the same sacks of cassava back to the scale and weighed them again. We did this about four times, until we achieved our quota.

The soldier just minded his work and did not realize that we were cheating him. Our Block Leader saw what we were doing, but he was in the same situation as we were and did not say anything. He just bowed his head and looked at his notebook and noted the amount of cassava each of us weighed. We wanted to finish our labor quota as soon as possible, so before long 400 prisoners were gathered around the two scales. We pushed each other and competed to weigh our sacks. Since we crowded around the scales in such an unorganized manner, it was easy for us to cheat.

The result was that the work was done at 11:00 AM, and the soldiers and prisoners were happy. Some of my group were even credited for more than their labor quota, because they forgot to count the amount of cassava they weighed in and brought it back too many times.

Nevertheless, when we considered the pile of cassava that 400 people harvested, we looked at each other and laughed. We knew that this heap should be over 40 tons, but it would have had to be five times larger than it was to weigh that much.

For three days, we weighed the cassava we harvested this way. Then, at the beginning of the second week of July,

our Block Leader told us, "The division and camp adminis-
trations have complained about us. They said we reported
harvesting more than 40 tons of cassava each day, but when
the cadre weighed it again it was not even 10 tons. They
asked where the other 30 tons of cassava went."

We realized that our Block Leader had been chastised
for our laziness. What a pity, I thought; but when I looked at
him, I could only laugh. The other prisoners laughed also. Then
our Block Leader bowed his head and said, "You cheated and
I got in trouble. It was hard on me!" We looked at each other
and laughed again.

After this, the cadre changed their method of weighing.
We now had to be in one line and wait our turn. After the
cassava was weighed, we had to pour it onto a pile near the
scale. We could no longer cheat by weighing the same sack
several times.

I entered the cassava farm and harvested my first
sack. I carried it to the weigh station. It weighed a little over
20 kilograms. As I walked back, I saw a few members of my
group at the edge of the farm.

They had discovered a new method of cheating. They
dumped the cassava out of their sacks, dug some dirt up, and
mixed it with the cassava. They put the mixture back in their
sacks and took it to be weighed.

I wanted to complete my labor quota as soon as possible, so I copied them and mixed dirt with my second sack
of cassava. It weighed around 30 kilograms.

On my way back to the farm, I saw some prisoners
mixing stones with the cassava. I copied them, also. First I
mixed dirt with the cassava and put it in my sack, then I
looked for two stones and put them in the middle. This sack
weighed about 40 kilograms.

I thought this method worked well and helped me
finish my labor quota quickly, so I continued to do it. All of
my group members did this also.

A week later, there was a different soldier, a woman, in

place of the male soldier at the scales. She was about 21 years old and spoke with a North Vietnamese accent.

That day while I mixed dirt and stones with cassava to fill my first sack, I did not think she would catch us. Then some of my group members said to me, "The new soldier caught all the people putting stones in their sacks. She caught Mr. Dung. After his sack was weighed, she ordered him to dump the cassava out and she found a large rock. She made Mr. Dung weigh the rock on the scale. It weighed eight kilograms."

I did not want to get caught, so I took the two stones out of my sack and only mixed dirt with my cassava for the rest of the day.

The next day, all the people who had been caught cheating were punished. For one day, they had to do hard labor in the camp. The cadre ordered these men to go into the forest and cut down trees, remove the branches from the trees, then carry the logs back to the Camp Administration Section. After my group members and I saw this, we did not dare put any more rocks in our sacks, but we did continue to mix dirt with the cassava. We called the place where we mixed the dirt and cassava "the mixing section."

Each of our sacks now weighed about 30 kilograms, and we all collected three sacks of cassava a day, totaling about 90 kilograms per person. We almost met our labor quota, so the cadre did not complain.

After a month of this, there were about 40 holes in "the mixing section." A man could sit, neck deep, in each of the holes. I thought the cadre probably knew about the dirt, but they did not say anything to us and we continued to do it. We often finished working by 1:00.

At the beginning of August, the cadre gave us another newspaper, which read that a meeting of 70 nations had taken place in Geneva. Lau Van Ha had spoken at the meeting on behalf of the Vietnamese government.

A few days later, we heard a rumor that our fate had

been decided at this meeting. By the end of the year, the United Nations would come up with a plan to take us out of Vietnam.

These rumors circulated continuously. We all discussed them and hoped that we would be deported soon. Many of us studied English. Our hope of being deported was the main reason why the majority of us waited and did not try to escape.

One day in mid-August, as I headed back to camp after work, I saw an old man in the visiting house. We had not had many visitors lately, and I wanted to find out more about the deportation. I went into the visiting house, got acquainted with him, and asked him about the rumor.

He said, "Three incidents took place already: the Secretary General of the United Nations visited Vietnam, the free side and the Communist side held a top meeting, and delegates from 70 nations met together. The Secretary General of the United Nations did not come to Vietnam to discuss deporting reeducation prisoners. None of the meetings discussed deporting reeducation prisoners from Vietnam."

I regretted having been tricked again. Obviously, the cadre had spread rumors that sounded good to us so that we would forget our weariness from the hard labor.

By the last week of August, no one studied English any longer. Everyone knew we had been tricked and stopped preparing for deportation.

On the afternoon of August 30, our entire camp mustered on the soccer field. Camp Political Officer Quy reported, "The majority of you worked well and obeyed the camp rules. You planted new seeds in May and June, cultivated all the young plants and trees, and harvested a large amount of cassava roots in July and August. The cadre applaud you. Nevertheless, there were a small number who were stubborn and did not obey the rules. Six of them escaped during the last four months."

Two of the escaped prisoners had been in my block: Mr. Hy and Mr. Trang. I did not know the other four.

Twenty-six

SEPTEMBER and OCTOBER 1979

On September 1, we did not go to work because 50 prisoners were moving to a new camp. My friend, Mr. Cuong, had his name on this list. His group had 30 minutes to prepare to leave.

At 10:00 AM, the cadre needed three people to bring food to the area where the 50 prisoners were waiting for further orders. I wanted to see my friend, so I volunteered.

I intended to visit with Mr. Cuong after I delivered the food, but the transport vehicle arrived and Political Officer Quy ordered the prisoners to muster before I even had a chance to look for Mr. Cuong.

Political Officer Quy then spoke to the prisoners. "Gentlemen, we have been following your progress over the long period in which you have lived in this camp. We found you to be very progressive, so we put your names on a special list and reported it to our superiors. We suggested that they consider yours to be a special case. Today our superiors have done just that. They have ordered us to take you to a new camp, where you will work for a short time and then be released. You are luckier than the others still in our camp, because your names are on the consideration list, and you will be released soon. Those who remain here will not be considered yet. We hope you will do well at your new camp, and we wish you good luck in being released soon."

The prisoners clapped enthusiastically. Some of them quickly ran to Officer Quy just before they boarded the vehicle and thanked him for his help. When they got on board, the driver covered the back of the vehicle with an iron net, and locked them in. When the vehicle began to move, some of them waved and shouted, "Good-bye, Mr. Quy. Take care." Officer Quy waved back and said good-bye to them.

When the transport vehicle was gone, I returned to camp with the other two prisoners and Officer Quy.

That evening, the remaining prisoners mustered on the soccer field. Political Officer Quy addressed us. "Gentlemen, during the last period, we kept track of all the reeducation prisoners in our camp, and we discovered 50 stubborn people who did not obey the reeducation policies and continued to oppose the government. Today we have arrested them and escorted them to jail, where they will be punished. We realize that all of you are very progressive and work very well, so we have reported you to our superiors for consideration to be released soon. We now suggest that you try your best and work well. Then we can close this camp and you can return to your families."

I was surprised by Officer Quy's message. The other prisoners were glad. They clapped their hands because they thought that they were progressive and were not going to be taken to jail where their activities would be carefully controlled by Public Security.

Officer Quy announced a new plan. During the next two months, our entire camp would harvest cassava only and supply it to the Reeducation Division Administration Section where it would be ground into powder.

Officer Quy finished his speech, and we returned to our quarters. On my way, one of the men who also had heard both of Officer Quy's speeches shook my shoulders and said, "This morning, when we took the food to the prisoners leaving camp, Political Officer Quy gave them a different message. I do not understand. Why did he say that? What a pity for them!"

When he said this I laughed at his naïvete, but I did not say anything to him because I did not know him well.

Later, my friends and I discussed Quy's speech. We agreed that the Camp Political Officer was smart. He had lied to both groups of prisoners. He had also created a special atmosphere. The 50 prisoners who had left were optimistic as they boarded the transport vehicle. Those who remained were also encouraged and believed themselves to be luckier than the others.

The next morning at 7:30 we collected at the gate. None of the soldiers were there and our Block Leaders counted us and were in charge of us as we worked.

We harvested cassava until we completed our daily labor quota of 110 kilograms per person. We finished around noon, then returned to camp and rested.

In the afternoon, I noticed the camp gate was left open and unguarded. We were free to do anything we liked. Some of my group went into the civilian zones to buy food. Others fished at the stream, and some played music or gambled at cards.

At 7:00 the gate was closed and locked. At this time, all the prisoners who had relatives visiting them were escorted out the gate by a soldier. The prisoners were allowed to see their relatives in the visiting house for two hours.

The next day our block leaders told us that from now on, our camp would have soccer matches every afternoon. Each group and each block had to form a soccer team and these teams would play against each other.

The next afternoon a soldiers' team from the Reeducation Division Administration came to our camp to play soccer against one of our teams. Our block leaders announced the match and we were all invited to watch.

My group members and I went to the soccer field. The soldiers' team lost. Afterwards, the cadre and soldiers said they had tried their best, but could not beat the prisoners and they praised us for playing so well. We all felt encouraged because our team had beaten the soldiers.

Later that day, the cadre gave out two pounds of green beans per group, and four sugar cubes to each person. Our Block Leader told us that the cadre would supply these items once a week so that we could use them to bet on the soccer matches.

The next day we began betting. Each group member

bet one sugar cube and a few green beans. My group's team won. We got all the sugar cubes and two pounds of green beans from the losing team. Each of us then added one additional sugar cube and we cooked a sweet soup. While we ate the soup, we congratulated the soccer players. Afterwards, we hoped our team would win more matches so we could cook more soup.

The next day, as soon as we came back from the cassava farms, I heard some of my group asking each other, "Which soccer team will they play today?"

Many of my group practiced with soccer balls instead of taking a nap. That afternoon we went to the soccer field to see the match.

Two days later, 10 minutes before the soccer matches were to begin, soldiers walked around the camp. If they saw someone playing music, they cursed at him and said something like, "You have been in the reeducation program for four years, but you are not progressive and still play music from the Old Regime!"

They would then seize the musical instrument and break it. Several prisoners from my block had their guitars broken that afternoon. But later that evening, I saw several prisoners playing music, and the soldiers did not bother them.

Because we were allowed to play music at night but not in the afternoon, I guessed that the cadre wanted to keep us at the soccer field. They did not want music to divert us.

The following day, while we prepared to go to the soccer field for a match, I heard three bullets fired. I walked toward the noise to investigate. I found that some prisoners had been playing guitars and drums in a room near the kitchen of Block 3. Political Officer Quy saw them playing, got mad, and shot three bullets into the air, complaining that they had been playing music from the Old Regime. After that, Political Officer Quy ordered all the guitars and drums in that room to be taken to the Camp Administration Section and stored there.

A few days later, my group's soccer team played again and some of the players cheated. Both teams began quarreling.

The match turned into a fist fight on the soccer field and was never finished. Fighting occurred several more times during the third week of September. Right at an exciting point the players would start fighting, because no one wanted to lose the game and his sugar cube.

From the end of September until the end of October, soccer matches became the favorite afternoon pastime. In the evening, I would sit with several of my friends and talk. No one discussed political topics anymore. We only talked about the soccer matches being played that week.

At the end of October I realized that the cadre had not reviewed our work for the last two months, so I reviewed them in my own mind. Two prisoners from my group, Mr. Thu and Mr. Lap, had escaped. Some prisoners from other groups had also escaped. Every week I heard of prisoners escaping. I did not know the total number, because the cadre did not count us or talk about the escapes during this period.

Twenty-seven

NOVEMBER 1, 1979 to NOVEMBER 19, 1979

On the last day of October, our Block Leaders told us that we would receive one meal of millet in the morning, then we would begin to harvest the rice. Our individual labor quota was 20 kilograms of paddy per day. We would stop working at 3:00, weigh our bamboo paddy baskets, yoke them on our shoulders, then carry them to the storehouse at the Regiment Administration Section. Upon our return to camp, the kitchen would provide us with a second meal of millet.

I began preparing for the next day. I walked out the gate into the cassava farm near camp and pulled up some cassava roots and boiled them for my breakfast tomorrow. I also boiled my drinking water.

At 7:00 AM, I awoke and ate my breakfast. Afterwards, I went to the kitchen to get my millet. I would take it with me for lunch.

At 8:00 AM, our entire camp mustered at the gate. One cadre and four soldiers guarded my block. They followed us to the paddies, but our Group Leader supervised our work.

After I'd been working for about 15 minutes, my Block Leader approached my Group Leader and told him that each cadre and soldier had hidden six sacks in the bushes. They wanted us to fill them with paddy, then put them back in the bushes. They were going to take the paddy to the civilian zones to sell for their own profit.

When I heard this, I gladly filled the sacks with paddy. I thought that if the cadre and soldiers stole paddy and sold it for themselves, then they would be easier on us while we worked. And we would be allowed to steal some for ourselves, too.

When we finished filling the sacks, all the guards disappeared. I knew that they were taking their paddy sacks to the civilian zones and that they did not care what we did.

After our noon lunch break, I poured out my drinking water and filled the bottle with paddy. I put some more in my small lunch bag. I saw other prisoners doing the same thing.

At 3:00, we stopped working. We yoked a basket of paddy between every two prisoners, then carried it to the scales near the edge of the rice field. Our block leader weighed each basket and recorded the weight in his notebook.

When another man and I brought our basket to the station, it weighed 25 kilograms. But my Block Leader noted it as 40 kilograms. All of the baskets weighed from 20 to 25 kilograms but our Block Leader always noted each one as 40 kilograms. He was helping us meet our quota because he was in the same situation as we were, and there were no guards around.

We left the field at 4:00. We yoked the paddy baskets on our shoulders, then walked about two miles to the Regiment Administration Section. We dumped the paddy in the storehouse, then brought the empty baskets back to our camp to use tomorrow.

We arrived in camp around 5:30. I took a bath at the stream, ate dinner, and prepared my food and drinking water for the next day.

At 7:00, a soldier came to my barracks and announced a list of reeducation prisoners who had relatives visiting. These prisoners were then allowed to go to the visiting house.

I began to prepare the paddy seeds I had stolen. I picked up a steel helmet a friend had given me when he was released. I used the helmet for a basin whenever I needed to wash something. Now I used it for a mortar, and I pestled the paddy seeds in it. I needed to separate the husk from the edible seed inside. Once husked, the seeds would be ready to cook.

I pestled paddy from a little after 7:00 until midnight, when I went to sleep. The others in my group did the same. Some did not have an steel helmet and I heard a couple of them say that they planned to go to the Montagnard hamlets on Sunday and asked for a wooden mortar. (We did not work on Sunday, so they would have time to do this then.)

The next morning, before I went to work, I collected containers to put paddy in. The day before, I took a small, half-gallon bottle of water to the rice paddies. Today I took a gallon bottle. It was the largest bottle I had. I filled it only one-third of the way with water. I also put my lunch in my largest lunch bag, because after I ate I would fill it with paddy, as well.

Everybody in my group was carrying larger lunch bags and bottles. Some even carried two-and-a-half-gallon pots. When I saw them, I said, "I can't imagine how big their stomachs are, that each one can drink two-and-a-half-gallons of water in seven hours!" My friends laughed.

The guards did the same as they had the day before. They brought their sacks to the paddies. Then, after we filled the sacks for them, they disappeared for the rest of the day. We did the same also and stole even more paddy than we did before.

That evening, we pestled paddy again, and the walls echoed with the sound of pestles beating against the mortars.

Some prisoners were too weary to pestle paddy and slept instead, surrounded by three or four others grinding paddy in their mortars. They were tired enough that they slept through the noise.

No one played his guitar during this time. Even if someone had wanted to, he would not have been able to hear it. No one played chess or dominoes or cards either, because our stomachs needed rice.

At 10:00 PM, I stopped pestling for about half an hour and took a walk outside. The sound of pestling thundered from all the barracks in camp, and I was sure the cadre could hear it. They must have known we stole the paddy, but could not stop us, since they were equally guilty. Both sides understood, and no one said anything. We were dependent on each other to be silent, so that the Regiment Administration did not find out.

The next day I woke up early and cooked rice. I planned to steal more paddy when I went to the fields, so I would not have to eat cassava root anymore. I also planned to save any rice that I did not cook during the harvest period. My group members were saving part of their rice, as well.

Before I left for work, I overheard some of my group complaining. They were angry because they had reported being sick a few days ago and the nurse would not allow them to rest. I realized that the cadre were using the same method for controlling the sick as they had used during the last period. They allowed a limited number of patients each day, and the nurse had to maintain that number. I did not pretend to be sick because I wanted to get more rice.

A day later, while on break, some of my group told me that our camp would soon be closed and we would move to Reeducation Regiment 2 in Bui Gia Map Zone.

The next day, the cadre gave each of us 10 dried fish and 15 sugar cubes. When we went to the storehouse to pick these items up, the supply cadre also told us we would be moving to a new camp, six miles away in the Bui Gia Map Zone. He said he owed us money for our food ration, so he was paying us with the fish and sugar.

My group discussed the rumor and the increase in our supplies. Others thought we would move to a camp in the Bui Gia Map Zone, but I had my doubts.

I said, "During the two previous harvest periods, we heard rumors that we would move to a new camp, but we did not move."

Some of my group did not agree with me. One said, "In the war, when we fought against the Communists, they spread rumors that they would attack our bases. We believed the rumors and always prepared for it. Nevertheless, sometimes they attacked, and sometimes they did not. It was better to take precautions when we heard the rumors. This is the same situation."

A few days later, the cadre gave each of us another 10 dried fish and 15 sugar cubes. The supply cadre told us again that he was paying his debt before we left.

Three days after that, a group of prisoners working in the regiment storehouse saw an unfamiliar cadre there. The stranger told them that he was the supply cadre for Regiment 2. He was at our storehouse preparing supply documents for us so we could all move to Regiment 2.

And three days after that, each of us again received 10 dried fish and 15 sugar cubes. The supply cadre said again that he was repaying his debt to us.

As a whole, my group continued to believe that we would move to a new camp in the Bui Gia Map Zone. Many prisoners killed most of their chickens so as not to have to carry them to the new camp, saving out perhaps only one hen.

Many harvested all their vegetables and ate them. They took down their garden fences and hen houses and burned the wood in their stoves. Many dried vegetable seeds in the sun, intending to plant them in the new camp.

All of this preparation and the discussion that accompanied it took our minds away from our weariness.

Finally, we finished harvesting the rice. During this period, two prisoners from my group and several others had escaped. I did not know the total number because the cadre did not review our work.

On the morning after we finished the harvest, a vehicle convoy came to our camp, and I realized we would really be leaving. Some of my group said, "I did not think we would move to Bui Gia Map Zone by vehicle. If I had known, I would have saved some of the chickens to take to the new camp and raise there."

There were 50 of us on each truck. As the last prisoner boarded, the driver closed and locked the back of the truck with an iron net.

As soon as we were all in, we began to move. We took

Crossroad 205; the convoy turned left and moved to Phuoc Long City. We realized then that we were not going to Bui Gia Map Zone. One of the prisoners on my truck said, "This is stupid. The supply cadre lied. They said we were moving to Bui Gia Map Zone, but we are not going there."

We then went on National Road 13 and bypassed Ho Chi Minh City. We continued onto National Road 15 and passed through Ba Ria City. At 10:00 that night, we arrived at Xuyen Moc Reeducation Center. Each truck backed up to a concrete building with all the lights turned on. We got off the trucks and walked about 20 yards between two lines of Public Security agents to the building. With no welcome or greeting, they waited until we were all inside, then closed and locked the door. Iron bars were over the windows. Armed Security agents patrolled around the building. We were in a Public Security reeducation camp.

Twenty-eight

NOVEMBER 20, 1979 to JANUARY 15, 1980

We slept in Camp C the first night at Xuyen Moc. The next morning, I was placed in a group of 190 reeducation prisoners who moved to Camp B, 500 yards away.

Camp B had two sections. The administration section had houses and barracks for the guards working and staying in the camp. The other section was the camp itself, where the reeducation prisoners stayed.

The prisoners' section was 150 yards by 150 yards and surrounded by three barbed-wire fences and several fully manned guard posts. There were electric lights on the fences, and I could see a road just beyond them.

As I entered the camp, I saw two rows of five barracks each. Between the rows of barracks, I could see a yard in which were two wells. At the end of the yard was a small house.

Each barracks had only one door, and the barracks sat in the middle of a lot. Barbed wire surrounded each lot. Each barbed-wire fence had one gate. One hundred fifty prisoners were assigned to each barracks.

As we neared our barracks, I saw some guards wearing Public Security uniforms and about 10 prisoners acting as security guards, or "trustees." Both guards and trustees were waiting in front of our barracks. As soon as we entered the gate, the guards had us muster, then checked our luggage. They took all of our money, which they said they would keep for us.

They assigned each of us to a company. Each company consisted of 30 prisoners. I was assigned to Company 18.

One of the guards told us that this camp had a crew of 20 prisoners who assisted the cadre in its operation. These were trustees who would explain and enforce the camp rules. They had the authority to arrest and beat prisoners who did not obey the camp rules. He also said that all of the guards in

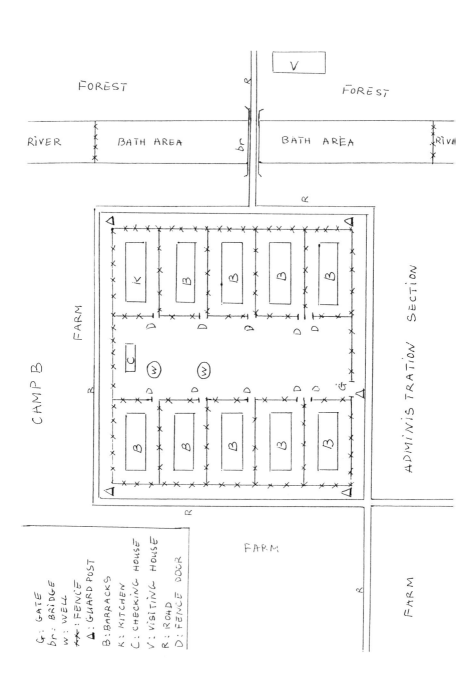

our camp were Public Security agents. Some of them were political cadre. I could not tell the difference by looking at them, because they all wore the same uniform. Only their actions let us know.

The guards left and the trustees showed us where to put our luggage, sleep, dry our clothes, cook our food, store our firewood and water containers, etc. These barracks were different from those in the other camps I had been in, because these had a latrine and electric lights suspended from the ceiling. Also, the walls were made of concrete and the windows were covered with iron bars.

After we prepared our sleeping areas, we were allowed to rest in our quarters for the remainder of the day. We talked to some of the trustees. They explained that there were four types of reeducation prisoners here.

The first type was the criminals. They were thieves, murders, drug dealers, etc. The cadre gave several of them jobs as cooks or trustees.

The second type was the political prisoners who had participated in political organizations after 1975 and opposed the Communist government.

The third type was Old Government personnel. They had worked for the Old Government as congressmen or assistant administrators of the province or district, etc.

The fourth type was us, military officers under the Old Government. All 190 of us had been lieutenants in the Old Government Army. There were 1,100 prisoners in this camp.

The next morning, all of us former lieutenants were gathered into a barracks. One of the cadre told us the camp rules. We had to obey the guards' orders. We had to be enthusiastic about working. Those who worked well and obeyed the camp rules would be released soon. If we heard three gun shots while we were working, we had to sit down in one group, and wait for the cadre's orders. If anyone tried to escape, the guards would shoot to kill. When we were in camp, we had to stay on our lot. We were not allowed to visit other barracks. We were not allowed to stand near the fence and talk to prisoners in other barracks.

Camp life began on our third day. I woke up at 6:30 AM. I took down my mosquito net, cleaned up my sleeping area, then waited for the cadre to unlock our barracks door.

At 7:00, a cadre and a trustee came to our quarters. The trustee unlocked and opened the door. We mustered outside in front of our barracks and sat down in 10 lines. The cadre counted us. We then went back into our barracks and brushed our teeth. Each group of 10 men chose one man to get breakfast from the kitchen. He took the food back to the barracks and divided it into individual portions.

At 7:08 AM, the bell rang. Two minutes later, a cadre and 10 trustees burst into our barracks shouting, "Hurry up and muster! All the people from the other barracks have already mustered!"

They ordered us to leave our food containers, saying they would return them to the kitchen for us. Some of the groups had already divided the food and were eating and some of the groups were still dividing their food. The trustees picked up all the containers, even the ones with food left in them. Some groups had not even divided their food yet, and they lost all of it. The trustees left with our containers and we ran to the gate and mustered inside the fence.

At the gate, many people were flustered. Some were still in their pajamas. Some had not put on their shoes yet, but were still wearing their sandals. Some people forgot their hats or their pots of drinking water.

The cadre complained that we were late, then he ordered each company to sit in two lines inside the fence, facing the gate. At the head of each line were the Company and Deputy Leaders. One cadre stood at the gate guard post. We waited for a cadre to call our company, then we stood up, and our Company Leader reported the number of prisoners working outside camp that day. We walked in two lines, and the cadre counted us as we passed through the gate. Three armed guards waited outside the gate for us. They escorted us to the farm.

At the farm, we mustered again. One of the Security agents informed us that his name was Thuy. He was the cadre responsible for our company each day. The other two Security agents were responsible for guarding us while we worked. We would have to ask their permission whenever we needed to urinate or defecate. However, we were not allowed to come any closer to them than six yards. Anyone who came closer than that would be shot.

Cadre Thuy ordered my company to get to work. The trees here had been cut down and burned, but the stumps were still standing. We had to dig up the ground, cut the roots, and pull the stumps out to level the surface. We used hoes, shovels, knives, and axes.

One prisoner was our Company Leader. Another was our Deputy Leader. These two men did not work. They stood and watched us as we worked. They counted us every 15 minutes and reported the number to the two Security agents guarding us. The rest of us worked in an area about 30 yards in diameter.

The two guards stood on large tree stumps and guarded us. They had their fingers on the triggers of their guns and were prepared to shoot us, if necessary.

Cadre Thuy watched us. In the first hour of work some of my company got in trouble because they were weary and rested for a moment. The cadre reprimanded them and told them to get back to work.

I was hungry and I began to look for ways to save energy. I wondered, "If I am only supplied a small amount of food and have to work hard, how will I survive?"

I could not think of a way out of my situation. Then suddenly my thoughts were interrupted. I saw another prisoner stand up and ask permission to move his bowels. The guard agreed, and the prisoner took a hoe, walked about 50 yards away, dug a small hole, defecated, then buried his stool. I saw that he was able to rest while he did all this. Then a second man stood up and asked permission to move his bowels and the guard again agreed.

I stood up. However, five more prisoners stood up at the same time. We all asked for permission to move our bowels. The guard said, with surprise, "Due to camp rules, I can allow only two people to move their bowels at one time. If you want to do it, wait until the first two people finish. You can take turns and do it later."

After that, we continued to take turns pretending to move our bowels. We had from 15 to 20 minutes rest each time. I decided to do it once per hour until the end of the work period.

At 9:30, we all gathered in one place for a 15-minute break.

An hour later, while we were working, we heard three gun shots pierce the air. This was the signal that a prisoner was escaping. The cadre ordered us to stop working and sit close together. Ten minutes later, he ordered us back to work.

At 11:30, we stopped working. We walked in two lines to a bathing area near our camp, escorted by armed guards on either side.

The bathing area was in a river, which I estimated to be 30 yards wide, 200 yards long, and four feet deep. At both ends was barbed wire. Security agents stood in rows on both banks of the river, watching us. A machine gun was set up at each end of the bathing area.

We had 10 minutes to bathe. At the end of our 10 minutes, none of us had finished. Many were still washing their clothes and had not yet taken their bath. Others were only now applying soap to their bodies. However, we still had to leave the river. After we had mustered, the cadre complained that we had taken too long. He suggested that we bathe faster next time.

We returned to our barracks at 12:00 PM, dried our

clothes on ropes, then went to the well to fetch water. We could take the water from one well only, and we had to use the pail that was there. We were not allowed to use our own pails, so if we wanted to get a pail of water from the well, we had to stand in line. I did not draw water from the well that noon, but others did. They waited 15 to 20 minutes to use the pail.

After I hung my clothes to dry, I spent a little time talking with my friends. We exchanged experiences from our first morning of labor in this camp. Some revealed how they avoided work by moving their bowels often. Some said that they observed the cadre as they were working. If he looked at them, they would work. If he looked away or left their company, they would rest. I thought these two methods of resting were good, and I intended to use both that afternoon.

At 12:20, the cooks announced lunch. One of my group members got our food from the kitchen, brought it to our barracks, and divided it into individual portions. We had learned from our experience this morning, when we lost our food. This afternoon we put our food in our own dishes.

At 12:30, a cadre and 10 trustees came to our quarters. "Go into your barracks. The cadre will count you." They said that they would return our food containers for us today, but tomorrow we would have to do it ourselves. Some prisoners were still dividing their food, so they quickly put their food in their own dishes, and we all carried our food into the barracks with us.

We sat on our sleeping mats, then the cadre walked in and counted us. After the cadre left, the trustees closed and locked the door and the fence gate.

We took 15 minutes to eat lunch. Afterwards, we did not have any water to wash with, because we could not leave our quarters, so we lay on our beds. We dozed off.

At 1:30, while we were all asleep, a cadre and some trustees stole into our lot. They stood around our barracks and outside the windows. They quietly unlocked and opened the door. The bell rang, then as soon as the bell stopped, the cadre shouted, "Muster! Quickly! Why do you sleep so late?"

I woke from a deep sleep. The trustees were shouting. I was startled and embarrassed, and I fell into a panic. I jumped up, seized a couple of sandals, and ran outside. Many others panicked also. Some grabbed a coat and a couple of sandals, then bolted out of the barracks. Some took a shoe and a sandal. Everyone crowded towards the door, pushing and shoving to get out.

When I got outside and was calm again, I saw one man holding a dirty cooking pot. I overheard him say, "This is stupid. This pot is not necessary." He ran back to our barracks and threw the cooking pot outside the door. He shoved the other prisoners out of his way and entered the barracks, seized a couple of shoes, and ran back in line.

I realized I was wearing just a T-shirt and shorts. I had not thought to change into my work clothes. I had also forgotten my hat and my drinking water. I noticed that some of my company had on a coat and shorts, but no pants. Many had forgotten their hats or drinking water also. Some prisoners wore a shoe on one foot and a sandal on the other. Then I heard the cadre complain that we were late and had mustered too slowly.

That afternoon when we walked out the gate, Cadre Thuy and two Security agents escorted us to the farms. They guarded us with the same attentiveness that they had this morning. We did the same tasks again, but now we had found a few ways to rest.

While we worked, we paid attention to the cadre. Every time he turned his head and looked away from us, we all rested. When the cadre turned back, we began working again. Some prisoners were careless and when the cadre looked back, they did not notice and continued to rest. They got in trouble right away.

Sometimes our cadre went to another company nearby and sat down to talk to a cadre there. We all rested when he did this. Then he would suddenly step out of the forest and shout, "Work! Why do you take a break?" It would startle us and we would begin working again. A minute later we would go back to resting. We did this every time the cadre visited another company. The two guards did not say anything. I supposed that the labor was not their responsibility, and they only had to make sure that we did not escape.

I asked permission to move my bowels once each hour. This allowed me to rest for about 15 minutes. Other prisoners did this, too.

At 5:30, we stopped working and mustered. We walked to the bathing area. After our bath, Cadre Thuy complained that we took too long and told us to do it faster next time.

At 6:00, we returned to camp. When we reached our quarters, we hung our clothes out to dry. Then some prisoners waited in line at the well or cooked food. Some of us did not have anything to cook, so we rested and waited for dinner. While we rested, some trustees came to us with interesting news. They told us the three shots we heard in the farms today were because a prisoner had tried to escape from Camp C. He had been shot and killed.

At 6:20, the cooks announced that dinner was ready. We came to the kitchen, took the food to our quarters, and divided it into individual portions.

At 6:30, a cadre and ten trustees came to our quarters and shouted, "Muster! The people in the other barracks are already lined up!" The trustees said they would return our food containers to the kitchen.

Some of us were still waiting at the well or cooking our food. Others were still preparing their food to be cooked. Some were still dividing up their food. We all had to stop what we were doing and run to where we had to muster in front of our quarters. We sat there as the cadre complained that we were too slow.

After we mustered, the cadre did not count us; instead, he stood at the well and talked to the other cadre. We sat and waited for 30 minutes.

Finally, the cadre counted us and we returned to our quarters. One of the trustees closed the door and locked it. All the electric lights were on, however, and we were still able to eat our dinner. Two Security agents patrolled outside our barracks, watching us.

After dinner, some of my friends and I gathered to talk. We all realized that there were no opportunities for us to try to escape. If we tried and failed, we would be killed. We had also experienced many difficulties. There was such a short time for us to eat, and while the camp held 1,100 prisoners, there was only one pail at the well; each of us was lucky to get even one pail of water. We collectively made plans to deal with our new situation.

At 7:30, the cadre switched on the loudspeakers. They broadcast a health program from the Hanoi Broadcasting Station. There were many loudspeakers wired onto the fences and utility poles. At first, the volume was just low enough for us to hear. Fifteen minutes later, the cadre began to turn the volume up.

A half hour later, a number of groups had gathered together to drink water, smoke, and talk. By then, the loudspeakers were turned up all the way, and it was very noisy in the barracks. Two people, sitting close and facing each other, could not hear each other talk at a normal volume, so they had to shout.

Since it was so difficult to talk, we hung our mosquito nets over our mats and lay down. I wanted to sleep, but for the past four years, I had slept in the dark, quiet jungle. Now I had to try to sleep in a place that was too noisy, and with electric lights shining in my eyes. I could not sleep and I frequently got out of bed to urinate. The other prisoners reacted in the same way.

At midnight, the cadre turned off the electric lights and loudspeakers, but there were still two petroleum lamps outside, shining on opposite corners of our barracks. Two armed Security agents continued to walk around the barracks. Despite all the distractions, we were tired and soon fell asleep.

November 23 was our fourth day in this camp and our second day of work. We had learned from our experience and we prepared for difficulties before they occurred.

At 6:00 AM, half an hour earlier than the day before, we all woke up and washed our faces and brushed our teeth. We then stood in line and waited to move our bowels. We prepared our supplies for that day's work and waited for the cadre.

He came to our barracks at 7:00 and we mustered outside. Before he counted us he said, "From now on, when you muster, each group will have one man who will not muster. Instead, that man will run to the kitchen and get the food."

During this period, we received three meals of sweet potatoes each day. At breakfast, we each received two to three sweet potatoes, about the width of my big toe and two to four inches long. At lunch and dinner, we received a double amount.

Two hours after breakfast we were hungry again. Before, when we were hungry, we would divide our food, then assign portions to each person by lottery. But now we were busy in the morning and did not have enough time to set up a lottery system. However, we found a faster method to divide our food.

The man who got our group's food from the kitchen divided it into 10 parts. He then stood and turned his back to the food. Another man pointed his hand at one of the portions and asked, "Whose food is this?" The first man would then name someone in our group, who would take that portion. This method would continue, until all 10 portions were distributed. This method kept us from fighting over the food, because we trusted him to divide it all equally.

After the food was divided, the man who got the group's food took some sweet potatoes and quickly returned the containers to the kitchen. He ate the potatoes as he ran back to the barracks.

As soon as we finished dividing the food, the bell rang. Everyone seized their sweet potatoes and ran to their barracks, grabbed their water pots and ran to the gate to be counted. We ate as we ran.

Several of my company members and I grabbed our water pails. We intended to take water from our bathing area today, so we wouldn't have to wait in the long line at the camp well.

When the bell rang, I saw a cadre and a few trustees standing outside our fence. They observed us, but did not complain about anything we did. I guessed that it was because we finished on time.

At this time, I concentrated all my efforts and thoughts on dealing with the difficult tasks the cadre had forced on us. Because of this, I was busy and felt that the morning had passed quickly so far.

At 8:00, we walked out the camp gate. A cadre and two guards escorted us to the farms and guarded us while we worked. I watched the cadre closely and rested when he was not looking. I also pretended to move my bowels once an hour. Other prisoners used these same techniques.

This morning, I observed that from the beginning to the end of our work time we always had two people moving their bowels. When one finished his turn, another took his place. Some prisoners moved their bowels four times in the morning alone. However, no one moved their bowels when we took our breaks.

Some prisoners always held a piece of paper in their hands when they asked permission from the guard. After they moved their bowel, they did not wipe with the paper. Instead, they saved it and put it back in their pocket. I thought to myself, "How dirty they are!"

Some prisoners took too long, so the guard would ask the Company Leader, "There is one man who requested permission to move his bowels. Three more people just asked for permission also. Do you know where the first man is?"

The Company Leader would call that man to stand up. He was usually startled. Sometimes he would raise his hand as he stood up and shout, "Here I am!" Then he would sit down again and quickly finish. Usually, a minute or two later, most stopped trying and returned to work. Sometimes, someone would stand up right away and shout, "I am here! I am done! I finished already!" Then he would pull up his pants and return to work.

Some prisoners who were on their way to move their bowels heard the cadre say, "It's break time." They automatically turned around, came back to the company, and took their break with the rest of us.

I could tell that my Company and Deputy Leaders wanted to laugh at us when they realized we avoided the hard labor by pretending to move our bowels a lot. But they tried their best to contain their laughter and keep their composure.

I realized that sometimes Cadre Thuy also struggled to keep a straight face when several of us asked to move our bowels.

One of my company, Mr. Tan, moved his bowels four times in one morning. Then, at noon (about five minutes before we left the farm) Mr. Tan asked if he could move his bowels again. Cadre Thuy could not hold back this time. He smiled and looked at his watch. Then he jokingly said, "It's time to go home. There is no time for that now, so please save it for this afternoon."

When we all heard these words, we laughed out loud. After that, we elected Mr. Tan to be the bowel-moving champion. He was famous for this incident, and we made up a new name for him. Everyone in our barracks called him Tan-Ia, the word "ia" meaning "to move the bowels" or "shit".

I paid attention to my work and watched the cadre. Everybody in my company looked for any opportunity to avoid work. Time passed quickly, and I forgot about my hunger.

At 11:30, we stopped working and walked to the bathing area. Because I was unable to finish my bath on the previous day, I began to think of ways to take a bath and wash my clothes in just 10 minutes. On the way, I thought about what

I would do first, second, third, etc.

When the cadre ordered us to start our baths, I quickly ran to the river bank, took off all my clothes, and ran naked into the water. I then drew a pail of water and placed it on the bank. I intended to take the water back to camp to wash with during our noon break. That way I would save time by not having to wait in line at the well.

I ran into the water again. I decided to wash one item of clothing each time I took a bath. This time I cleaned my pants. The next time, I would clean my coat, and so on. When the cadre announced that our bath time was over, I got out of the river, put on my clothes, and mustered. I had managed to finish within 10 minutes. All my company members did the same as I and also finished on time. We returned to camp. From the time we left our work area until we entered the camp gate, my mind was on how to take my bath quickly.

When I returned to the barracks, I dried my clothes on ropes and put my pot of water under my bed. When the cook announced lunch, we had only 10 minutes before the cadre and trustees came to our quarters to count us, so the man who got our food ran to the kitchen and divided it up the same as this morning. He waited until everyone else got their portion and took his food last. He ran back to the kitchen to return the food containers, then ran back to our barracks again. After the cadre counted us, we had 15 minutes to eat. Afterwards, I washed with the water under my bed, then took a 30-minute nap.

Everyone in my barracks got up 15 minutes before the labor bell rang. We dressed and prepared for the afternoon's work. When the bell rang, the trustees opened our door. We ran out, got our pails, and ran to where we were counted. My mind was busy, thinking about what I needed to do. I had to hurry, but I managed to complete my tasks on time.

That afternoon, we did everything the same as we had in the morning, taking our baths after work, and so on.

At 6:00 I returned to my barracks with the rest of my company. Two of us carried back one pail of water which we would use to wash with after dinner and the next morning.

No one cooked his own food. When the cook announced dinner, one prisoner from each group hurried to the kitchen and got the food. We used the same procedures as we had at lunch because we still had only 10 minutes.

At 6:30, a cadre came by and we ran to muster in front of our barracks. We sat there for half an hour.

At 7:00, the cadre counted us and we entered our barracks. Then we ate dinner in our quarters.

Two Security agents stood outside our barracks. I noticed two guards at each of the other barracks as well.

At 7:30, as we finished our last few bites of food, we began gathering in small groups and talking. I heard the loudspeakers being turned on, but the noise was very faint and we could easily talk over it. They were turned up a little at a time.

By 8:00, the loudspeakers were turned up all the way and it was very noisy in our barracks. It was difficult to talk, so we hung our mosquito nets over our mats and lay down. None of us could sleep because it was so noisy and bright. I frequently got out of bed to urinate.

Some prisoners refused to listen to the health program. Mr. Thao wanted to go to sleep early, so he stuffed his ears with cotton and held a blanket around his head. But I could tell he was uncomfortable, because sometimes he got angry and cursed out loud.

Some who could not sleep lay on their beds. When they heard singing on the program, they added funny words to the songs and made the rest of us laugh.

At midnight, the electric lights and the loudspeakers were turned off. The two petroleum lamps were still on, but it was now quiet and dark enough for us to sleep.

The next day our work was the same. But that evening, our Barracks Leader announced that the cadre wanted all the prisoners to be quiet at night so we could sleep and improve our health. The cadre complained that a few prisoners who were not polite lay on their beds and quarreled and cursed, or joked and laughed out loud. These people were noisy and made trouble for everyone else. The cadre, therefore, suggested that anyone who could not sleep should be quiet and not disturb the others.

We realized that the guards had heard us and reported us to their superiors. We agreed that it was too difficult to talk over the noise of the loudspeakers anyway, so we decided to keep quiet at night. Still, we could not sleep that evening, and I noticed several people get up to urinate frequently.

From the end of November until mid-January everything stayed the same. We were busy all day, six days a week. On Sunday we were allowed to rest in our quarters.

On the first Sunday, I used my free time to talk with my friends. There were a lot more guards in this camp than there were in any of the others we had been imprisoned in before. The other camps usually held about 600 prisoners and were controlled by 20 cadre and soldiers at most. Here we estimated that 200 guards controlled 1,100 prisoners.

Among the guards were two officers. One was a 55-year-old captain. The other was a 50-year-old lieutenant. The others were Public Security agents and did not wear rank on their collars. I could not tell which was which just by looking at them. Instead, I guessed their rank by the way they acted. Five were from 22 to 30 years old. Most seemed very young, 18 to 22.

I figured that most of them were newly hired. When the Communists conquered South Vietnam in 1975, they probably did not have enough Security personnel to guard all the reeducation camps, so they used soldiers. Then, as they recruited and trained Security agents to guard the camps, prisoners were transferred from the military to the Public Security camps.

The policies of this camp were different from those in the other camps. Here, Public Security imposed a high level of control and made our lives very difficult. They shorted us on food, scheduled little time for meals and bathing, provided only one pail at the well for the whole camp to use, and forced us to work continuously.

We managed as best we could. We rearranged our lives to try to ensure our survival. Our minds were occupied day and night with anticipating what we would need to survive. We forgot about our hunger and the time passed quickly.

After the first week of work, the kitchen stopped supplying us with drinking water. Our company provided one man to boil the drinking water and pour it into bottles for everyone else. I wanted to avoid the labor on the farms, so I volunteered for this job and my Company Leader agreed to let me do this.

In the middle of December, I was tired and pretended to be sick again. I walked into a barracks where a doctor examined and treated patients. At 7:30, we gathered in one of the other barracks to rest. At noon I returned to my own barracks for lunch, then I went back to the patients' barracks for my afternoon rest. It was easy to be sick, so I pretended for three more days, then went back to work again.

There were from 90 to 100 prisoners in the patients' barracks every day. My company had 30 people, but only 18 to 25 of us worked each day. The others pretended to be sick.

On the afternoon of January 15, 1980, my company attended a meeting at the farm. Cadre Thuy reviewed our work. "You have been in this camp for two months. The cadre realize that all of you have obeyed the camp rules and have enjoyed living here. No one escaped. We are satisfied with your progress." He did not mention anything about our avoiding labor by moving our bowels so much or by our resting when no one was looking. I thought we must have reacted according to their intentions, so they did not complain.

Twenty-nine

JANUARY 16 1980 to APRIL 30, 1980

The camp rules allowed our relatives to visit us once every two months. Every afternoon before we went to work the cadre announced a list of prisoners whose relatives had come to visit. Those prisoners did not go to work that afternoon, but spent the time with their relatives.

During the fourth week of January 1980, my mother and a younger brother visited me. On this day, about 40 other prisoners had visitors as well. We all sat at the gate and waited our turn. One cadre led eight prisoners at a time to the visiting house. After he brought the first eight back to camp, he took another group of eight to the visiting house. This continued until everyone had visited his relatives.

The visiting house was 300 yards from camp. When I walked inside, I saw a long, narrow table with a bench on either side of it. The prisoners sat on one bench and our relatives sat on the other. A Security agent stood at one end of the table, and a trustee stood at the other end.

When we sat down, the Security agent announced it was time to visit. Our relatives brought supplies from the waiting room to the visiting room. Then they sat down and we talked. The Security agent and the trustee listened to our conversation.

After 15 minutes, the Security agent looked at his watch and announced that the visiting time was over. We stopped talking, our relatives stood up and said goodbye, then they went back to the waiting room. We took our supplies to a room inside the camp. Everything was carefully checked, then we took it all back to our quarters.

Other prisoners from my barracks who were also being visited had received a large amount of supplies from their families. Later that afternoon they did not eat their food from the kitchen and announced to the other people in our barracks, "Whoever needs more sweet potatoes can have mine."

Sometimes I saw leftover sweet potatoes. No one wanted them because most of us had been visited by our relatives and had extra supplies.

On the morning of February 1, a change occurred. The cadre came to our barracks at 7:00. They counted us, then we got our food from the kitchen. We ate in a hurry, because we thought we had only 10 minutes for breakfast. Then we sat on our beds and waited. To my surprise, we waited for half an hour, and the bell did not ring.

It finally rang at 7:45, and we mustered outside. At 8:00, we walked out the gate and went to work.

At work, the cadre told us we would stop digging up stumps on the farms, but would move to the edge of the forest to clear a new area there. The cadre stopped forcing us to work when we were tired, and allowed us to rest.

The Security agents no longer guarded us. When we reached the work area, they looked for a big tree, sat at its foot, and rested. They told our Company Leader to stop reporting our numbers. Before, he had to report every 15 minutes; now he reported only when we were ready to leave the farm.

At 9:00, the guards left our work area and did not return until the end of our labor period. The cadre was bored, so he went to other companies to talk to the cadre there, and we were left by ourselves.

Because the cadre and guards had changed toward us, we changed too. If we were healthy, we worked. If we were weary, we rested. And we stopped moving our bowels so often.

At break time, the cadre announced, "From now on, our break time will be 30 minutes instead of 15." Then he left us and went to visit a nearby company.

We sat down and rested. It seemed to me that the cadre was gone for much longer than 30 minutes. We rested all the time he was away.

When he came back, he looked at his watch and said,

"Oh! We took too long a break. Get back to work."

He had made a mistake and allowed us to rest for more than an hour. We worked for 10 minutes more, then it was time to stop for lunch. The cadre led us to the bathing area.

It was different today. Before, there were several Security agents on the river banks, guarding us. Two, armed with machine guns, stood at opposite ends of the bathing area. We were not allowed to swim past them and we had only 10 minutes to bathe.

Today there were only two guards altogether, one at each end of the bathing area. We still had to stay between them, but Cadre Thuy told us, "From now on, you can bath for as long as you want."

I was glad to hear this. I walked to the river with the rest of my company and we bathed with leisure. Then we took some pails of water from the river. When we were finished, we carried our water back to camp.

We reached our quarters at 12:00. Some trustees told us, "The cadre will now allow you to take water from the well with your own pails. You do not have to stand in line for water anymore. Also, from now on, you will have 40 minutes to eat."

Some of my company took their pails and ropes, and headed towards the well. It took them only a few minutes, and they were back again.

At 12:20, we got our food from the kitchen and ate.

At 1:00, the cadre did not come to our barracks to count us. Instead, a trustee counted us. Afterward he said, "Even though I will leave the door of your barracks open, you are still not allowed to leave your quarters."

He walked out and left the door open, but he closed and locked the fence gate. We stayed in our quarters and took a nap.

At 1:45, a trustee unlocked the fence gate. We got up and prepared for the afternoon's work.

At 2:00, the bell rang, and we went back to work. When

we reached the farms, the cadre and Security agents treated us in the same easy way they had this morning.

The cadre allowed us to stop working early. We walked to the bathing area, took a bath, then returned to camp. Before, we returned to camp at 6:00. Now we returned at 5:30.

As soon as we reached our barracks the trustees told us of another policy change. From now on, every afternoon when we returned to our quarters, we would have until 7:00 to cook our own dinner. However, the cadre gave us less than two hours to finish everything and they wanted us to be on time. We were not allowed to cook at noon or in the morning, except for Sunday when we could cook any time during the day.

As soon as the trustees left, those of us who had received food from our families began to cook. At 6:55 I finished but noticed that most of the prisoners had not finished cooking yet.

At 7:00, a cadre and a trustee came to our barracks. When we mustered outside, the cadre reminded us that we were allowed to cook, but we had to finish on time. Then he counted us and we went back inside and the trustee closed and locked the door of our quarters. Electric lights were turned on, and the two guards patrolled around our barracks.

Everyone finished dinner and cleaned up by 7:30. To my surprise, the loudspeakers had not been turned on.

We sat and talked about the policy changes and how we would adjust to them.

At 10:00, the cadre switched the electric lights off and we went to sleep. The petroleum lamps stayed on outside and the guards walked around our quarters all night.

The following morning, we woke up later than usual, most of us sleeping until 6:45. We did not hurry to clean up our sleeping area, brush our teeth, etc. When the cadre came, we mustered outside and leisurely ate our breakfast. Afterward we waited 15 minutes for the bell to ring, then went to work.

At the farms, we worked at our regular speed and

stopped taking latrine breaks so often. When we felt strong, we worked. When we felt weary, we stopped and rested. At break time, we gathered firewood to take back to our quarters to cook our food with.

We returned to our quarters at noon. Today, everyone took his own pail and rope and drew water from the well. We used this water to wash with after lunch. We ate lunch, then napped from 1:00 to 1:45. We went back to work at 2:00.

We returned to our barracks at 5:30. Because most of us had not finished cooking on time yesterday, today everyone hurried. I and three of my friends prepared our food together. We divided the work among ourselves. One man cooked the food. Another assisted the first. The third man fetched water from the well and brought it to the cooks. He also put a pail of water in the latrine so we could wash with it after dinner and the next morning. The fourth man dried our clothes on ropes and fetched our food from the kitchen.

Many of my company did the same, dividing the work up within small groups. Some cooked for themselves. They finished later than the others, but everyone still finished on time. But no one had any spare time. Nobody sat inside. The majority of us were outside, cooking. We all moved fast and concentrated on finishing everything on time.

At 7:00, a cadre and a trustee came to our barracks and counted us. We went back inside and formed into our groups again and ate our food together. Later, we went to the latrine and cleaned our cooking pots, bowls, and dishes. Then we gathered again, drank water, smoked, and talked.

I sat with several of my friends. We figured that we were the first former military officers from the Old Regime to stay in this camp. The cadre probably had believed we would try to escape, which explained why they had watched us so closely during our first two months.

Since none of us had tried to escape, the cadre now permitted us ample time to eat and bathe and to cook for ourselves in the afternoon. We were comfortable in this camp now.

A few days later, our diet was changed from sweet potatoes to dried corn. At first we had millet and we had an appetite for it, but I saw about ten corn kernels in each bowl. I thought one of the cooks had been careless and dropped the corn in our millet. But the amount of dried corn increased a little in our second meal, and the amount of millet decreased a little. By the fourth day our food ration was half millet and half corn, and by the seventh day our food ration was all dried corn and the millet had disappeared. By this time we had the same appetite for the corn as we did for the millet, and no one complained.

We ate corn for two weeks, then the cadre changed our rations again. At noon one day, when we came back from work, we were especially hungry. This time, the kitchen served us slices of dried cassava instead of corn. We took the food to our quarters, then some prisoners got mad. I heard someone curse, "This is stupid! This kind of food is for pigs! How are we supposed to eat it?"

Someone else said, "The longer we're here, the worse the food gets. The dried corn was okay, but how can we eat dried cassava?"

We were all unhappy about the food. Still, if we did not eat the dried cassava, we would have empty stomachs. We were not allowed to cook at noon, so we were stuck in this situation. Since we did not have an alternative, we added sesame salt and shrimp paste to the dried cassava and ate it. As we ate, some prisoners grew angry again and cursed again, but we all finished, and no one had any cassava left over. The prisoners who got mad and complained the most were the first to finish their food. That afternoon most of us cooked our own food and did not eat the dried cassava.

The next morning, we had a third meal of dried cassava. Since we still were not allowed to cook in the morning we had to eat the cassava, but this time no one complained. A week later, when we ate the cassava we had the same appetite for it as we had had for the dried corn.

At the end of February, the cadre began using rumors against us again. On the last day of the month, I pretended to be sick and was allowed to rest in the patients' house. While I was there, some "criminal" patients told me that the Communist Party was experiencing problems. The Party had split into several groups, and the conflict between them had resulted in each secretly killing members of other groups.

A few days earlier, rebel armies had tried to overthrow the Communist government at Hanoi, but had failed. Three of the rebel leaders were arrested and imprisoned. They were: General Giap Nguyen Vo, Minister of Defense; Mr. Trinh Duy Nguyen, Foreign Office Minister; and Mr. Nghi Thanh Le, Minister of Economics.

Three days later we were ordered to sit and listen to a prisoner from our barracks read the newspaper. This surprised me. It was the first time in this camp that the cadre had ordered us to listen to someone read the paper.

The man reading the newspaper said the Communist government had replaced three department ministers, but he did not mention anything about rebel armies trying to overthrow the government.

That evening I sat with several of my friends and discussed the rumor and the newspaper article we had heard read. We realized the cadre were taking advantage of the change in department heads. They were using this news and spreading rumors that corresponded to it. But none of us believed them. By this time, we were all familiar with this technique.

In mid-March, I pretended to be sick again. While resting in the patients' house, some of the criminal prisoners told me another rumor. They said that the Communist Party intended to change their political policy. They also claimed that the BBC had announced that leaders of the Communist Party were forced to change their political policy, even though some of them did not want to. Supposedly, the changes would begin in June or July of 1980. I heard the other patients discuss these rumors. They wanted the political situation in Vietnam to change, and they hoped the rumors were true.

One of them said, "Let's be patient and stay in camp for a few more months, then we will return home."

That evening, I mentioned the rumors to my friends. None of them believed it.

Mr. Uyen said to me, "Don't get your hopes up. We've seen this many times before in the camps in Phuoc Long Province. All those rumors were false, too."

At the end of March, because the military officers did not believe the rumors, all the other reeducation prisoners thought we were just being skeptical. They said to us, "Since you lost the war, you lost your fighting spirit." It was too hard to explain to them how the Communists were using rumors to control us, so we let them experience it for themselves. Only then would they understand.

At the end of April, my company gathered at our work area, and our cadre reviewed our work over the last three and a half months. He said, "All of you obeyed the camp rules well, enjoyed your living in camp, and no one escaped during this period...."

Thirty

MAY and JUNE 1980

May 1, we woke up at 6:30, and the cadre entered our quarters at 7:00. We stood in 10 lines outside our barracks and waited for the cadre to count us. Then we ate breakfast. The bell rang at 7:45 and we walked out the gate at 8:00.

Our morning was easy, as it had been, and I did not expect any changes. But when we reached the farm, I found out that things would be different.

Cadre Thuy announced, "Today, our company will begin 'The Rainy Season Plan'. We are responsible for this farm. We will plant cassava trees and finish by the end of May. We will cultivate the young cassava during the month of June. To accomplish our goal, I have decided to decrease your break time from 30 minutes to 15 minutes. I hope all of you will work hard and finish this work on time."

Cadre Thuy ordered us to stand in one line with two yards between us. We hoed the ground and planted cassava trees. He stood behind us and we worked without stopping. If anyone was tired and tried to rest, the cadre reprimanded that prisoner and immediately forced him to go back to work.

I did not have to stand in line and hoe like the rest of my company. The cadre picked me to boil our drinking water instead.

At our break, I and several others cut firewood to take back to camp at noon to use to cook our food.

After our morning work time, we took a bath in the river. Only two Security agents guarded us. We could take as long as we wanted.

We returned to our quarters at noon, and the cadre let us relax. We could use our own pails to take water from the well, and we had 40 minutes for lunch. However, the cadre no longer left our barracks door open during lunch. Now, when we took our noon nap, the door to our barracks was closed and locked.

At 2:00 we walked to the farm, and the cadre treated us the same as he had earlier this morning.

After we had worked for an hour, I noticed a black rain cloud approaching. The cadre ordered us to stop working and we returned to camp. When we reached our barracks the trustees locked us up.

At 5:00, the rain stopped and the trustees unlocked the barracks and we went outside and cooked our food.

At 7:00, the cadre counted us and we returned to our quarters. The trustees closed and locked our barracks door. The electric lights were on, and we ate dinner. Later, we gathered into small groups, drank water, smoked, and talked. Some of us played chess or music. As I looked out my window, I saw two Security agents walking around each of the barracks.

Several of us discussed the new program. We realized the cadre wanted us to finish on time, so they increased our labor, stopped us from resting during the work period, and decreased our break time. They were also afraid we would try to escape. If a rain cloud approached while we were on the farm, they brought us back to camp and locked us inside our barracks. They did this during our lunch break too. Still, they continued to be easy on us after our work period. We all agreed to try to adapt to the changes when we returned to work tomorrow.

At 10:00, the electric lights went out, and the petroleum lamps outside were lit. The two guards continued to patrol outside.

The next morning it was raining outside when we woke up and we sat in our barracks and waited.

At 7:00, it was still raining. A cadre and a trustee unlocked our door and the cadre entered; his raincoat was dripping wet. He counted us. Then we were allowed to get our food from the kitchen and eat.

At 7:45, a trustee came to our barracks and told us to

go inside. Then he locked us up again.

At 9:00, the rain stopped and the labor bell rang. A trustee opened our barracks door and we went to work.

When we reached the farms, we mustered. The cadre counted us. My company consisted of 30 reeducation prisoners, but only 18 were at work today. The day before, everyone had reported for work, but 12 prisoners were off sick today. I thought they must have decided to deal with the hard labor by pretending to be sick.

As I boiled our drinking water, I watched my company at work. There were always two people moving their bowels. It was the only way they could rest and conserve their energy.

We returned to camp at noon, and I heard from my friends who had been in the patients' house today that the cadre ordered one of the reeducation prisoners who had been a medical doctor to examine the other patients. The patients who were seriously ill would be allowed to rest all day. Patients who were not seriously ill could rest only in the morning and would have to go back to work in the afternoon. The twelve patients from my company would have to return to work.

When we mustered at the farm that afternoon, the cadre counted us. There were fewer prisoners present now than there had been this morning. Fourteen from my company were pretending to be sick. Even though the cadre limited the number of patients by forcing them to go back to work in the afternoon, the number of new patients equalled the number of those returning.

Early in the second week of May, some of my company who had reported sick that morning told me that they had heard that crowds of civilians were demonstrating in the Mekong Plain. Can Tho City was the most turbulent, and the government was getting a headache over it. They would stop a demonstration at one place, and another would start up somewhere else.

My experience with previous rumors made me believe this one to be false and my friends agreed. Mr. Uyen said,

"Don't get your hopes up about this rumor. I think most of what we hear are lies." No one from my company paid any attention to it.

A week later, another rumor had it that a large demonstration had taken place in the city of Bien Hoa. And right after the Communists stopped this one, others occurred in Ho Nai Zone and the city of Ba Ria. Traffic going from Ho Chi Minh City to Ba Ria on National Road 15 was delayed due to the crowds.

The following week there was still another rumor, this one saying that there had been an important meeting in Da Lat to discuss alternatives for coping with the demonstrations. A mine exploded during the meeting, and all of the 40 participants were killed.

At the end of the month we heard that demonstrations were taking place in Ho Chi Minh City. Crowds of civilians participated in the neighborhoods of Nga Ba Ong Ta, Xom Moi, Quoc Tu, and Ben Thanh. The Communists used guns to break up the demonstrations in Ben Thanh, and some civilians were killed.

I did not believe any of these rumors, nor did I pay much attention to them. When I discussed them with my friends, I found they thought the same as I did. None of us cared much about them.

On June 1, Cadre Thuy addressed my company at the farm. He told us we had accomplished our goal of planting cassava on time. Therefore, today our company would begin to weed the grass on the farm and cultivate young cassava trees. This work did not have to be done soon; our break time would be increased from 15 minutes to half an hour.

He ordered my company to stand in one row, side by side. I still boiled our drinking water. The rest of my company weeded grass, but the cadre no longer stood behind them or forced them to work continuously, as before. Instead, he and the two Security agents guarding us looked for a large tree nearby that they could sit under. If a prisoner was tired, he could stop working and rest for awhile, also.

When my company went to the farms the next day, everyone showed up. No one pretended to be sick that day and no one pretended to move his bowels.

Three days later, while we were working, we heard three gun shots. We stopped working and sat close together for about 15 minutes and waited for orders from the cadre. When we returned to camp, we discovered that a prisoner from our camp had escaped.

A couple of evenings later we heard another rumor. China had attacked Vietnam for a second time, and had taken over six provinces near the border. I did not believe the rumor, and all my friends ignored it, too.

The next day I felt sick and reported to the patients' house. I soon realized that other reeducation prisoners in camp believed the rumors; several sat together, discussing them. They thought the Communists were having a lot of difficulties because of the demonstrations taking place and because of the Chinese attacking Vietnam again. These prisoners believed the political situation in Vietnam would change soon. They hoped and waited for the day when they could go home.

In the evening, I mentioned these rumors to my friends who were old military officers like myself. None of us believed the rumors. We thought only about the food that we would cook and eat that day.

On the last afternoon of June, my company mustered on the farm. Cadre Thuy reviewed our work over the last two months. He told us we had done a great job. We had planted cassava trees in May and had finished on time. After that, we had cultivated the farms. Today, all the cassava trees were over half a yard high. He applauded us for this. He also told us we had all obeyed the camp rules well, and no one from our company had made any mistakes during this period.

Thirty-one

JULY 1, 1980 to AUGUST 30, 1980

On July 1, I woke up at 6:30. At 7:00, the cadre came into our barracks and counted us, then we ate breakfast.

At 8:00, we walked to the farms. The two Security agents guarding us looked for a shade tree to rest under. The cadre continued to be easy on us. If we were healthy, we worked; if we were weary, we rested.

Because our work was no longer unbearable, we did not pretend to be sick anymore. Twenty-nine out of the 30 reeducation prisoners in my company worked that day.

We were still allowed to take long baths, but the two guards continued to guard the bathing area. When we finished, we called out our names and got out of the river.

At 12:00, we returned to camp, retrieved water from the well and leisurely ate our lunch.

When we returned to the farms that afternoon, it began to rain. The cadre continued to take precautions against our trying to escape, and returned us to camp. We entered our barracks, then the doors were closed and locked.

At 5:30 we were allowed outside for an hour and a half to cook our food.

At 7:00 the cadre counted us and we were locked in our barracks again. We ate dinner, then sat together and smoked and talked.

The electric lights went off at 10:00, but the two petroleum lamps still shone outside and there were still two guards at each barracks.

This was our routine during the first week of July. But in the second week, things changed.

On the morning of July 8, we received fresh corn instead of dried cassava. Each of us received four ears of corn for breakfast, eight for lunch, and eight for dinner. After eating the fresh corn, I felt full.

Later that morning, two companies in my camp received new orders. (The other companies continued to cultivate the farms.) One company of Old Government staff and one company of Old Government military officers were ordered to cut thatch and bring it back to camp. My company was one of these. The guards led us to the edge of the forest. Each of us cut two bundles of thatch that the cadre would use to make roofs and walls for their barracks. The guards stood nearby while we worked.

That evening, some of my company who had stayed in the patients' house that day repeated to us a rumor they had heard. "The cadre will release all the reeducation prisoners by the end of this year. They will release us in turn, starting in the middle of July. When all the reeducation prisoners are released, they will close this center." They said that the criminal, political, and Old Government staff prisoners believed this rumor and were discussing it at the patients' house. They reasoned that the Communists had decided to change their policy because of the political situation in Vietnam and the civilian demonstrations that took place last month. They also believed that the Communists would release all reeducation prisoners before any government policy changes. Some of the patients said, "We will certainly be released by the end of this year, so it is better to wait a few more months, rather than try to escape."

The Old Government military officers thought this rumor was false. We all just ignored it. Mr. Uyen said, "I think there is nothing to this rumor. We've seen this many times before. If it does happen, the cadre will only release a few people. It is unlikely we will have our names on the list." We continued to think about what we were about to cook and eat each day.

Two days later, another rumor had it that the cadre were preparing documents for 160 reeducation prisoners who would be released in mid-July. These prisoners would come from Camps A, B, and C.

The next day, I felt lazy and pretended to be sick. At the patients' house, I talked to several other prisoners. All the reeducation prisoners except the Old Government military officers like myself believed this rumor was true. They were excited about it.

On July 15, the cadre released 160 Old Government staff members and military officers. Our camp, B, had 40 prisoners released. The rest of the released prisoners came from Camps A and C.

That evening, Mr. Uyen said, "The rumor was correct. I think the Communists will release us all soon. I hope that everybody will be released by the end of this year." We all hoped that we would be released soon.

The next day we heard a third rumor. Some patients said that the cadre would release another 200 prisoners at the end of August. When my friends and I heard this rumor, we were all hopeful; no one said the rumors were false this time. The cadre took advantage of this situation.

In the morning, before we went to work, we attended a camp meeting. The highest ranking cadre in our camp told us, "There are some reeducation prisoners who continue to oppose Communism. The cadre have a list of their names and these people will not be released during the next turn. Also, in the past week, many people did not finish their food and threw their corn into the trash. This is waste. From now on, the cadre will save it."

At lunch that afternoon, the cadre decreased our food rations by half. We now received only two ears of corn for breakfast, four ears for lunch, and four ears for dinner.

I hoped the cadre would consider releasing me soon, so I tried my best to obey the camp rules. I did not dare complain about the decrease in food. No one said anything about the new food policy, they just cooked more from the supplies their families brought.

The next day, when we walked outside the camp gate,

I saw that only one cadre and one Security agent were assigned to each company.

My company and one other were told to cut thatch again. The cadre led us to a place 300 yards from camp on a nearby road and said, "Now go and look for thatch. Cut it and bring it back here. Return on time so we can get back to camp at the same time as the other companies."

The cadre and the guard then disappeared until the end of our work period. I heard the men in my company talking to each other about using this time to look for crabs, snails, fish, etc. Then they all entered the forest.

I was the only one left at our designated rendezvous point. I boiled our drinking water and put it in pots for everyone else. When I finished, I made a fishing pole and fished.

Around 11:00 my company returned. Each man carried two bundles of thatch and a small bag. In the bags were crabs, snails, bamboo buds, and vegetables. Some also carried large pumpkins. I asked, "Where did you get that pumpkin?"

They smiled. "We walked on the road for about two miles. We came to Farm A2, which belongs to the military unit of Bien Hoa Air Base. They had a rice paddy and they had also planted a pumpkin patch. We did not see anyone around, so we stole all the pumpkins we could find."

Around 11:15, the cadre and the guard came back and counted us. We then walked to the Camp Administration Section where the thatch bundles were stored. After we dropped the thatch off, we walked to the bathing area. The Security agents who had guarded this area were no longer present.

At noon, I noticed some changes at our barracks. Before, the doors were closed and locked when we took our afternoon nap. Now the cadre left the barracks doors and fence gate open.

At 2:00, a black rain cloud covered the sky above us. We knew it would rain soon, and I thought we would stay in our quarters. To my surprise, the bell rang and the cadre told us to go to work. So we put on rain coats and went outside.

It rained while we were in the forest, yet we were not allowed to return to camp. All the other companies stayed at the farms also.

That evening when I looked out my window, I saw only one guard at each barracks.

My friends and I discussed the most recent changes. We thought that the cadre were taking advantage of our hopefulness. They had decreased the number of Security personnel guarding us, held us at the farms when it rained, and cut our rations by 50 percent. They also had allowed some of us to work alone, cutting thatch near the roadside, and had stopped guarding us at the bathing area. We were happy about these changes and agreed that it would be easy to escape now. But we all thought that it was not necessary, since we would be released soon.

On August 30, the cadre released another 200 reeducation prisoners. My name was on this list. My heart rejoiced. Exhilarated, I gathered my luggage and prepared to leave the camp.

That afternoon all the prisoners to be released stayed in one barracks. The cadre checked our luggage and told us that tomorrow we would receive our certificates of release.

That evening I lay in bed and thought how wonderful it would be to see my family again and to be free! I also worried a little when I thought about how I had been away for more than five years. I assumed that the Communists had achieved their political goals in the civilian zones and a lot of changes had taken place. When I stepped out of the reeducation center, I knew I would see a new society and I wondered how I would adjust to it.

Thirty-two

AUGUST 31, 1980 to SEPTEMBER 4, 1980
(Released into My Family's Custody)

I was one of 50 prisoners from my camp released on August 31, 1980. At 8:00, I walked to the Camp Administration Section and signed my documents. I received my certificate of release and money for a bus ride to my new home. My certificate stated that I would be confined to my family's custody for 12 months.

By 10:00 AM, all of the released prisoners had received their certificates, and the cadre told us to wait at the Camp Administration Section. Camp trucks would pick us up and take us to Ba Ria City, about 20 miles away.

We waited for 30 minutes, but the trucks did not arrive. I began to feel anxious. I heard a prisoner say, "These cadre often change their minds. If we stay here much longer, they will take our release certificates back."

Most of the prisoners around me stood up. They did not want to wait any longer, so they walked to the road and looked for a civilian bus. I and 11 others waited at the Camp Administration Section for the trucks. I did not think the cadre would change their minds or take our certificates away.

At 11:30 a truck came by and took all of us to Ba Ria. There we looked for the bus that would take us to Ho Chi Minh City.

In 1975, my family had left Ho Chi Minh and moved to Kien Giang Province. I would meet them there, but first I wanted to spend a few days in Ho Chi Minh, visiting my friends and cousins who still lived there.

On the way to Ho Chi Minh, Mr. Uyen, who had also been released today, invited me to his house. I accepted his offer.

As we traveled to Ho Chi Minh, I began to think. I had been away from this city for more than five years. Many things would have changed and I did not know what to expect.

When we arrived, Mr. Uyen and I walked around. We came to Le Loi Avenue. I remembered that before 1975 this street had been a bustling commercial section. Shops had lined both sides. Crowds of people walked on the busy sidewalks as cars and motorcycles drove by. Now as I walked down Le Loi Avenue, all the shops were closed. Most vehicles had disappeared. Only bicyclists rode on the avenue, along with an occasional bus. A few pedestrians walked on the sidewalks.

All the streets that I could see were the same. The government had already taken control of trade and commerce, and all the private businesses had been closed down.

After Mr. Uyen and I walked down a few streets, I followed him to his house. We walked inside and all his family members gathered around him. His brother's eyes were wet with tears of happiness. Everyone was so very glad to see him. His neighbors were also there, and they joined in congratulating him on his return home.

That afternoon, as we sat talking, Mr. Uyen's brother explained Communist policies to us.

If a civilian wanted to visit his cousin in another province for more than one week, he had to report to Public Security and put in an application for a visiting license. When a visitor arrived in the city, the owners of the house had to report to Public Security before the visitor spent the night. If a visitor slept overnight in someone's house and the owner did not first report it, the owner of the home and the visitor would both be in trouble with Pubilc Security.

In the Old Regime, civilians were free to go anywhere in the country without permission. Now the Communists carefully controlled the population, and people were confined to specified areas.

I gave my certificate of release to Mr. Uyen's brother and he took it to Public Security and reported for me. Public Security allowed me to stay for that night.

The next morning, I left Mr. Uyen's house and went to visit my friends and cousins. As I visited each of them, I noticed drastic changes in their situation. Before I went to the reeducation camps in 1975, I had seen many nice things in their homes: armchairs, beautiful cupboards, refrigerators, televisions, electric fans, radios, etc. Each family had one or two motorcycles. Now all of these things had disappeared and had been replaced with a bicycle or two, a wooden table and four wooden chairs. My friends and cousins were pale and thin. I realized that they were not able to earn enough money to live on and must have sold all their nice things to buy food.

By September 3, I had spent three days in Ho Chi Minh. I prepared for my trip the next morning to Kien Giang Province, where my family was living. My cousins told me that if I wanted to buy a bus ticket, I would have to get to the station early.

At 3:00 AM the next day, I left my cousin's house and went to the bus station.

I reached the bus parking lot an hour later. A wall 13 feet high surrounded the station. All the gates were closed. People lined the sidewalk around the station, waiting for the gates to open. A dense cluster of mats blocked each gate. People had spent the night sleeping on these mats and under mosquito nets rented to them by people who lived nearby.

I waited there for another hour and at 5:00 one of the gates opened. All the customers grabbed their luggage and ran to the open gate. They were pushing and shoving as they entered. I held my bag and ran too.

A few security guards stood at the gate and told everyone to sit down on the ground. As we sat, we shoved against each other, trying to move closer to the guard. When he pointed his finger at someone, that meant he could stand up and take his luggage inside the parking lot.

This method was very complicated and unorganized, and it provided an opportunity for thieves to steal the luggage of those customers who were careless in their eagerness to get inside. While I shoved other people out of my way and moved forward, I kept one hand on my shirt pocket over my wallet and my other hand on my duffel bag.

I spent half an hour inching my way to the front. Finally a guard pointed to me and I stood up with my bag in my hand and entered the gate. I walked to the ticket counter and found the line for tickets to Kien Giang Province. There I waited with the other customers.

Several merchants with food baskets yoked on their shoulders walked around the waiting area selling food. Once every 30 minutes, a voice came over the loudspeakers and announced, "Attention all customers, please watch your luggage. Thieves may steal unguarded luggage."

At 7:45, a couple of hustlers walked over and asked each of us in line if we would like to buy a bus ticket. One of them approached me and said he had some tickets for the first bus. He offered to sell me one and advised me to buy it if I wanted to get on the bus soon.

I was curious, so I asked, "How much for one ticket?"

He answered, "Five piastres for one ticket at the counter. Twenty-five piastres if you buy it from me."

I politely refused his offer and continued to wait patiently in line. He continued down the line, and I saw a few customers buy tickets from him.

At 8:00, they began selling tickets for the first bus at the counter.

Forty-five minutes later the hustlers were selling tickets for the second bus, and some people in line bought some.

At 9:00, they began selling tickets for the second bus at the counter. Forty-five minutes later, the hustlers were selling tickets for the third bus. A few more people bought these tickets.

I finally realized that the bus station employees were earning a little extra money by selling tickets on the black market 15 minutes before they were sold at the counter.

I waited for four and a half hours. At 10:00, I reached

the counter and bought my ticket to Kien Giang Province. I immediately boarded the crowded bus.

Half an hour later, the bus moved out of the station. As we left the parking lot, I saw several customers standing along the road with their hands raised. The bus stopped and they got on. They paid the driver 25 piastres, the black market price. There was no place for these people to sit, so they stood up during the entire trip.

While on the bus, I remembered what it had been like to ride a bus in 1975, before the Communists took control of South Vietnam. There were no walls or fences around the bus station. There were many bus companies, and I spent about five minutes buying a ticket at the counter. Now all the private bus companies had been confiscated and made public property.

The Communists had accomplished their goals in this city. The government controlled civil and commercial life. Individual freedom was limited. The standard of living was poorer for everyone I knew, and life was very difficult for civilians here.

I arrived at my family's home that afternoon, at Kinh 3B Hamlet, Tan Hiep A Village, Tan Hiep District, Kien Giang Province.

As soon as I reached the gate to my house, my youngest brother saw me. He shouted loudly, in surprise and joy, "Brother Tri returns home!"

All my family heard this and ran out of the house. They met me at the gate and gathered around me and welcomed me home.

My next-door neighbors also heard my brother shout, and they also came to my house to congratulate me on returning home.

Thirty-three

SEPTEMBER 5, 1980 to DECEMBER 14, 1985
(Living in the Communist Hamlet)

On September 5, 1980, I began my new life as a "confined man." I did not have civil status yet. I reported to Public Security in my hamlet; then I reported to the Public Security chief of my village; lastly, I reported to Public Security in my district.

One of the Security agents at the district office read my certificate of release, then told me to buy a notebook. Each week I had to note all my activities and any incidents concerning the security of my hamlet. I also had to report to all three places each week, at which time Security personnel would read my reports and sign them.

On September 6, I began to participate in the life of the hamlet. The entire hamlet was about four miles long. A river ran down the middle of it. Houses sat on both sides of the river, and behind the houses were rice paddies. Two concrete paths and an abundance of coconut trees ran along the river banks. Each path measured a yard wide, and was used by pedestrians, bicyclists, and motorcyclists.

The Communists divided my hamlet into several groups. My family was in Group 8, which consisted of about 20 families. I spent a few days visiting several of the families in my neighborhood and my group, and I saw that each family had from four to eight acres of farmland.

May, which is the beginning of the rainy season each year, is also the time for farmers to begin sowing paddy. The farmers here planted seven-month paddy, just as they had always done. They also planted beans, tomatoes, and cucumbers, and each family raised a few pigs, chickens, and ducks. In December, each family would harvest two to four tons of paddy. This was the old way, which the farmers had been following for a long time.

I asked my neighbors about Communist practices here. They told me that the Communists took control of this hamlet in 1975, and separated it into several groups. Since then, whenever someone wanted to visit another province or city for more than one week, he had to report to the district Public Security office and put in an application for a visiting permit. Also, anyone who visited this hamlet for more than a week had to report to hamlet Security and present his visiting permit.

My neighbors also told me that at the end of the rice harvest each family had to pay the Communists an agricultural tax of 200 to 400 kilograms of paddy.

The Communists had not taken over their farming methods yet, and the people here were currently living better than those I had visited in the cities.

In the second week of September, I began working in the rice paddies. Every day, I worked with my family. There were 10 people in my family: my mother, myself, five brothers, and three sisters. But my fourth oldest brother and two of my sisters did not live with us, so there were only seven of us working and living together. After working in the paddies, I usually had some leisure time, and I would play chess with my neighbors or fish by the river. I enjoyed living here for now.

The following week, Public Security announced over a bullhorn that all the men confined to our hamlet had to report to the village office. I reported for work with 30 other men. We had to spend three days repairing Security agents' houses.

Only one of the other men had also been an officer for the Old Government. The others told me that they had belonged to an anti-communist organization between 1976 and 1978. They told me that several people from this hamlet had joined this organization and secretly fought against the Communist government. Unluckily for them, spies infiltrated their organization and obtained a list of all the people in it; then the Communists arrested everyone in the resistance. Ten of them were sent to reeducation camps. The rest were confined to this hamlet.

They described some of their experiences here. Whenever village Security personnel needed paddy sowed or harvested, or grass weeded on their own fields, they ordered these men to work for them without payment. Sometimes Security also had them build or repair the village offices or the Security agents' houses, also without payment.

For my first three months, I obeyed orders and enjoyed my life here. At the end of November, the Security agent in my hamlet suggested that my report period be extended from one week to two weeks and district Security agreed.

In December, one of my younger sisters got married and moved away. Also, my second oldest brother decided he did not like rural life. Since he was single, he left my mother's house and moved to Ho Chi Minh City. My family now had five people living at home: my mother, me, and three of my younger brothers. Every day the five of us worked on the farm together.

In February 1981, my fourth oldest brother had an opportunity to escape from Vietnam, and he took it. I wanted to escape also, but I did not have enough money or gold to pay for my trip.

In the middle of 1982, my family received good news. My second oldest brother, who lived in Ho Chi Minh City, got married and got a job in the city. Also, my fourth oldest brother had arrived in the United States. He began sending money to my mother to help support our family. This made my family very happy.

During this time, I fell in love with one of the girls in my hamlet, Miss Phung. At the end of 1982, we decided to get married.

In February 1983, my two youngest brothers tried to escape from Vietnam. They failed and were imprisoned in reeducation camps. We now had three people left to work on our farm: my mother, me, and my third oldest brother.

In the spring, the Communists began to change the method of farming used in my hamlet. In early May, my group attended a meeting. Our Hamlet Leader told us that the government planned to create an "agricultural revolution" in our hamlet. Everyone would have farmland to work on. The government would supply us with fertilizer, gas, and oil. It would also plough the farms for us. We were responsible for sowing paddy, then cultivating and harvesting the plants. We would no longer plant seven-month paddy. We now had to plant three-month paddy. In previous years, we had harvested paddy once a year. Now, with the new agricultural plan, we would plant and harvest paddy twice a year. The Hamlet Leader added, "You will all have plenty of paddy in your houses. You will be rich and have a better life." When he finished his speech, everyone enthusiastically applauded.

The next day, May 3, all the farms in my group were confiscated "in the public interest." The Communists then re-divided the farms. Each family was given an equal area of land, and each person was responsible for about one acre.

A few days later, several government tractor ploughs came and ploughed all the farms. At the same time, government boats carrying fertilizer, insecticides, gas, and oil came. They sold these items to us at inflated prices. For example: one kilogram of fertilizer, called "ure," cost one and a half kilograms of paddy before; now the Communists were charging us three kilograms of paddy for it. All the other items were inflated, as well.

We did not have to pay cash for the plough, fertilizer, insecticide, oil, and gas when we received them. Instead, we had to pay the government in paddy when the harvest was finished. By the end of May, all the farms were ploughed and all the families had received adequate supplies.

At this time, Miss Phung and I were married. She moved in with my family and helped farm our land.

At the beginning of June 1983, all the families in my group began to sow paddy. Some people, like my neighbor, Mrs. Vinh, did not sow the new paddy plants, but continued to sow the old plants. Armed Security agents came to our hamlet and spoke with the heads of these families. They warned them that the government no longer allowed us to sow the old plants. Then the tractor ploughs came and ploughed their farms a second time, and these families had to pay for the ploughing again.

A week later, Security agents came to Mr. Canh's house. They chained his wrists and arrested him, then put him in jail. We were told that Mr. Canh had continued to plant the old paddy; therefore, he was imprisoned. Everybody knew about Mr. Canh's case, and no one dared plant the old paddy anymore. By the end of June, all the farms were sowed with the new paddy.

By the first of July, the rice plants were six to twelve inches high. All the families weeded grass, spread fertilizer, and sprayed insecticides. Each day, my mother, my third oldest brother, my wife and I all worked from 8:00 AM to noon. After a two-hour break, we worked again from 2:00 to 5:00. By the end of August, the rice was ripe enough to harvest.

We began harvesting in September, and by the middle of the month we had about half a ton per acre. By the end of the month, all the families in my group had finished the harvest.

On October 1, we were told the amount of paddy we had to pay the government for ploughing, fertilizer, insecticides, oil, and gas. Everyone also had to pay additional paddy for a "land tax" calculated on the amount of land they cultivated.

The next day government agents came to collect. My family collected all the rice paddy we had harvested and used it to pay our debt, but it was not enough. I checked with the other families in my group and found that no one had harvested enough to pay their debt. We all owed the government more than we had grown.

Because none of us had paid off our debt, in mid-October armed Security agents and officials from the district and the village offices came to my hamlet. They entered each house and yelled profanely at the occupants, "Why don't you pay what you owe!" They checked the houses and seized anything of value: a beautiful bed or dining room set, a pumping machine, or a small amount of paddy. They would sell these and apply the proceeds to that family's debt.

I watched these families, their eyes swollen with tears, as the officials took everything they owned. They were left with nothing; even the rice they had held back to eat was taken. In my group, Mrs. Vinh had her table and chairs confiscated and Mr. Chien lost his pumping machine. All the groups in my hamlet experienced this, but no one dared speak out for fear of being arrested.

My family was in debt also, and we did not want this to happen to us. We were raising a pig, which weighed about 65 kilograms, so we sold it and used the money to buy more paddy to pay off our debt.

Some of my neighbors also looked for ways by which to raise money. They sold their pigs, gold rings, or gold necklaces and bought enough paddy to pay off their debt. Then they were able to recover their beds, tables and chairs, pumping machines, etc. from the government.

When my family had paid our debt in full, we had no more paddy in our house. My neighbors did not have any paddy either. We became depressed, thinking about the government's "agricultural revolution."

A week later, while we were all still feeling depressed, the Communists consoled us by spreading a rumor. One of my neighbors said that Chin Le Quang, the Communist Party Leader for this District, had lost his job, because he was too harsh when he implemented the new agriculture plan. He went too far when he ordered his crews to collect people's furniture, and so he was punished.

I was intrigued by the rumor. I went to my neighbors' houses to see how they had reacted to it. They were happy and felt vindicated for what they had lost.

A month later I found out that the rumor was false. Chin Le Quang had not lost his job. Nevertheless, the rumor worked. It cheered the villagers.

In November, government boats began to carry fertilizer, gas, and oil to our hamlet. They supplied every family. I realized that the Communists had finished their first six-month agricultural plan, from May to October. Now, they were beginning their second. I guessed the second plan would be the same as the first.

My family continued to plant three-month paddy. In March 1984, we harvested it. During the first weeks of April, government agents came to our hamlet and took all our paddy. We paid them everything we had harvested, but it still was not enough. Most of my neighbors did not harvest enough to pay their debt either.

In the third week of April, government officials and Security personnel came again and checked several houses. They collected beds, tables, chairs, pumping machines, and everything else of value.

My family did not want this kind of trouble, so we looked for ways to keep the Communists from taking our furniture. Luckily, my fourth oldest brother was in the United States and sent a little money to help my mother. She used this money to buy rice to feed our family and to pay our debt.

My family had participated in the "agricultural revolution" for one year, and the Communists had implemented two agricultural plans. We had worked hard but could not earn enough to feed ourselves. We lost all the money we had previously saved, trying to pay our government debt. We tried desperately to think of ways to deal with our situation.

In May, my mother and third oldest brother left our hamlet and returned to Ho Chi Minh City. They moved in with my second oldest brother and his family. Then they looked for jobs. My wife and I wanted to leave the hamlet too, but could not because I was still a "confined man."

At this time, there were about 20 families in Groups 3, 4, 5, and 6 who sold their houses and moved away. One of my group, Mr. Thong, moved his family, too. They left because they could no longer survive here.

Over time, I saw many families move out of the hamlet. When I talked with my neighbors who were still here, they told me they were too poor to move away. They felt horrible when government officials and Security agents cursed at them and confiscated their furniture, but they could do nothing. They knew they would be imprisoned if they spoke out.

My neighbors did what they could to survive. Mr. Hieu's wife had a small boat. She bought piglets, dogs, cats, and other things, then rowed the boat to other hamlets and sold these to earn a little money for food for her family. They ate some rice at each meal, but they had to eat a lot of sweet potatoes and bananas to fill themselves.

For another year, my wife and I worked hard every day. We harvested twice more but we never had enough paddy to pay our debt to the government.

After each harvest, the government sent officials to collect. My mother did not want me to get into trouble, so she gave me the money to pay off my debt. She also gave me a little extra money for food.

The other families in my group were very poor. They did not have even a small amount of rice for food. The Communists got nothing more from them.

My group participated in the "agricultural revolution" for two years. We all worked in the rice paddies every day, but by the end of April 1985, many families in my group were still in debt to the government. Each family owed at least a half ton of paddy. Mr. Thanh's family had the biggest debt. They owed four tons. The total debt of all the families in my group was about 40 tons.

About this time, I received a notice from the district Public Security office stating that because I had obeyed their orders for the last 56 months I was no longer "confined." Although the Department of the Interior had ordered me confined for only 12 months, the local authorities had confined me for 56 months.

Even though I was no longer confined by Public

Security, my family and I were still discriminated against in all matters concerning the Communist government, because of my previous position as an officer in the Old Government. For example, if my wife or I put in an application for a factory job or a government office position, we would not even be considered. Under the Communist regime, all businesses were under the control of the government.

In May 1985, the government implemented its "agricultural plan" in my hamlet for the fifth time, supplying fertilizer, gas, oil, etc., and ploughed the farms for us. We planted three-month paddy in June, July, and August. In September we harvested.

During the first two weeks of October, government agents came to each house and collected paddy from the farmers. We also had to pay back loans from the previous two years.

The result of the loan payment was that most of the families in my group did not have enough paddy to pay off their debt. Some owed the government as much as two or three tons now. Mr. Thanh's family owed five tons. The total debt for all the families in my group had increased to 50 tons.

My family was in the same situation as the others. We paid all the paddy we had to the government, but we still did not have enough.

Many families had nothing left that could be sold or taken to pay off their debt. The Communists could not do anything more to these poor people, so they let them stay in debt. My family was one of these.

The Group and Deputy Group Leaders came to my house and told me it did not matter to them whether or not I was in debt. But they feared I would get in trouble if they reported me to the government as being unable to pay. I told them I had already done all I was capable of and could not do anything more.

In mid-October, Government officials and Public Security agents came to my hamlet again. They found that no one could afford to pay their debt, and there was nothing more that could be taken from them. The officials did not collect anything except for a little rice that had been put aside for food. But when they came to Mr. Binh's house they removed his tin roof. They told the other villagers that Mr. Binh was dealt with in this way because he had been a military officer for the Old Government and had not paid enough on his debt.

There were only two men living in my hamlet who had been officers for the Old Government, Mr. Binh and me. I guessed that in a few days, when the government officials came back, they would remove my tin roof also.

Luckily, while I was worrying about losing my tin roof, my mother came to visit me. She had heard about Mr. Binh's case and gave me enough money to pay my debt. So the officials did not come to my house.

When the government agents returned, they took all of the paddy that had been harvested since their last visit. All of the villagers were depressed.

Later that month, a rumor spread through my hamlet. Radio and television stations and newspapers from foreign countries had announced that a comet, ten times bigger than Earth, was moving towards our planet and would strike it in February 1986. The earth would explode upon impact. All the superpower nations such as the USA, Russia, England, and France were concentrating their rockets and atomic bombs. They intended to shoot the bombs into space and destroy the comet. If they could not do this, our planet would be destroyed and everyone would die.

Everyone discussed the rumor. Mrs. Hai said, "We will live for a few more months, then the end of the world will come and we will all die."

When I was in Mr. Dau's house, they were discussing it also, and his mother said, "On the day of reckoning, God and our Lord Jesus will come for the judgement. So let's do good things and prepare for our death. Don't forget to go to church and see the priest for your confession by January 1986." Everyone soon forgot about the government's collecting paddy from them.

In the middle of November, an explanation for the rumor of the comet was typed and hung on the door of my church. It said that the rumor was not correct. The comet that would appear in February was Halley's Comet. It was discovered by an English astronomer, and every 76 years it can be seen as it passes near the earth. I believed that the Communists had used this rumor to accomplish their goals, but they did not want it to spread to other hamlets. That is why they finally explained it to us.

The government had conducted its "agricultural revolution" in my hamlet for two and one half years now. I had farmed and worked hard every day, but I was not able to earn enough rice for my family to eat. If my mother had not helped me, the Communists would have taken the tin roof off of my house. I wanted to move my family back to Ho Chi Minh City, but I could not. Because I had been an officer for the Old Government, the Communists would refuse my application for permanent residence in this or any other city. I decided to try to escape.

My father-in-law told me that his brother was secretly preparing a boat in which he intended to escape from Vietnam. If I wanted to participate in the escape, I should ask him about it.

My wife and I realized that we needed to better our lives. If we tried to escape and failed, we could die at sea or be imprisoned. If we succeeded, we would live in another country; we would have freedom and our lives would be easier. We decided to take the risk.

We saw my wife's uncle and he agreed to let us join his crew. Because we were so poor, he said he would help us with the payment. We would pay him one ounce of gold up front. Then, if we came to the United States and got jobs, we would pay him 3,000 dollars. We agreed. We borrowed an ounce of gold from one of my cousins and used it for payment.

Thirty-four

DECEMBER 14, 1985 to MARCH 1987
(Escaping from Vietnam)

On the evening of December 14, 1985, those of us fleeing Vietnam with my wife's uncle hid at predesignated points on the river bank. My family and 20 other refugees hid in a cottage in Mong Tho Village, in Kien Giang Province.

At midnight, a boat moved silently along the river and stopped at each point. Hidden in a veil of darkness, we quietly boarded the boat which was only about 10 yards long and two yards wide.

Half an hour later the people at the last point boarded the boat. We started the engine and headed towards the sea.

There was a guard post on the river bank and Security agents were on duty 24 hours a day. Anyone who took a boat from the river to the sea had to stop at the guard post so Public Security could inspect the boat and check his papers showing authorization to go out to sea.

At 1:00 AM, our boat came to this guard post. We did not stop there, but continued to move on. A Security agent shouted only once, "Hi, come here." Then he was quiet. We did not stop.

I wondered why he didn't try harder to stop us, so I asked the boat pilot why the Security agent had not shot at us. He told me that by 1:00 AM all the Security agents at this post were sleeping soundly, except for the one on guard. My wife's uncle had secretly given this one some gold so he would allow our boat to pass the control point.

That day the sea was rough and the waves crashed high above our heads. The waters were void of any other boats until 3:00 PM, when a large government boat came by and arrested us. They threatened us by shooting repeatedly into the sky, and ordered us to head back towards the continent.

When we began heading back toward land, they

stopped shooting. After five minutes, my wife's uncle took an ounce of gold and packed it in his handkerchief. He added a small piece of iron, to make the package heavier. Then he stood at the head of our boat and raised his hand, motioning for them to come closer.

The crew of the other boat understood his meaning, so they maneuvered close to us. Our uncle threw the package onto the other boat. Then they moved their boat away from ours. But a few minutes later, they moved close to us again and returned the package. One of them used his hands to express his disagreement, then the boat backed off again.

My wife's uncle opened the package and saw that they had returned his gold, so he solicited help from the other people. He needed more money to bargain for our freedom. Many of the people in our boat gave him their gold rings and cash. He packed all the gold and cash together, stood at the head of our boat, and signaled the government boat to return.

They moved their boat close to ours. Our uncle threw the package onto their boat. They took the package and moved their boat away.

A few minutes later, one of them raised his hand to demonstrate their acceptance of the gold and money and motioned us to move on. Then they moved away.

The following day the sea was still very rough, and our boat almost sank many times. None of us thought we would survive. We all sat on the floor of the boat and prayed to God for our deliverance.

At noon, on December 17, 1985, a Thai Air Force plane circled over us several times. We were all thankful and waved happily at the plane.

Early that evening, a Thai Navy boat came by and towed us for four hours. Finally they pointed us in the direction of the continent and left.

Now alone, we continued to move in that direction; and at 1:00 AM, on December 18, 1985, we arrived on land. As soon as our boat hit the shoreline, the waves turned us over, and I quickly ran to some nearby houses. I saw a lady and asked her, in English, "Where are we, Thailand or Malaysia?"

She did not understand English, but she understood my question. She said, "Thailand." I quickly returned to the others and gave them the good news.

The people here were very glad to see us, but I was surprised when several men with knives and axes started running towards our boat. They shouted threats at us, then ordered us to get away from the boat. They boarded it and took everything that could be removed.

Afterwards, they led us to their Buddhist Temple. There, they took anything of value we had left, such as watches, gold rings, and gold necklaces. We lost all our remaining possessions, except for the clothes we were wearing.

Sometime after daybreak, the people changed their manner towards us. They came to the temple and invited us to come to their houses. They cooked and served us delicious food.

In the afternoon, police came in two trucks and took us to Songkhla Refugee Camp. All 52 of us were very glad we had arrived safely. I thought, now we can live our lives in freedom.

We stayed in Songkhla Refugee Camp for three months and in Sikieu Refugee Camp for another month. We were then transferred to Pananikhom Refugee Camp for three more months.

In June 1986, a U.S. delegate interviewed my family and accepted us for immigration to the United States.

The next month, we left Thailand and moved to Bataan Refugee Camp in the Philippines where we studied English.

On March 19, 1987, my family and I arrived in the United States.

Lê Hu'u Trí was a young lieutenant in the South Vietnamese army when Saigon fell to the North Vietnamese in April 1975. Shortly afterward, he was imprisoned and spent nearly six years in "reeducation camps," actually labor camps where he was one of thousands of Vietnamese forced to clear forest land for agriculture. In December 1985, he and his wife escaped from Vietnam by boat. He has lived in the United States since 1987.